Democracy
and Socialism
in Sandinista
Nicaragua

Democracy
and Socialism
in Sandinista
Nicaragua

Harry E. Vanden
Gary Prevost

Lynne Rienner Publishers ❖ Boulder & London

Photographs by Harry E. Vanden

Published in the United States of America in 1993 by
Lynne Rienner Publishers, Inc.
1800 30th Street, Boulder, Colorado 80301

and in the United Kingdom by
Lynne Rienner Publishers, Inc.
3 Henrietta Street, Covent Garden, London WC2E 8LU

Library of Congress Cataloging-in-Publication Data
Vanden, Harry E.
  Democracy and socialism in Sandinista Nicaragua / by Harry E.
  Vanden and Gary Prevost.
      p.   cm.
  Includes bibliographical references and index.
  ISBN 1-55587-227-1 (hc)
    1. Nicaragua—Politics and government—1979– 2. Democracy—
Nicaragua. 3. Socialism—Nicaragua. 4. Elections—Nicaragua.
5. Frente Sandinista de Liberación Nacional. I. Prevost, Gary.
II. Title.
JL1616.V36 1992
972.8505′3—dc20   92-24289
                                                                          CIP

British Cataloguing in Publication Data
A Cataloguing in Publication record for this book
is available from the British Library.

Printed and bound in the United States of America

The paper used in this publication meets the requirements
of the American National Standard for Permanence of
Paper for Printed Library Materials Z39.48-1984.

For David, Jonathan, and the coming generations
in all of the Americas
who long for a politics that empowers them

❖ Contents ❖

List of Illustrations   ix
Acknowledgments   xi

1   Introduction: On Democracy   1
      Capitalist and Socialist Conceptions of Democracy, 6

2   The Genesis of Sandinismo   23

3   Democracy and the Development
    of Mass Organizations   49
      Neighborhood Organization:
          The Sandinista Defense Committees, 57
      Women's Organization: AMNLAE, 58
      National Union of Farmers and Ranchers: UNAG, 62
      Labor Organizations: CST and ATC, 64
      Religious Organization: The Popular Church, 66

4   The 1984 Elections and the Evolution of Nicaraguan
    Governmental Structures   71
      Democratic Elections, 74
      Constitution Making, 83
      The New Governmental Structure, 86

5   Sandinista Thought and Action   89
      Principles of FSLN Political Philosophy, 89
      Political Pluralism, 92
      Mixed Economy, 97
      Nonalignment, 100

6   The Evolving Structure of the FSLN   109
       The National Directorate, 110
       Departments of the National Directorate, 112
       The Sandinista Assembly, 115
       Regional, Zonal, and Local Organization, 116
       Organizational Changes After 1987, 117

7   The 1990 Elections: Capitalism and Western-Style
    Democracy Stop the Revolution   129
       The Costly Campaign, 131
       The Economic Realities, 137
       The Final Outcome, 143
       Conclusion, 146

    Appendix: Chronology of the FSLN   153
    Bibliography   155
    Index   163
    About the Book and Authors   172

❖ Illustrations ❖

Photographs

Tomás Borge   37
Mural Formerly in Front of AMNLAE Headquarters   59
Billboard Announcing Election Results   81
The National Assembly in Session   87
Sandinista Leaders Campaigning   132
FSLN Campaign Poster on Temporary Dwelling   139
Closing UNO Rally in Managua   142
Lining Up to Vote in Monimbó   145

Map

2.1   Sandinista Guerrilla Warfare, 1961–1970   38

Figures

3.1   Structure of the National Union of Farmers and Ranchers
        and the Sandinista Defense Committees   63
6.1   Pre-1990 FSLN National Party Structure   111
6.2   Current FSLN National Party Structure   118
7.1   Ballot for President and Vice-President   133

Tables

4.1   1984 Election Results   81
7.1   Parties in the 1990 Election   134

ix

❖ Acknowledgments ❖

Many individuals and organizations made this book possible. We are particularly indebted to Andrew Reding, senior fellow at the World Policy Institute in New York. Andrew was originally to be a coauthor, but other commitments made that level of participation impossible. We profited greatly from his comments and assistance in various stages of the project. Gary Prevost wishes to acknowledge the financial assistance of the Fulbright Program's Central American Republics Research Grant that supported his sabbatical research in Nicaragua in 1990–1991. He also wishes to acknowledge the Bush Foundation for support of an earlier research trip to Nicaragua. Harry Vanden gratefully acknowledges travel and field support grants from the Division of Sponsored Research and the College of Social Science of the University of South Florida. St. John's University and the Department of Government and International Affairs of the University of South Florida funded numerous trips to professional meetings where the authors presented various chapters of the book as panel papers and gained valuable feedback from fellow Nicaraguanists, particularly Thomas Walker of Ohio University. Valuable comments from John Britton, Lou Pérez, and Steve Watrous were helpful, as was the assistance of Gary Ruchwarger, Martha Morgan, and Rose Spalding.

In Nicaragua the authors are indebted to many individuals and institutions who facilitated their research. These individuals include Vanessa Castro, Patricia Elvir, Edgar Parrales, Ramón Menneses, Tomás Borge, Carlos Vilas, Sixto Ulloa, Rafaela Cerda, Francisco Campbell, Carlos Tünnerman, Miriam Hooker, Mariano Fiallos, Murielle Vigil, Julio Valle Castillo, Victor Tirado, and Alejandro Martínez Cuenca. Organizations that provided assistance include the Secretariat of the FSLN, the National Assembly, the Institute of Nicaraguan Studies (IEN), the Supreme Electoral Council (CSE), the Institute for the Development of Democracy (IPADE), the Nicaraguan Women's Association (AMNLAE), the International Relations Department of the FSLN, the Valdivieso Center, and the Foundation for the Global Economic Challenge (FIDEG). The Departments of Government at St. John's University and the University of South Florida provided material assistance to complete the work. Research assistants Tom Ricker, who made the index, and Linda Alegro were particularly helpful. Research assistants Garrett Chapman and Kevin Schooler prepared the bibliography. We especially wish to thank Shirley Zipoy at St. John's University for her office assistance and to acknowledge the support of Kate Watts and Lynne Rienner at Lynne Rienner Publishers. Both authors wish to acknowledge the support of their compañeras, Catherine Kocy and Vera Vanden.

Harry E. Vanden
Gary Prevost

❖ ONE ❖

Introduction: On Democracy

With the deepening of the struggle . . . only the workers and the peasants will go all the way.

—Augusto César Sandino[1]

Do not be frightened into their surrender by the alarms of the timid, or the croakings of wealth against the ascendancy of the people.

—Thomas Jefferson[2]

When it took power in July 1979, the Sandinista government of Nicaragua did not have any well-developed theory of Marxist democracy on which to draw. Nor did it have fully democratic Marxist models on which to base its praxis or on which it could rely for support, sustenance, and encouragement to develop its own democratic Marxism. There were few real-world examples and little support from actual nation states to develop a democratic form of socialism, and even fewer to do so within the specific historic conditions in Nicaragua.[3] The absence of these factors made the construction of such a democratic socialism difficult. It also retarded the development of sufficient confidence to sustain truly unique democratic institutions in the face of increasing external pressure from the United States and decreasing support from the Eastern European countries.

Both the United States and the Soviet Union thought their respective model was the best for the Nicaraguans. Even though the Soviets were more subtle, both superpowers were to some degree uncomfortable with a uniquely Nicaraguan road to development and democracy that would break radically from the Eastern and Western models. Ironically, each side believed that developments in Nicaragua were wholly inadequate and indicative of either dominance by Western influences (from the perspective of the socialist East) or communism (from the perspective of the capitalist West). The socialist states were, however, clearly more willing to support Nicaragua because the ideology was nominally Marxist (even

1

though the economic and political systems were very different from those in Eastern Europe). The socialist states also realized that Nicaragua's newly found independent, nonaligned stance threatened the traditional hegemony that the United States had exercised in the Caribbean Basin.[4]

The popular insurrection that swept the Sandinistas to power in 1979 initially endowed the emerging political system with a strong participatory dimension. It did not, however, coincide well with either Western representative democracy or Eastern bureaucratic socialism, since both of these systems had either diminished or never adequately evolved mechanisms to insure or facilitate direct, ongoing participation by the people.

The Marxist tradition is more diverse than the now-failed socialist states in Eastern Europe would suggest. As with Jeffersonian democracy, theoretical Marxism allows for real or direct democracy as well as non-participatory forms of governance that claim to be participatory. The first relies more heavily on innovative theoretical interpretations, while the second is based on Leninist conceptualizations of the party and actual socialist practice.

Before Stalinism poisoned the international socialist movement, Marxism was not a fixed dogma; it was a means of understanding events and a theoretical guide for developing *all* aspects of socialism.[5] Among these were ways of assuring that democracy developed under socialism (see Megill 1970, p. 54). In his now widely quoted essay, "What is Orthodox Marxism?" (originally published in the early 1920s), Georg Lukacs (1971, p. 1) argues that Marxism "does not imply the uncritical acceptance of the results of Marx's investigations. It is not the 'belief' in this or that thesis, not the exegesis of a 'sacred' book. On the contrary, orthodox refers exclusively to *method."*

Thus Marxism can and should be developed in light of new and different conditions. The Russian Marxist dissident Roy Medvedev (1975, p. xx) argues that "Marxism, in my view, is not some kind of dogma but a science that should be developed and enriched by new ideas and theories, while propositions that prove to be obsolete, one-sided, or even wrong must be discarded." And as to democracy, he is even more specific: "It is absolutely not true that Marxism and socialism are incompatible with democracy." He does note that "the works of neither Marx and Engels nor Lenin adequately deal with the complex problems involved [with democracy]" (ibid.), and calls for the development of democratic Marxist theory to fill this gap. Lamentably, this task has not yet been accomplished.

As Marxists like Lukacs strove to assert their independence and develop democratic theory and practice in Hungary in 1956 (Lukacs was minister of education in the short-lived Nagy government and was imprisoned and exiled for his involvement), they were brutally crushed by the Soviet juggernaut that had been fashioned by Joseph Stalin. Even more to the point, the vibrant, experimental, and very democratic Marxism (socialism with a human face) that was led by Alexander Dubcek in the Prague Spring of 1968 was also crushed by Soviet tanks before any of the theoretical or practical problems of democratizing Marxism could be resolved. A similar fate seems to have met many others who attempted to democratize Marxist theory or practice. For instance, when Rudolf Bahro (1978, esp. part 3) wrote his now famous work *Die Alternative* in 1977 and called for an emancipatory alternative to the bureaucratic socialism that had developed in Eastern Europe, he was first forced from the party in the German Democratic Republic and then forced into exile. The generally negative reception that such calls for a democratic, participatory alternative in Eastern Europe received made it difficult for creative Marxist thinkers everywhere and further retarded the development of democratic Marxist theory.

No form of democracy has been easy to achieve in the Latin American context. Although most Latin American nations have been republics for some 170 years (Brazil was an empire until 1889 and Cuba did not gain its independence until 1902), few have been able to achieve any consistent democracy and many have been influenced as much by outside forces as by the will of their own people. Nicaragua, for instance, experienced long periods of dictatorial rule, the frequent intervention of the Marines, and the seizure of power in the 1850s by a Yankee mercenary, William Walker, who declared himself president and designated English as the official language. Like most of Latin America, its history, institutions, and political culture were heavily imbued with authoritarianism and often influenced by some of the least democratic aspects of its large neighbor to the North.

If the first, nineteenth-century (bourgeois democratic) revolutions did not firmly root nominal Western democracy in all of Latin America, many hoped that the second (socialist) revolutions would break the authoritarian tradition and interject vibrant forms of people's democracy into the political milieu. Indeed, Fidel Castro and Ché Guevara dreamt of a continental revolution that would forge free and independent socialist republics in which the people could rule their destinies. But their dream has been difficult to realize. First, other socialist revolutions were not immediately triumphant. Second, as Cuba gained more autonomy and freedom as an independent nation, the constant economic and political pressure from the United States combined with other factors to prevent it from transcending its authoritarian political culture or setting aside the antidemocratic influences from Eastern Europe. Cuba did not begin to hold elections or provide other forms of democratic participation for more than a decade after the revolutionary triumph. Reforms in the mid-1970s did, however, institutionalize regularized local elections and initiate a series of new structures and procedures (popular power in particular) that facilitated greater participation and decisionmaking power for the Cuban masses, though mostly at the lower level (see Harnecker 1980). These reforms and the participation they engendered represented a new and different attempt to keep alive the democratic ideal in Latin America— this time in a state that was well along the path of socialist construction. Michael Lowy (1986, p. 270) observed that "popular power in Cuba represents a real democratic advance in the transition to socialism and an example that should be carefully studied." But like its Eastern European counterparts, Cuba was still struggling with authoritarian and bureaucratic party rule. Nor did the constant pressure from the United States diminish the perceived need for an authoritarian state. The popular power movement did interject an element of democracy at the local level. Decisionmaking at the national level, however, was still far removed from direct control by the people. No national leaders were elected directly by the people or by their mass organizations.

This reality and the growing bureaucratization of Cuban society led many to wonder if the construction of socialist states in Latin America would actually enhance the practice of democracy. The triumph of progressive forces in Chile in 1970 suggested that even more traditional forms of Western-style democracy might allow some Latin American nations with more firmly established democratic political cultures and institutions to use these to construct socialism and stimulate even greater participation by the popular masses. The flowering of democracy and socialism during the Allende years proved inspirational for many Latin Americans. In the eyes of many, Chile even began to serve as a model of democratic socialism in Latin America. However, the bloody 1973 coup and the Pinochet dictatorship that followed suggested that Western democracy and socialism might not be compatible at all and that more authoritarian measures might be necessary to ensure the continuation of socialism and even the possibility of more expansive democracy at a later time.

The triumph of the Sandinista revolution in Nicaragua in July 1979 established a state that valued its freedom and independence highly. The Sandinista revolution was clearly under the hegemony of a Marxist vanguard party, but it was also dedicated to the democratic incorporation of the Nicaraguan people and—because of the broad-based, multiclass composition of the coalition of forces that toppled Anastasio Somoza—to democratic pluralism. Although buffeted by the residual effects of the revolution against Somoza and the increasing hostility of the United States after 1981, there was (in varying degrees) a commitment to building both democracy and socialism in the new state.

The case of Nicaragua thus posed an important question: can a Latin American—or Third World—nation, struggling to achieve a larger degree of freedom and independence, sustain relatively high degrees of both democracy and socialism? And more specifically, can democracy exist within a state that is based on a nationalist variant of Third World Marxism? Even some writers who are sympathetic to the socialist enterprise are ready to acknowledge the difficulty of achieving democracy in this context. Orlando Núñez Soto and Roger Burbach (1986, p. 106) admit that the "majority of socialist countries . . . have not been ideal political or cultural democracies." They note that such regimes have been plagued by authoritarianism, vertical bureaucratic tendencies, and elitist behavior (ibid.). Recently, even some Soviet writers—enlivened no doubt by perestroika—suggested that the reason Joseph Stalin was able to impose an absolute authoritarianism on the Soviet nation so easily was that the original Bolshevik Party contained centralized tendencies that facilitated this process (see Keller 1988). One writer went so far as to suggest that "the sternest indictment of state socialism is its stifling of grass-roots initiative" (ibid.). Writing from a critical perspective, Medvedev (1981, esp. chap. 2) suggested that such tendencies may even be inherent in some, though not all, of Lenin's thought. Further, and perhaps more precisely, the initial variant of Latin American Marxism that was championed by the Comintern and eventually adopted by virtually all the orthodox Marxist parties in Latin America was that of a rather traditional Soviet authoritarian conception of socialism that left little room for democratic initiative of any kind (see NACLA 1987, Caballero 1987, Vanden 1986). It emphasized the centralization of power and the key and unchallenged role of the vanguard party. The advocates of this position were hesitant to concede too much power to the people themselves and were thus less than trusting of peasant-led revolutionary movements or populism generally (see Vanden 1986, Hodges 1986).

In Latin America there were a few early Marxist innovators like José Carlos Mariátegui (Peru, 1894–1930), but they had not been successful in breaking away the Latin American Marxist movement from Soviet-centric (if not Stalin-dominated) dogmatic authoritarianism. Half a century later Carlos Fonseca Amador and the other Sandinista leaders were finally able to enjoy a great deal more success in a very different historical period. Formulating theory and praxis in a small peripheral society in the 1960s, 1970s, and 1980s, a second generation of Sandinista leaders broke with this past (and the orthodox Nicaraguan Socialist Party) to develop a different kind of Marxism—one that was much less constrained and could take full advantage not only of polycentrism and Eurocommunism, but of the democratic, participatory dimension of the New Left in the West, the experiment with socialist democracy in Chile, and the popular power movement in Cuba. The historic reality in which the construction of socialism in Nicaragua occurred was thus radically different from that of other Third World nations.

Unlike the stolid, bureaucratized state socialism that Stalin and his followers had developed in the Soviet Union and Eastern Europe, that which was developing in Nicaragua was much more in touch with the democratic, popular dimension of Marxism. As such, it offered many new possibilities. Founding Sandinista National Liberation Front (FSLN) members Carlos Fonseca Amador and Tomás Borge had brief, problematic associations with the pro-Soviet, Nicaraguan Socialist Party but had not stayed with the party because they believed its (Stalinist) version of Marxism was not a viable example of how Marxism should be developed in Nicaragua. When Borge was exiled in Peru, Fonseca Amador told him to seek out Esteban Pavletich. The Peruvian had served as Augusto César Sandino's secretary and had been the primary link between Sandino's struggle and the iconoclastic group of Peruvian Marxist-Leninists led by Mariátegui. In talking with Pavletich about Mariátegui, Borge was utilizing one of the few sources of authentic Latin Marxism and symbolically laying the groundwork for the development of a non-Stalinist Marxism in Nicaragua. Indeed, Borge's view of Mariátegui (who was eventually condemned by the Soviets in the 1930s) was that "he was the most important Marxist that Latin America produced." Conversely, he was openly critical of other Latin American Marxists who had dogmatically followed the Soviet line.[6] The Sandinistas hoped to break with the old authoritarian Marxism that had dominated the movement in and outside of Latin America. To do so they realized that they must infuse their ideology and politics with a strong dose of popular democracy. However, it was not always easy to decide just which forms of democracy were optimal or applicable.

Capitalist and Socialist Conceptions of Democracy

"Democracy" derives from *demos,* the people, and *kratos,* the exercise of power. In its original sense it means power of the people (Medvedev 1975, p. 31). American academic Samuel Huntington (1989, p. 12) suggests that "democracy can be defined in terms of who rules, for what ends and by what means." In its most radical sense, it is, as Abraham Lincoln said, a government of the people, and by the people, and for the people. Unlike other types of government, it claims to allow the people themselves to rule, to make the decisions that govern their lives, and "all reasonable people, when they speak of democracy, mean a system in which collective decisions, i.e., the decisions which affect the whole community, are taken by all interested parties" (Bobbio 1976, p. 111). They are to decide their own destiny through their participation in the political process.

Although democracy in the abstract has few detractors, there is no unanimity of opinion on exactly which forms of political participation are essential for democracy or precisely which political institutions best allow the demos to have a say in the governmental process. Richard Fagen (1986, p. 258) believes that there must be effective participation by individuals and groups in the decisions that most affect their lives, a system of accountability such that leaders and officials can be monitored and changed if necessary, and political equality so that all have an equal opportunity to participate in the political process.

Upon closer examination, one finds not one, but several visions of democracy.[7] These include representative democracy as practiced in Western nations, people's democracy as practiced in many Marxist-Leninist states, and direct or participatory democracy as practiced by young students and workers in Paris in 1968 and by the people of Prague in the spring of 1968. There is also growing interest in grass-roots democracy, especially as manifest in the worker self-management and neighborhood control movements. But as different types of democracy proliferate, agreement on what is essential to democracy is more difficult to achieve. Thus, groups that hold one form particularly dear are often loath to admit that other forms might also tap other dimensions of democracy.

In North America and Western Europe some have been very skeptical of the kind or degree of democracy allowed by governmental structures that are not identical to their own. Thus many believed that Nicaragua, because it was guided by a party that considered itself socialist, could not possibly harbor democracy (see U.S. Dept. of State 1987). Socialists have been equally critical of Western-style representative democracy. Lenin (1971, pp. 295–296), for instance, argued that the real essence of bourgeois parliamentarianism was "to decide once every few years which member of the ruling class is to repress and crush the people through parliament." Accordingly, he and many Marxists believed that elections and formal parliamentary institutions did not guarantee democracy either. Rather, they believed such formal institutions must be transformed into working bodies—like Marx's original vision of the Paris Commune of 1871 or the original local soviets in 1917—that allowed the people to have a direct say in the making of policy (ibid., pp. 296–297; see also Marx 1960, 1978).

As we examine what democracy means, it may be possible to find some similarities in the ways in which democracy is conceived and practiced in socialist and capitalist states. Like John Locke, Marx did not like government and planted the idea—which Lenin developed—that the state apparatus should disappear ("wither away" in Lenin's words). Like Jefferson, he saw government as a necessary evil to be endured only in a transitional stage of socialism while the material bases of class differentiation were eliminated. As the polity moved to a more advanced stage of socialism (communism) it would no longer be necessary to have a government, and the people would rule directly. Indeed, he thought he saw the seeds of such rule when he observed the popular assemblies in the Paris Commune in 1871.

Both Marx and Jefferson trusted the people and thought that they would rule wisely and justly under the right conditions. Neither thought that rule should be far removed from the people, and both believed the interests and opinion of the majority should be the final arbiter. Although their modern-day disciples have often found themselves in opposition, Marx and Jefferson shared a similar view of human nature and democracy, if not government as well. Like the French thinker Jean-Jacques Rousseau, both men saw an inherent goodness in all human beings. This led them to place their faith in the people and their inherent ability to control their affairs. They did not think that others should be forever ordained to govern for them. Responding to Rousseau's introductory remarks in *The Social Contract,* that while born free people are everywhere in chains, Marx ends the *Communist Manifesto* with his now-famous observation that the proletariat has a world to win and nothing to lose but its chains. Nor did Jefferson—who thought rebellion every twenty years or so was salutary to the body politic—believe that the freedom of the people should be usurped by an elite.[8] As he put it shortly before he died in the summer of 1826, "the light of science has already laid open to every view the palpable truth that the mass of mankind has not been born with saddles on their backs, nor a favored few booted and spurred ready to ride them ..." (in Padover 1956, p. 344).

Jefferson hated monarchy and aristocracy and believed in the people: "My most earnest wish is to see the republican element of popular control pushed to the maximum of its practicable exercise." Only then could government be "pure and perpetual." The writer of the Declaration of Independence thought government should be minimal and always under the control of the people. Although he accepted representative government (as contrasted to direct rule by the people) as a necessity, because he believed it was not possible to have direct government in entities that were much larger than New England townships, he thought that such governing should be by the citizens "acting directly and personally, according to rules established by the majority." Further, the degree of rule by the people should be judged in proportion to the "direct action of its citizens," and the next best thing to pure democracy is where people in branches of government "are chosen by the people more or less directly" (in Padover 1939, p. 39).

At one point Jefferson went so far as to propose a ward system for Virginia, wherein everyone could be "an acting member of the common government, transacting in person a great portion of its rights and duties" (in Lobel 1988, p. 824). In that tradition, many nineteenth-century American radicals rejected the whole system of representative government and argued that laws should be passed by referendum. They believed that the population should participate directly in the governmental decisionmaking process (ibid.).

The origins of this pure view of democracy extend back through Rousseau to classical Greece where it was assumed that all qualified individuals would not only vote but would directly engage in government through selection by lot or through voluntary participation. Initially, however, the enfranchised demos was a very select group comprised of men who were large landowners or had other means of wealth that allowed them the time to pursue the affairs of state (all women, slaves, and those of lesser means were excluded). When democracy was reborn and developed after the American Revolution, the categories and numbers of those so enfranchised were gradually widened. As European systems were reformed to include more political participants, the idea of some type of rule by the people gained legitimacy and wider acceptance. Gradually its forms (though not necessarily its radical essence) spread to more distant parts of Europe and Latin America in the nineteenth century. By the second half of the twentieth century, the concept of participation in elections and other democratic enterprises by virtually all the citizens was widely accepted.

Classical or orthodox theories of democracy are strongly premised on real popular participation in the governmental process. Commitment to this theory of democracy therefore implies a belief in the desirability and necessity of widespread popular participation. Likewise, the corollary is that low levels of political interest and participation result from inadequacies in the structures or opportunities for participation that exist in a particular polity and not from any inherent inadequacies in the people themselves (see Osbun 1985, p. 29). Classical democratic thinkers like Rousseau (as well as Jefferson) are therefore seen as theorists par excellence of participation as an integral part of democracy. They also hold that equality and economic independence are the minimum conditions necessary for such democratic participation. For thinkers like Rousseau and John Stuart Mill, "participation has far wider functions and is central to the establishment and maintenance of the democratic polity" (Pateman 1970, p. 20).

This vision of democracy runs through American history and was manifest in populist leaders like Andrew Jackson and in populist movements. It also can be seen in the widening of the voting franchise and in the institutionalization of and recourse to initiative, referendum, and recall that blossomed in the late nineteenth and early twentieth centuries (see Goodwyn 1976, Salvatore 1982, Hahn 1983). In his work on direct democracy, Thomas Cronin (1989, pp. 19–20) finds that these reform movements gradually opened up the American political system to allow more direct democracy and that such manifestations "have been a lasting and generally positive part of the American landscape" (p. 2). Recent manifestations include the calls for direct democracy by students in the 1960s and the current movements in favor of grass-roots, neighborhood, and workplace democracy. Although not as prevalent as Jefferson might have hoped, democracy based on widespread popular participation has its advocates and supporters (see, for instance, Bachrach and Baratz 1962 and Bachrach 1967). It is still practiced in the New England town meeting and in isolated areas like the Swiss Canton of Apenzell, where the local populace meet around an ancient tree once a year to decide what will be done in the twelve months that follow (Woodstock 1971, pp. 12–13).[9]

But there is another strain of democracy that emerged in the West. In the United States, the writers of *The Federalist Papers* did not think that direct participation of the mass of the people in government was always possible or desirable. Rather they believed that the people should be represented by those who understood the true needs of the republic (those with wealth and/or position). James Madison did not even think that representatives had to be tied directly to the interests of the electorate (Lobel 1988, pp. 828–829).

When arguing for strengthening the federal government, Alexander Hamilton (*The Federalist Papers, Federalist 35,* 1952) is even more clear: "The actual representation of all classes of the people by persons of each class, is altogether visionary." Hamilton further assumed a commonality of interest between all those who labored in a particular sector of society regardless of their particular wealth. To his way of thinking, the poorest tenant and wealthiest landlord had a common interest (Lobel 1988, pp. 828–829). As suggested elsewhere in *The Federalist Papers,* there have been those who did not think direct democracy was necessary and further believed that chosen representatives (who might come from the well-heeled) could represent the interests of all. Democracy was thus equated with representative government. And after 1787–1788, many held that "democracy meant not government by and of the people, but simply representative government" (ibid., p. 830).

On the other hand, there was considerable concern that the new, more centralized constitutional structure of the United States government would remove power from the hands of the people. *The Federalist Papers* were in large part written to calm such popular fears. The author of *Federalist 57* (*The Federalist Papers* 1952, pp. 176–179) spends a considerable amount of time answering the charge that the leadership of this new government "will be taken from that class of citizens which will have least sympathy with the mass of the people, and be most likely to aim at an ambitious sacrifice of the many to the aggrandizement of the few." *Federalist 55 (The Federalist Papers* 1952, p. 172) also attempts to refute the charge that the House of Representatives "will be taken from the class of citizens which will sympathize least with the feelings of the masses of the people, and be most likely to aim at a permanent elevation of the few on the depression of the many." John Adams wanted forms of government that stressed avoiding the excesses of pure or direct democracy (Cronin 1989, p. 15). The constitutional structure provided the framework for a system of indirect democracy and minimized the tradition of direct democracy that was as old as the English settlements in North America (ibid., p. 1). Popular concerns about such exclusionary visions of democracy did not, however, stop the constitutional structure from being implemented in 1789. This set in motion an emphasis on indirect forms of democracy and a deemphasis on popular participation. Over time this has evolved into a system where there is less and less popular participation.

In a current version of Hamilton's thinking, George Will argued that the "people are not supposed to govern; they are not supposed to decide issues. They are supposed to decide who will decide" (in ibid., p. 21). But even participation in elections (deciding who will decide) is declining. In recent local elections in the United States, an average of fewer than 20 percent of those registered voted. In the presidential election of 1984, only 53 percent of the eligible voters participated. In the 1988 election the figure was reduced to 50 percent, meaning that some 26 percent of the eligible electorate in the United States chose the president. Only 36 percent of the electorate voted in the 1990 midterm election. This evolution has prompted many writers to be critical of what is currently termed democracy in the United States and to suggest that it is far from majoritarian rule (Parenti 1983).

In his recent article "America as a Model for the World? A Skeptical View," Ted Robert Gurr (1991, p. 665) notes that "empowered political minorities can block concerted action" on major policy issues such as medical care and social services for those in need. In *America: What Went Wrong?* Donald Barlett and James B. Steele (1992, p. ix) note how the concentration of wealth and power has derailed American democracy. They observe that the "wage and salary structure of American business, encouraged by federal tax policies, is pushing the nation toward a two-class society. The top 4 percent make as much as the bottom half of U.S. workers." Such trends at least suggest that some care should be taken in holding up this form of democracy as a perfect model that should be emulated at all cost by developing nations like Nicaragua. Indeed Greider (1992) finds that American democracy has been betrayed.

Revisions of classical democracy have found their theorists in more modern times. In his well-known work *Capitalism, Socialism and Democ-*

racy, Joseph Schumpter (1943, p. 283) argues that the "electoral mass is incapable of action other than stampede." Similarly, he believes participation no longer has a central role in the democratic process (see Pateman 1970, p. 5). Another revisionist theorist even suggested that limited participation and apathy have a positive function because they cushion the shock of disagreement, adjustment, and change.[10]

These writers were expressing unease with that manifestation of the beliefs of the masses that Rousseau (1952, esp. book 2) termed the popular will (*volonté populaire*), which is sometimes equated with unreflective or unenlightened public opinion. It is assumed that there is also a general will (*volonté général*) that represents a (more enlightened and) more informed common interest. "The general will alone can direct the State according to the object for which it was instituted, i.e., the common good" (ibid., p. 395). And, "what makes the will general is less the number of votes than the common interest among them" (ibid., p. 397). The democratic revisionists believed that different forms of indirect, representative democracy could express the interest of the people (represent their general interest) as well as or better than direct democracy. But there is more to Rousseau's thinking. He stipulates that the will is only general if it is the will of the entire body of the people, while it is not when it is only the will of a part of it. And further, "there is often a great deal of difference between the will of all and the general will; the latter considers only the common interest, while the former takes private interest into account, and it is no more than a sum of particular wills . . ." (ibid., p. 396). Thus many of the democratic revisionists assume that a class of representatives may be able to ascertain the general will for the people even though the government itself may not precisely be of the people. That is, a group not of the people can decide for the people.

The idea of a small group deciding for the many is not limited to revisionist theorists of Western democracy. This concept has perhaps its most perfect articulation in Lenin's conception of the vanguard party as that entity that best understands the needs of the majority (the working class in the modern, increasingly industrialized world) and is therefore most competent to implement policy that benefits it. The theoretical underpinning of the Leninist party is premised on the assumption that the vanguard can know the general will of the people. With the revisionist thinkers in the West, little attempt is made to distinguish between a general will that—no matter how hard to know—considers only the common interest and a will of all that *is no more than a sum of particular wills* (ibid.).

One is here reminded of the work of Robert Dahl, one of the most prominent current revisionist theorists of democracy. Dahl (1956, p. 143) found that as long as there are representatives of each group involved in the decisionmaking process in some (not necessarily effective) way, representative democracy is alive and well: "In American politics, as in all other societies, control over decisions is unevenly distributed; neither individuals nor groups are political equals. . . . Thus the making of governmental decisions is not a majestic march of great majorities united upon certain matters of basic policy. It is the steady appeasement of relatively small groups" (ibid., p. 164). In Dahl's original conceptualization of democracy (polyarchy), the rule of multiple minorities was presented as a model of what works in the American political system (and what is therefore desirable).[11] Under Dahl's system, all the people were not involved in the decisionmaking process, only some of their representatives were consulted on some issues. This is a far cry from the classical vision of democracy that sees all of the demos participating in the vital decisionmaking processes of government. Yet this view has been widely accepted as an accurate description of representative democracy in the United States and (implicitly) as a model for democratic government. In such systems, participation has no central role. All that is necessary is that enough citizens participate to keep the electoral machinery working (Pateman 1970, p. 5).[12]

This commonly accepted view of democracy in the West is problematic. First, it contradicts the clear participatory dimension of democracy found in classical Greece and in Rousseau's and Jefferson's writings; second, it assumes that educating the masses for their central role in the decisionmaking process is not necessary or important. Writers from Rousseau to John Dewey have underscored the importance of education, informed deliberation, and participation in the democratic process and hold them essential to the effective functioning of democracy. L. Davis (1964, pp. 40–41) underscores the importance of these processes and argues that participation has an ambitious purpose:

> the education of the entire people to the point where their intellectual, emotional, and moral capabilities have reached their full potential and they are joined freely and actively in a genuine community. . . .

Systems that do not achieve such education, popular deliberation, and involvement do not, we believe, realize their full potential and therefore could be considered singularly ill-suited as models of democratic government. The bureaucratized socialism of Eastern Europe—though it did provide education—afforded little popular deliberation and less meaningful participation. In the United States, there is much popular deliberation, but the quality of education often diminishes its effectiveness. Over the past few decades, there has been less and less participation in most forms of governance, while economic and political power has become more and more concentrated. Gurr (1991, p. 666) has noted that policymaking in the United States has not made for the most egalitarian of societies:[13]

> Between 1977 and 1988 the after-tax income of the poorest fifth dropped 10%, of the next poorest fifth, it dropped 3%. At the other end of the scale the household income of the richest fifth increased 34%. And for the top one percent it increased 122%.

Barlett and Steele (1992, esp. chap. 9) suggest that the political process in the United States is increasingly responding more to wealth and influence than popular need or participation. According to federal statistics released in early 1992, the top 1 percent of households in the United States had greater net worth than the bottom 90 percent of households by 1989 (*New York Times* 1992, p. 1).

In contrast to the concentration of wealth and influence and declining participation in the United States, classical or full democracy considers participation essential. Moreover, democracy that is participatory is founded on two complementary notions: "that people are inherently capable of understanding their problems and expressing themselves about these problems and their solutions" and that "real solutions to problems require the fullest participation of the people in these solutions, with the development of freedom from dependency on authorities and experts" (Oppenheimer 1971, p. 277). The idea is to create a polity in which everyone will participate to the fullest in decisions that concern their everyday or long-range affairs. The process of decisionmaking, therefore, is as important as the actual immediate decision made.

Thus one is led to ask the more difficult questions of if and where adequate models of full democracy exist. As he explored this question along the way to the formulation of a new democratic theory, Megill (1970, p. 44) observed that, in different ways, the liberal democrats in the West and the Stalinists in Eastern Europe have each "diverted democracy from its basic tradition of rule by the people." In the socialist countries, the people have been replaced by the party, which is in turn controlled by the party organization (ibid.). Leninist and therefore Communist views of democracy flow from the model of the Marxist-Leninist Party that developed in Russia and the relation of the party to the society. This party was successful in seizing power, but it failed as an instrument for the thoroughgoing democratization of society, particularly as it developed under Stalin's rule (ibid., p. 43). This is ironic because, from his earliest writings, "Marx was committed to the idea of direct democracy. His early conception of such democracy involved a Rousseauesque critique of the principles of representation . . ." and he held the view that "true democracy involves the disappearance of the state and thus the separation of the state from civil society" (Bottomore et al. 1983, p. 114).

Marx was greatly inspired by the Paris Commune of 1871, which took the management of the revolution into its hands. In it, "plain working men [and women] for the first time dared to infringe upon the Governmental privilege of their 'natural superiors' [in Jefferson's terms, those who thought themselves born "booted and spurred" to ride the masses] and, under circumstances of unexamined difficulty, performed their work modestly, conscientiously, and efficiently . . ." (in Marx 1978, p. 636).

In Marx's mind, the Commune—which was more advanced than the communes that developed in the Middle Ages and was in part inspired by the first French Commune of 1792 (which Jefferson championed)—was the first glimpse of how democracy might work in a socialist society. It was formed by municipal councillors who were chosen by universal suffrage in each ward and were "responsible and revokable at short terms." The majority were working people or their acknowledged representatives. The Commune itself was to be "a working, not a parliamentary body, executive and legislative at the same time" (ibid., p. 632). And (ibid., p. 633)

> In a rough sketch of national organization which the Commune had no time to develop, it states clearly that the Commune was to be the political form of even the smallest hamlet, and that in the rural districts the standing army was to be replaced by a national militia, with an extremely short term of service. The rural communes of every district were to administer their common affairs by an assembly of delegates in the central town, and these district assemblies were again to send deputies to the National Delegation in Paris, each delegate to be at any time revocable and bound by the *mandat impératif* (formal instructions) of his constituents. The few but important functions which still would remain for a central government . . . were to be discharged by Communal, and therefore strictly responsible agents. The unity of the nation was not to be broken, but, on the contrary, to be organized by the Communal Constitution. . . .

The people would decide most issues directly at the commune level and would send their direct, recallable representatives to provincial and national assemblies that would in turn decide those issues that could not be handled at the local level. The legitimate functions of government were to be restored to the responsible agents of society, the common people. This system would be very different from old representative institutions, where every three or six years it was decided "which member of the ruling class was to misrepresent the people in Parliament" (ibid.). Lest there be any misunderstanding, Marx explicitly states that "nothing could be more foreign to the spirit of the Commune than to supersede universal suffrage by hierarchical investiture" (ibid.). Throughout history there have been a few other examples of direct communal rule, starting with the original Christian communities and including the communes formed in Republican Spain by the socialists and anarchists during the Spanish Civil War. The *kibbutzim* in Israel are perhaps the most widely known and successful example (Woodstock 1971, p. 21).

In socialist thought, democracy is thus conceived as popular democracy in which—as with Rousseau and Jefferson—the majority rules. According to the Marxist conception of democracy, majority rule means rule by the poorer classes (in those societies that have not yet achieved advanced socialism) since they are by definition the majority (see Kiss 1982, chaps. 1, 2). Some analysts go on to say that democracy is class determined and thus does not exist if the popular classes (where there are still classes) do not rule (ibid., pp. 11–12). But others, who followed Lenin's ideas and were influenced by Stalin, did not see democracy as an end in itself. It was a means of achieving social emancipation. Like the socialist revolution, it was a means of achieving liberation (ibid., p. 122). The revolution was to break down the machinery of class domination and allow a dictatorship of the proletariat to rule for the working people while the structure of the new society was developing. Such a class dictatorship was only considered necessary until the old bourgeois state could be replaced by the classless society, at which time the people would rule directly as the state withered away.

According to Lenin, the vanguard party was to lead the people in the socialist revolution and guide the state while the new society was being constructed. But Lenin's ideas very much flowed from the Russian political culture that produced his thought. Hannah Arendt (1958) notes, for instance, that the revolution occurred in a country with a well-established centralized bureaucracy. Russia had a very authoritarian culture, and "it stands to reason that if any aspect of social life can directly affect government it is the experience with authority that men [and women] have" (H. Eckstein as cited in Pateman 1970, p. 12). The historic conditions in which the first experiment in socialist rule developed influenced not only Soviet Marxism, but—because of the influence of the Soviet Union—the way in which socialist thought and praxis developed elsewhere. Commenting on the relative lack of democracy in the Soviet Union and Eastern Europe, Mihailo Markovic (1982, pp. 171–173) also notes that the political culture included elements of "Byzantine-Oriental societies" that did little to instill the libertarian values that foster democracy. Rather they added to the authoritarian influences that imprinted the development of Marxism.

The first days of the Russian revolution were exciting and dynamic. Workers' councils or soviets took control of neighborhoods and factories in St. Petersburg, much the same way the people had formed communes in Paris during the first days of the French Revolution of 1792 and the

Paris Commune of 1871. Democracy was alive, direct, and vibrant. The people themselves were exerting their rule. As the revolution raged on and foreign powers cut off the infant socialist state economically and sent expeditionary forces to overthrow it, conditions were considered to be such that more authoritarian measures were needed. Democracy became restricted as the people ruled less and less directly. Lenin, however, believed that democracy could be reinstituted after the revolution was no longer threatened (Medvedev 1975, p. 43). He held that if "during the transition period from capitalism to socialism there are some restrictions on democracy (and the extent of these restrictions must be gradually reduced), nonetheless with the full victory of socialism all restrictions on political democracy fall away" (in ibid., p. 31). Indeed, Lenin said, "The victory of socialism is impossible without the realization of democracy" (ibid.).

But for Lenin the structure and the vanguard role of the party were fundamental. In the 1920s there was considerable discussion of how the party would be organized and exactly what relation it would have to the exercise of power by other segments of the society. Before he died in 1924, Lenin had already begun to express concern about the role of bureaucracy. In this context, the question of party organization was central, but by then what had come to be called democratic centralism had been accepted. Ironically, although designed to democratize the functioning of the party, in reality it did not allow any real discussion of the issues or contact with the revolutionary movement as manifest in the toiling masses (Megill 1970, p. 43).

After Lenin's death there was even less opportunity for discussion. As Stalin consolidated his power, he came to view any opposition as a hostile bourgeois influence that had to be resisted (Medvedev 1975, p. 44). Thus not only was popular democracy discouraged, but dissent was not tolerated. The heady democracy of the first days of the revolution was increasingly replaced by bureaucratic authoritarian party rule. The Left opposition tried to resist these trends inside the Soviet Union. They were not successful and, like Leon Trotsky, many were killed.

Although many other socialists objected to Stalinism, they did not object to the "paternalistic justification of systematic antidemocratic measures of some form" (Cunningham 1987, p. 274). Lenin believed that the Communist Party was best equipped to know the general will of the people and rule on their behalf. Stalin evidently came to believe that he was best suited to decide important issues in the party. Thus a party bureaucracy that was increasingly dominated by one person began to rule in the name of the people. These decisions were ostensibly made to safeguard if not save the revolution from its internal and external enemies. Practical necessity was cited as the rationale. In theoretical terms, it was argued that certain tactical decisions were necessary but that their implementation and effect were temporal. Megill (1970, p. 62) holds that the effects were much more far-reaching: they led to a theoretical failure of Stalinism that in turn crippled the democratic Marxist tradition because it failed to "distinguish between purely tactical considerations—practical considerations, which may be more or less correct at a given moment—and the theoretical development of Marxism."

The Hungarian Marxist Georg Lukacs is equally clear on this issue: "In other words: instead of following the true method of Marxism and developing a strategy and tactics from an analysis of events, tactical decisions—right or wrong decisions—were decisive, and a theory was built on these" (cited in ibid., p. 62). Lukacs further argues (ibid., p. 55) that

> The tremendous historical guilt of Stalinism exists in the fact that not only was scientific development not followed up, but this development went backwards. Stalin hindered just those tendencies which would have been capable of developing Marxism.

As Marxist theory and practice developed in the Soviet Union and those areas of the world that were modeled after it, its democratic and participatory dimensions were generally neglected if not directly subordinated to immediate concerns as defined by the party leadership. In the West, representative democratic institutions became bulwarks against direct and majority participation in government, which in turn laid the basis for the transformation of these institutions into paternalistic organs of minority rule (Cunningham 1987, p. 276). In socialist countries similar processes occurred (ibid., p. 356). The paternalistic vanguardism of the party was substituted for the direct rule of the people that Marx glimpsed in the Paris Commune. Although party congresses and even elections were held in the peoples' democracies, the demos was ruled much more than it ruled. Milovan Djilas (1957, 1962) has suggested that a "new class" of rulers had developed in such societies and that they had usurped popular rule. The state did not wither away and democracy did not develop. Stalin even argued that the state must be strengthened greatly before it could wither away (Bottomore et al. 1983, p. 463). Elaborate rationalizations attempted to show how the people were actually being served because the party was deciding on their behalf by setting the agenda and limiting the number of candidates for whom the people voted in elections.[14] As had been done by Dahl and other revisionist theorists of democracy in the West, theory was elaborated to explain how (some) democracy actually did exist in the status quo, even though that reality was lacking when it came to real democracy and democratization. In both instances, it seemed it was much easier to change, modify, or reinterpret the theory than it was to change the status quo and actually allow the people to have power.

Many who wrote from a Marxist perspective did not realize that there was a confluence of interests and perspective on the part of the hierarchies of both Eastern socialism and Western capitalist democracy. They were both heavily invested in the status quo and reluctant to allow any change. As with the bureaucratization of the state and party in Eastern Europe, several scholars have noted that there has been an historical proliferation of bureaucracy and bureaucratic thought in U.S. institutions. Decisions and initiatives for problem solving have come more and more from the center, thus discouraging local participation (see, inter alia, Wiebe 1967, Higgs 1987, and Lasch 1979, 1991). The elite in Eastern Europe criticized the economic and political marginalization of the majority in capitalist democracy but would not institute genuinely democratic institutions at home. The establishment in the West would criticize the elitist rule in socialist states while allowing economic and political elites to exercise increasingly more power at home and the masses to participate less and less. Neither moved to increase democracy. Both argued that the people were better off in their respective system and insisted theirs was the model to copy.

Despite the poverty of democratic examples in both the capitalist West and socialist East, Nicaragua had set about the process of constructing real democracy within a socialist state. The Sandinista revolution had rediscovered Nicaragua's popular history and thus its popular consciousness; it had indeed unleashed the power of the masses. Unlike other revolutionary experiences, there was enough understanding among the Sandinistas, members of the popular church, Nicaraguan and internationalist youth, and others involved with the revolutionary process to set up institutional structures that included and channeled mass participation. The masses had not only been mobilized, they had found ways they could continue to express their will. But the reality was complex. On the one hand the Sandinista leadership was delighted to see "the people" (which was how they conceived the diverse, multiclass popular revolutionary force in Nicaragua) fully mobilized. On the other hand they feared that if they immediately held elections, the formal Western facade of institutional democracy that Somoza and many other traditional Central American leaders had manipulated to foreclose real and effective participation might well be the only democracy that would be allowed to develop. The Sandinista leaders were also well acquainted with Leninist thinking as to the vanguard role of the party and thus felt they had a special obligation to prepare the people by ensuring that their political consciousness was developed. The dominant role the party had assumed in the decisionmaking process in Cuba also helped to incline their thinking in more authoritarian directions. Because they also feared the influence of bourgeois elements inside the country, and in part because they could not totally break away from unconscious authoritarian beliefs (which resulted principally from Nicaraguan political history and culture), the Sandinista leadership, as principally manifested in the National Directorate, reserved a substantial amount of power to itself.

In the early 1980s, the creation of Western representative institutions was postponed and direct participation was encouraged. But an authoritarian decisionmaking trend was developing inside the party and among those Sandinista leaders who held key governmental posts. These tendencies and the increasing military and economic pressure exerted by the United States worked against the further empowerment of the demos through direct and continued participation. Nor were traditional models of democracy in Eastern Europe or the West helpful in this regard. Subsequent chapters will show how these factors interacted to produce a unique development of democracy within a socialist state. Like the mixed economy in which it developed, both representative and participatory democracy eventually operated side by side under the guidance of the democratic centralism of the FSLN. Indeed, it seems that there was continued competition among Western representative democracy, participatory democracy, and democratic centralism. It remains to be seen if the confluence of these factors actually caused democracy to flower in Sandinista Nicaragua, or if it stifled the construction of what might have been the first full-blown example of direct, participatory Marxist democracy.

Notes

1. Augusto César Sandino in *El pensamiento vivo,* Vol. 2 (1984, p. 72).
2. Thomas Jefferson in Padover (1939, p. 34).
3. The problem of existing models of socialism is explored in Lowy (1991).
4. Thus, the socialist states were willing to continue to support Nicaragua not only because they hoped it would eventually become more like their own systems, but because the Sandinistas proved to be a thorn in the side of U.S. hegemony, much the same as Yugoslavia (which was a founder of the Nonaligned Movement) had been for the USSR and the hegemony it exercised in Eastern Europe.
5. By the late 1920s, after V. I. Lenin's death in 1924, Joseph Stalin (1879–1953) consolidated his rule in the Soviet Union. By the early 1930s he emerged as the unchallenged Soviet leader. His increasingly dictatorial rule thwarted any attempts at democracy in the USSR. He continued in power until his death in 1953, his authoritarian version of Marxism continued to haunt the Soviet regime and those patterned after it in Eastern Europe and elsewhere. See Bottomore et al. (1983, pp. 460–464) and Deutscher (1949).
6. Vanden interview with Tomás Borge, Managua, December 7, 1984.
7. For an establishment understanding of democracy, see the opening editorial, "Why the Journal of Democracy," by Diamond and Plattner (1990, pp. 3–5). The journal was funded and established by the National Endowment for Democracy.

This definition includes peaceful competition for all effective positions in government through elections, independent political participation, and a high level of civil and political liberty as necessary conditions for democracy. It does not seem to require that all the people be involved (directly or indirectly) in the actual governmental process, or that decisions in government be representative of majority interests or even majority opinion. Some might even observe, cynically, that such a definition could classify as democratic a system in which the majority of those eligible to vote do not vote for their national leaders and in which many decisions seem increasingly to favor the interests of the wealthy and powerful over the poor and powerless: that is, a system that appears to have a representative democratic form but lacks actual democratic content and is no longer run by or for the majority of the people.

8. Writing to Madison in 1787, Jefferson observed: "I hold it, that a little rebellion, now and then, is a good thing, and as necessary in the political world as storms in the physical" (in Padover 1939, p. 19). Writing to William Smith that same year: "God forbid we should ever be twenty years without such a rebellion" (ibid., p. 20).

9. It should be noted, however, that in Switzerland the franchise was limited to males until 1971 and that this decision was resisted in Apenzell. Apenzell is a relic of one of the few successful peasant revolts (1408) in which the masses were able to rid themselves of their overlords.

10. Pateman's (1970, p. 7) assessment of B. R. Berelson.

11. In "Two Faces of Power" (1962), Bachrach and Baratz demonstrated how this form of democracy does not even include each group's representatives in the agenda-setting process and may only consult them on nonessential issues. See also Bachrach (1967).

12. Given the continual low voter turnout through the 1980s in the United States, it remains to be seen if even this minimalist definition of democracy has been met. See William Greider, *Who Will Tell the People: The Betrayal of American Democracy* (1992).

13. Interestingly, Gurr does not address the decline in electoral participation; nor do other authors in the special section of *PS,* "America as a Model for the World" (December 1991).

14. Ironically, Bachrach and Baratz argue that the elite in the United States uses similar tactics by limiting the range of choices that people actually have. See Bachrach and Baratz (1962, pp. 947–952).

❖ TWO ❖
The Genesis of Sandinismo

We could say that we did not invent the fundamental elements of our liberation ourselves. The vanguard gathered these ideas from Sandino, from our own people, and this is what enabled us to lead the people toward their liberty. We found political, military, ideological, and moral elements in our people, in our own history. . . .

—Humberto Ortega Saavedra[1]

The ideas that inspired the revolution in Nicaragua did not emerge full blown in the politically charged atmosphere that characterized Latin America after the Cuban Revolution. Rather, over the years, Sandinismo became an ideological vehicle through which a popular vision of the national past could be recaptured by the Nicaraguan masses. It became a means of empowerment and mobilization.

Before Sandinismo—and Sandino—Nicaragua was often reminiscent of García Márquez's (1971) tragic town of Macondo, a place where the people could not comprehend—let alone change—their present reality because they had lost their sense of history (see also Taylor 1975). Much of the time it seemed that many of the country's leaders did not even realize that the development of the nation was not the same as the aggrandizement of personal interest, or that cooperating with an expanding imperial presence would ultimately compromise national dignity and the nation itself. Even many who fought for the Liberal cause were like Colonel Aureliano Buendía in *One Hundred Years of Solitude*—they became mired in the struggle itself and lost sight of what they were fighting for. As suggested by García Márquez (in ibid., p. 110), "a consciousness of history is a necessary precondition for a society's survival and autonomous development."

The beginning of a modern national consciousness in Nicaragua that included the Indian and mestizo masses only emerged toward the end of the nineteenth century. This was more than a generation after the proslavery adventurer William Walker carried out the first in a long series of U.S. interventions in national affairs. Only then could a few intellectuals begin to look toward their distant indigenous past to rediscover their nation's historic identity and thus transcend the narrow Hispanicism that had often constrained national politics, thought, and literature and the masses generally.

Although the Liberal reform movement did not develop in Nicaragua until the late nineteenth century, it carried a vision of society similar to movements in Mexico (under Benito Juárez) and elsewhere in Latin America. José Santos Zelaya's Liberal Revolution of 1893 marked the beginning of the modern Liberal movement in Nicaragua. Although constrained by traditional European-style liberalism, he introduced some progressive ideas and began to challenge the traditional oligarchy and the power of the Catholic Church. His successful drive to recover the Atlantic Coast from British colonialism also stimulated the growth of a national consciousness. Supported by elements of the national bourgeoisie, Zelaya introduced reforms that soon alarmed the Conservative forces and threatened the interests of U.S. capital (which was evidently antagonistic to the growth of a vigorous, independent national capitalist class in Nicaragua).

As Zelaya faced increasing internal and external pressure, his regime degenerated into a dictatorship. In 1909, Washington forced him to resign before he could implement his plans to modernize Nicaragua. Thus the national bourgeoisie did not achieve the changes necessary to develop a modern nationalist capitalist system. Using various pretexts, the United States sent Marines in 1909 to reinstate Conservative rule and ensure the dominant position of U.S. capital. As U.S. intervention increased over the next years (the Marines were again landed in 1912 to prop up the puppet regime of Adolfo Díaz, and did not leave until 1925), anti-interventionist sentiment grew among the Nicaraguan people. This tended to radicalize many supporters of the Liberal movement, and even prompted a few Conservatives to join some thirty armed uprisings between 1906 and 1926 against U.S.-installed governments (Ortega 1980c, p. 10).

With the outbreak of a new Liberal uprising against a Conservative coup in 1925 and the U.S.-inspired reinstallation of Adolfo Díaz as president, the struggle began to take on clear nationalist and anti-imperialist overtones. The Marines once again intervened. It was at this point that Augusto César Sandino returned from Mexico and joined the now strongly nationalist Liberal struggle. Although Sandino (a mechanic) encountered open hostility from the upper-class head of the Liberal army, José M. Moncada, he was able to arm and organize his own Liberal band and participate in the increasingly successful offensive. The Liberal struggle was meeting with enthusiastic support from the masses, who were participating in growing numbers. But as these forces were in sight of a clear military victory, the United States arranged a compromise solution that was accepted by Moncada and eventually supported by all the Liberal generals, save one—Sandino. None of the bourgeois leaders supported Sandino. But large numbers of the peasants, miners, artisans, workers, and Indians who had fought with him followed him to the Segovias, a remote mountain region in the north.

From its inception, Sandino's struggle inspired and was supported by many members of the lower classes in Nicaragua. Sandino and his Army to Defend National Sovereignty were often forced to rely on little more than their own ingenuity and assistance from Nicaraguan popular sectors. Their fight became a popular national struggle.

Sandino (Ramírez 1979, pp. 87–88) articulated the movement's ideology when he argued that

> The tie of nationality gives me the right to take responsibility for my actions regarding Nicaragua, and therefore, Central America and the entire continent that speaks our tongue.... I am a worker from the city, an artisan as they say in my country. But my ideal is to be found on the broad horizon of internationalism, in the right to be free and demand justice.... That I am a plebeian, the oligarchs (that is, the swamp rats) will say. No matter—my greatest honor is to arise from among the oppressed who are the soul and nerve of the race, from those of us who have been left behind to live at the mercy of the shameless assassins who helped to inspire the crime of high treason: the Conservatives of Nicaragua....

Although a Nicaraguan who clearly identified with the Nicaraguan masses, Sandino also realized that Nicaragua's struggle was part of a larger movement: "at the present historical moment our struggle is national and racial [ethnic Latin American], it will become international as the colonial and semicolonial peoples unite with the peoples of the imperialistic nations" (in Macaulay 1967, p. 113; see also Conrad 1990). Sandino thus enjoyed an internationalist vision of a popular revolutionary nationalism that was linked to other revolutionary movements throughout the world: "It would not be strange for me and my army to find ourselves in any country of Latin America where the murderous invader had set his sights on conquest" (in Benito Escobar 1979, p. 5).[2]

The movement's leader was born in Niquinohomo, Nicaragua, in 1895, the illegitimate son of a reasonably successful landowner of Spanish descent and an Indian woman who worked for the Sandino family. Several experiences in his formative years contributed to his revolutionary outlook. One important incident was the mistreatment of his lower-class mother and her subsequent miscarriage in a horrid prison cell, where the young Sandino was forced to care for her. In 1912 Sandino witnessed the humiliation of General Benjamín Zeledón, who unsuccessfully fought against the U.S. Marine invasion. Sandino later recounted that the latter experience was crucial to the development of his strong Nicaraguan nationalism and his opposition to North American domination.

When Sandino shot and killed a man during an argument in 1920, he was forced to flee the country; in the process he came into contact with political movements that would shape his development. From 1923 to 1926 Sandino worked in a U.S.-owned oil company near Tampico, Mexico, first as a mechanic and later as a bookkeeper. It was a time when he became acquainted with the Mexican Revolution, the organized workers movement, and the role of North American companies there.[3] Political development in Mexico was far advanced from Sandino's native Nicaragua. When he arrived in the summer of 1923, the Mexican Revolution was only twelve years old, and political activity was alive in the seaport city. The anarcho-syndicalist Industrial Workers of the World (IWW) and Communist-led trade unions dominated the Tampico labor movement. In addition, religious currents, such as Freemasonry, that were favorable to the Mexican Revolution were active in the city. In Tampico there was a lodge of Freemasonry with a particularly radical bent, the Bolshevik Grand Lodge. Donald Hodges (1986) speculates that in Tampico Sandino developed a religious philosophy grounded in Freemasonry and spiritualism. For his part, Sandino (in ibid., p. 7) wrote:

> Around the year 1925 I succeeded in surrounding myself with a group of Spiritualist friends with whom I discussed daily the submission of our people in Latin America to either the hypocritical advances or violent interventions of the Yankee imperial assassin.

In Hodges's view, the single most important political influence on Sandino may have come from the writings and activities of one of the most radical of the Mexican revolutionaries, the anarcho-syndicalist Ricardo Flores Magón. Flores Magón was a leader of one revolutionary current of opposition to the dictatorship of Porfirio Díaz. In 1921 the General Confederation of Workers (CGT) was formed under the influence of Flores Magón's ideas, a blend of anarcho-communism and revolutionary syndicalism. Strongly influenced by earlier anarchist thinkers, such as the Russian Peter Kropotkin and the Italian Errico Malatesta, Flores Magón believed there was a common enemy of progress in the alliance of property, state, and church. He advocated a thoroughgoing social revolution based on economic equality, political liberty, and universal love. As a syndicalist, Flores Magón saw the possibility of achieving this revolution through the efforts of the workers' own organizations, their trade unions. Like other anarcho-syndicalists of that era, Flores Magón was favorable to both the Mexican and Russian revolutions. He was strongly supportive of Lenin and gave his backing to the Mexican peasant leader Emiliano Zapata.

While never rejecting his anarcho-communism, Sandino apparently gravitated more toward spiritualism in the last years of his life. In 1929 Sandino was drawn to both Freemasonry and to the "Light and Truth" doctrines of the magnetic spiritual school. Even as he was entrusting the archives of his Defending Army to the Masonic Grand Lodge he was embracing the rational philosophy of Joaquín Trincado and the spiritualist's philosophy of liberation that Trincado developed in the Argentine magnetic spiritual school.

Strongly rejecting established religion, Trincado developed a philosophy based on world communism, unitary law, and the universal presence of magnetic spiritualism. Opposed to the class division of society, magnetic spiritualism called for a communal fraternity with equal rights and duties to work and to consume. Such a society was to be achieved by the creation of worker-managed cooperatives. Sandino came in contact with these ideas in Tampico and later established a chapter of Trincado's organization in Nicaragua during his armed struggle. Hodges also demonstrates that Sandino's efforts to establish an agricultural cooperative in Wiwili during 1933–1934 were part of his attempt to implement the anarcho-Communist objectives of the school. Sandino's comments (in ibid. 1986, pp. 43–44) on the Wiwili efforts demonstrate the class-conscious nature of his views.

> Here I am dedicated to the founding of a society of mutual aid and universal fraternity. I want to put my grain of sand in favor of the emancipation and social well being of the working class which has always been exploited and looked down upon by the bureaucratic bourgeoisie.

Sandino's commitment to such radical social change and his affiliation with the anarcho-communism of the magnetic school demonstrate the inadequacy of any description of Sandino that labels him as simply a Nicaraguan nationalist and patriot.

While Sandino's personal political and intellectual development came primarily through the aforementioned philosophies—anarchism and magnetic spiritualism, his efforts to conduct a guerrilla struggle against the United States Marines also led him to have important contacts with the Communists and their organizations. Sandino was not a Communist, but he shared their desire to abolish exploitation and the capitalist system through a worldwide revolution of the oppressed. Actually, according to Neill Macaulay (1985, p. 157), three groups struggled for influence with Sandino's movement—the Mexican revolutionary government, the Communist International, and the Mexican-based American Popular Revolutionary Alliance (APRA). The APRA was founded in May 1924 in Mexico by Peruvian exile Victor Raúl Haya de la Torre. For a time, a Peruvian Aprista, Esteban Pavletich, served as Sandino's secretary.[4] However, the APRA was never a fully serious contender for Sandino's loyalties because it was not ideologically close to him nor did it succeed in raising much material aid in comparison to the Comintern or the Mexican government.

During the time when the APRA actively recruited Sandino, it was outmaneuvered by the Comintern acting through the Anti-Imperialist League of the Americas and the Mexican-based Hands Off Nicaragua Committee. The League saw Sandino as the leader of the most important liberation movement in the Western Hemisphere in the twentieth century and gave him all of the support they could muster. The League's representative to Sandino was the Salvadoran revolutionary Agustín Farabundo Martí, who reached the rank of colonel within Sandino's army and served for a time as Sandino's advisor. Martí's role as a representative of the Comintern was to convince Sandino to ally himself directly with the Comintern and to carry out its full program. Up to 1928, the Comintern pursued a broad alliance strategy that included solidarity with non-revolutionary forces in pursuit of bourgeois-democratic and nationalist goals. Sandino was in agreement with that strategy, and it was the basis of his unity with the Comintern. However, at its Sixth Congress in September 1928 the Comintern adopted a new strategy that abandoned cooperation with non-Communist elements. The shift was prompted by the failure of collaboration with the Kuomintang in China and imminent worldwide economic crisis which—it was believed—would allow the triumph of worldwide socialism. The policy ushered in the "ultra-left" period of the Comintern that would see Communists in Western Europe denounce the Social Democrats as "social fascists" and in Germany divide the workers movement, thus paving the way for Nazi power.

The Latin American Communist parties ratified the shift in policy in June 1929; soon after, Sandino, like his Peruvian supporter José Carlos Mariátegui, came into sharp conflict with Comintern representatives. In particular, the Mexican Communist Party—which broke with the Mexican revolutionary government in line with the new Comintern policy—looked with disfavor on Sandino's appeal to that government for support in the spring of 1930. Sandino was immediately attacked by the Mexican Communist Party as a "traitor to the cause of world anti-imperialism"(Hodges 1986, pp. 102–103). Realizing the importance of Comintern assistance to his movement, Sandino tried to restore friendly relations with the Communists, but they had chosen to cut him off. The Comintern denounced him in 1933 for agreeing to a truce and even attacked him posthumously in 1935. The final attack is ironic because at its Seventh Congress in August

1935, the Comintern rejected its own strategy of class confrontation and adopted a new strategy of popular front. In this reversal, the Comintern was self-critical of its earlier policies, but no apologies were made to Sandino. It is important to note that Fonseca Amador was fully aware of Sandino's problems with the Comintern. In writing of that period (1984b, p. 103) he blames the breakdown of solidarity with Sandino on the "inflexible sectarianism" of the Mexican Communist Party, which demanded that Sandino make statements against the Mexican government and then attacked him when he refused.

Sandino did not reject Marxist methodology or a commitment to communism, but only the self-defeating ultra-left strategy of the Comintern. He favored a broad alliance strategy that was needed if his movement for social revolution and national liberation was to succeed. Sandino not only challenged the Comintern's claimed monopoly on revolution in the Western Hemisphere but also its claim to be the sole representative of communism in the region (Hodges 1986, p. 71). In that regard Sandino's challenge to the Comintern bears striking resemblance not only to José Carlos Mariátegui's struggle with the Communist International in 1929 and 1930, but to the FSLN's successful challenge to the established Marxist-Leninist Party of Nicaragua a generation later.

The struggle continued from 1927 to 1933, and Sandino's growing army of miners, Indians, peasants, artisans, and workers made life very difficult for the Marines. Their political work and the increasing sophistication and tenacity of their popular guerrilla war had gained the support of many of the Nicaraguan masses, growing numbers of Latin Americans, a few informed North Americans, and many Latin American intellectuals.[5] The ferocity of the conflict with the Marines forced Sandino and his followers to upgrade their military tactics and strengthen their ties with the rural masses who supported their struggle. As they fought on, the Sandinists received little assistance from outside. They thus had to become more and more self-reliant and learn how to make optimum use of their only abundant resource—the Nicaraguan people. Rifles from the Spanish-American War, war matériel captured from the invaders, bombs made from the sardine cans the Marines discarded, and a sea of machetes wielded by ever more determined *campesinos*—such were the armaments used to confront machine guns and dive bombers (see Macaulay 1967, chaps. 4, 5; Selser 1981).

This was one of the first modern examples of the power of a guerrilla army with mass popular support against a technologically superior invader, even when the latter was supported by local Quislings and the mercenary military forces at their disposal. Mobile guerrilla bands as the components of an egalitarian people's army, political as well as military organization, integrated political and military actions, close ties to the peasants, and, most importantly, popular support and involvement—such were the lessons to be learned from Sandino's people's war against imperialism. These lessons were not forgotten later by the leadership of the FSLN.[6]

Tragically, although Sandino's political support had enabled him to gain a military victory, he disbanded his army before he could achieve far-reaching political and economic change. At the height of his power (late 1932), he had written (Ramírez 1979, p. 254) that "Our Army is preparing to take the reins of national power to proceed with the organization of large cooperatives of Nicaraguan workers and peasants, who will exploit our own natural resources for the benefit of the Nicaraguan family in general." He began to set up agricultural cooperatives in the Segovias, employing methods his Indian ancestors had used centuries before (see Selser 1981, chap. 12; Ramírez 1979, pp. xiv, xv). He had also become fully cognizant of how little the traditional parties served the interests of the Nicaraguan people and, at the time of his death, he was planning to start a national political movement designed to protect and empower the Nicaraguan masses—to serve the demos. After his treacherous death at the hands of Somoza's National Guard (1934) the cooperatives were attacked and most of Sandino's followers were soon slaughtered by the U.S.-trained National Guard. Some Sandinist columns fought on for a few more years in remote areas, but they too were eventually forced to abandon systematic armed resistance. All that remained was the spirit of Sandino and the example of his army, which lived on in the popular mind for some time, nourished by eyewitness accounts and first-hand stories from Sandinist survivors.

By exploiting his close ties to Washington and his position as head of the National Guard, Anastasio Somoza García soon emerged as the most powerful political figure in the country. The Nicaraguan people were restricted from power and disenfranchised. Somoza realized that Sandino and his Army to Defend National Sovereignty favored popular rule and thus represented the greatest threat to the reestablishment of rule by a U.S.-backed elite. No doubt he also sensed that Sandino was a symbol of and a possible key to the rediscovery of popular history and popular participation by the Nicaraguan people. Not content to have ordered Sandino's execution, he attempted to distort the popular memory of Sandino and his followers by having a slanderous anti-Sandino book published under his name (Somoza García 1936).[7] Somoza's efforts achieved some success, in that it was soon very difficult for the masses of Nicaraguans to obtain any favorable written accounts of the Sandinist struggle within the country.

After Somoza took direct control of the government in 1936, he instituted an increasingly repressive family dictatorship that—mostly because of its close ties to the U.S.—would endure until militarily defeated by the FSLN in 1979. However, despite bloody repression and the intense vilification of Sandino and his followers, sporadic popular struggle continued through the 1930s, 1940s, and 1950s, though clearly at a relatively low level. This period of struggle included military actions by both old Sandinists and younger patriots such as the "Generation of '44" (see Blandón 1980).[8]

By the 1940s the full force of the Somoza dictatorship was being felt. Somoza had proven to be one of the best "good neighbors" of the United States and had been lavishly received by Franklin Roosevelt in Washington. By the 1950s Nicaragua was a fully dependent producer of primary goods (mostly coffee and cotton), and an integral part of the U.S. system of political and economic control in the Western Hemisphere. Sandino's anti-imperialist popular struggle seemed to have been for naught. The guerrilla hero and the revolutionary struggle seemed to be slowly disappearing from the popular mind as the people had less and less access to power. There were occasional armed actions or putsch attempts by old Sandinists and other Nicaraguans who could no longer countenance the heavy-handed political and economic manipulation that characterized the Somozas and their friends. Students and workers (as in 1944) occasionally demonstrated against the regime, but lacked any clear ideological perspective in which to place their struggle. There was neither ideology nor organization for popular mobilization. Opposition to the dictatorship came to be symbolized by the sincere, but elitist, Conservative Party. Even the Nicaraguan Socialist Party (founded as a pro-Moscow Communist Party in 1944) often collaborated with traditional bourgeois politicians and Somoza-controlled unions, at the workers' expense. Somoza had taken over the Liberal Party and even went so far as to make pacts (1948 and 1950) with the Conservative Party, in an attempt to co-opt the only major focal point of opposition to his regime. Without even the militant liberalism that had initiated Sandino in his struggle, it was difficult for the diffuse opposition forces to gain the political perspective necessary to mobilize the masses again against the forces of dictatorship and imperialism.

But Nicaragua is a land of poets, and poets often reflect the popular will. Rigoberto López Pérez was one of the Nicaraguan intellectuals who directly felt the far-reaching cultural implications of a dependent dictatorship that was subservient to U.S. imperialism. He, like the Cuban poet José Martí, felt compelled to exchange pen for pistol to liberate his country. In 1956 the young poet assassinated Somoza. In so doing he not only avenged Sandino, but spurred a much-needed reexamination of national conscience that would increasingly challenge the status quo and free the Nicaraguan people from their lethargy.

"Rigoberto López Pérez's action, and the different armed attacks and popular uprisings that the Nicaraguan people unleashed from 1956 to 1960, in great part reflect the gradual loss of Conservative political control over the popular masses. Somoza's assassination and the subsequent series of armed movements that developed occurred outside of the tutelage of the bourgeois opposition, and came to be the first attempts to reintegrate the revolutionary Sandinist movement" (Ortega 1980a, p. 81). Little by little the spirit of Sandino's struggle was once again being felt across the land and the demos began to stir. A new wave of guerrilla activities broke out in the countryside; one of the more famous of these was even led by Ramón Raudales, a veteran of Sandino's army. The university students also began to show a new militancy and, for the first time, a small group began to study Marxist theory (ibid., p. 83).

The development of Marxism in Latin America before the advent of the Cuban Revolution did not facilitate the application of that ideology to national conditions. José Carlos Mariátegui was one of the few who attempted to creatively apply Marxism to Latin American reality. After the international Communist movement changed directions in 1928, his efforts in Peru were met with the most caustic criticism from the Communist International and many Latin American Communists. After this, the type of Marxism that was espoused by the Communist parties in Latin America generally tended to be dogmatic, sectarian, and not particularly well-suited to Latin American conditions; it was far from democratic. The development of Nicaraguan communism was no different. The Nicaraguan Socialist Party was founded in 1944 and maintained the closest of ties to the Soviet Union. Like most Latin American Communist parties prior to the 1960s, its ideology was modeled after that of Soviet Stalinism. It was thus ill-equipped to creatively fuse Marxism with the national reality of Nicaragua. Nonetheless, the party was virtually the only institution in the country where Marxist ideas were taken seriously. As such, it attracted the attention of emerging young student radicals like Carlos Fonseca Amador and Tomás Borge.

Fonseca Amador was born in Matagalpa in northern Nicaragua. His mother was a cook, his father a worker in an American-owned mine. Borge was a secondary school classmate and close friend. Fonseca Amador was a political activist at an early age. At sixteen he participated in a strike at his school demanding the removal of a medallion depicting Somoza from the school's crest. At seventeen he and Borge discovered the writings of Marx and Engels in the bookstore of poet Samuel Meza, and read and studied these philosophers. In addition, José Ramón Gutierrez Castro, a friend of Fonseca Amador and former classmate of Borge, lived in Guatemala from 1950 to 1953, where he became familiar with Marxist writings. Gutierrez Castro later wrote of Fonseca Amador's reaction to the new ideas: "Marxism fit him like a suit he had been awaiting for a long time" (in Blandón 1980, p. 184–185).

Fonseca Amador was initially sympathetic with UNAP, an organization that tried to recruit youth into the existing political parties, but he quickly found UNAP inadequate and drifted toward the Moscow-aligned Nicaraguan Socialist Party (PSN). First he sold *Unidad,* the PSN's paper, throughout Matagalpa and then in 1955, at the age of nineteen, he joined the party (Borge 1984, p. 28). Fonseca Amador enrolled in law school in León the following year and, with Silvio Mayorga and Borge, formed a cell of the PSN's youth group. Fonseca Amador saw the assassination of the elder Somoza in 1956 as an indication that a new revolution was developing, but he also recognized that the fight was not simply against Somoza but also against the United States and those Nicaraguans who tied their existence to the United States.

Fonseca Amador began studying Nicaraguan history in this era, and later traced the roots of the FSLN to the numerous attempts of the Indians to resist Spanish conquest. He also identified with the rebellion in 1821 led by Cleto Ordoñez against the annexation of Nicaragua by Augustín de Iturbide, Emperor of Mexico. He demonstrated his class consciousness by noting that the Ordoñez rebellion was a popular struggle based in the poorer classes against the local reactionaries led by Crisanto Sacasa. Other nineteenth-century Nicaraguans that Fonseca Amador identified with included those who sought a united Central America, particularly Francisco Morazán; those who fought the American adventurer William Walker in the 1850s; and those who participated in the War of the Indians in 1881. Fonseca Amador saw the latter, an uprising of Indian and mestizo people against the ruling elite of Matagalpa, as a forerunner to Sandino's war. He characterized the rise to power of Zelaya and the Liberals in 1893 as a bourgeois revolution and, like Sandino, strongly identified with the efforts of Benjamín Zeledón and his followers to resist its subversion by the conservatives and the U.S. Marines (Fonseca Amador 1984b, pp. 9–38). Of course, Fonseca Amador also studied Sandino and found great inspiration in his struggle against the Marines and also in his strong class consciousness and internationalism. Apparently it was Gregorio Selser's *Sandino, General de Hombres Libres* that most influenced Fonseca Amador (Borge 1984, p. 22). Later he met Santos López, a veteran of the Sandino struggle who was the living link between their revolutionary generations.

Although enthralled with the revolutionary actions of the Nicaraguan people, Fonseca Amador did not limit his study to Nicaraguan history. He was becoming a Marxist and an internationalist. In 1957 he traveled to the Soviet Union and wrote *A Nicaraguan in Moscow,* a positive, almost uncritical acceptance of the Soviet model of socialism (ibid., p. 24).

However, he began to be disillusioned by the reformist approaches of the PSN and sought a new vehicle for change based on the methodology of armed struggle. The key turning point was the shooting of four UNAP students during anti-Somoza demonstrations in 1959. His disenchantment with the PSN did not involve a rejection of Marxism but rather a belief that the PSN was abandoning the use of Marxism as a dynamic philosophy. He thus saw in the July 26th Movement in Cuba the playing out and renewal of the revolutionary traditions of Sandino, and Castro's triumph showed that victory was possible. Deported to Guatemala in April 1959, following student demonstrations in León, he went briefly to Cuba. Then, with advice from Ché Guevara and practical assistance from the Cuban government, he joined up with the "Rigoberto López Pérez" column in the Honduran border region, a group of fifty-five Nicaraguans, Cubans, and other Latin Americans. The column was surprised and massacred; Fonseca Amador was wounded but made his way to Cuba for convalescence. By then Cuba was clearly becoming both the inspiration for and the basis of practical assistance. As Borge (ibid., p. 28) said at the time, "the victory of the armed struggle in Cuba, more than a joy, was a lifting of innumerable curtains, a flash of light that shone beyond the simple and boring dogmas of the time. Fidel was for us the resurrection of Sandino."

In many ways Fonseca Amador was in the process of arriving at a broad and important theoretical break with the strategy of the PSN and with almost all of Latin American Marxism at the time. The Nicaraguan PSN argued that, in the absence of fully developed capitalism in Nicaragua and an industrial working class, the main task of the revolutionary party, outside of trade union work in the embryonic working class, was to seek alliances within the "national bourgeoisie" in pursuit of a "bourgeois-democratic" era in Nicaragua. As noted above, the PSN was founded in 1944 while Nicaragua was an ally of the Soviet Union as part of the Allied war effort. Thus the party initially enjoyed the tolerance of the government. During 1944–1948 the PSN allied itself with the populist stance adopted by Anastasio Somoza García and gained considerable influence in the fledging trade union movement. However, after a deal with the Conservatives and because he saw the rightward, anti-Communist drift of U.S. policy, Somoza broke his alliance with the PSN and the party was outlawed by the 1950 constitution. The PSN then sought alliances with other anti-Somoza parties such as the Conservatives who fell out of favor with Somoza during the 1950s.

This strategy, which denigrated the revolutionary potential of the Nicaraguan masses, led Fonseca Amador to break with the PSN and return to Lenin and Trotsky's theory of continuing or permanent revolution, which also had a profoundly democratic basis and had been adopted by Ché Guevara (see Liss 1984, pp. 258–259). As Lenin and Trotsky had done in Russia, Ché and Fonseca Amador rejected the idea that the bourgeoisie had any significant revolutionary role to play in twentieth-century semicolonial countries like Cuba and Nicaragua. Rather, they believed that the key to achieving fundamental change lay in the creation of a revolution based in the working class and the peasantry and committed to armed struggle. Here there is a definite convergence with the often-quoted phrase from Sandino: "Only the workers and the peasants will go all the way, only their organized force will attain victory" (in Fonseca Amador 1984b, pp. 99–100).

Another element crucial to the revolutionary philosophy of Fonseca Amador and Ché, in contrast to that of the PSN and Soviet Marxism, was its emphasis on will and the belief that to some degree revolution could be improvised. They turned to the Peruvian Marxist José Carlos Mariátegui and to the Italian Antonio Gramsci to craft a philosophy based on revolutionary action, the importance of the subjective factor in making revolution, and the role of ideology in motivating the masses (Hodges 1986, pp. 182–184). Mariátegui believed that the revolutionary was motivated by a "myth" and not any narrow personal interest—a theme echoed often in the speeches of Ché and Fidel. Mariátegui also believed that myth could be turned into revolutionary action through careful political education of a broad segment of the people.[9]

The example of the Cuban Revolution had already helped to inspire other guerrilla activity in the late 1950s. As the Cuban revolutionaries responded to U.S. pressures and threats by deepening the social transformations on the island and openly adopting Marxist-Leninist ideas, their example became increasingly attractive to the young militants in Nicaragua. Like many young Latin American revolutionaries, they were much taken by Fidel Castro's 26th of July Movement and believed that guerrilla warfare—as outlined by Ché Guevara (1969)—was the best method of implementing political change. Their sympathies thus moved from the Stalinist outlook of the PSN to the dynamic and revolutionary Marxism being developed by the Cuban leaders. Ché's theory of rural guerrilla warfare had borrowed from Sandino. The Sandinistas would, in turn, borrow from the Cuban example to continue Sandino's struggle.

The efforts to create a Marxism in both Cuba and Nicaragua that was based in their own national conditions met with considerable resistance in Moscow. Ché's ideas were labeled "tropical communism" by Soviet ideologues, and during the 1960s there was virtual open warfare between the established Moscow-oriented Latin American Communist parties and the Cuban revolutionary leaders and their allies like the FSLN. When, at the end of 1959, the PSN again declared armed struggle premature, attacked the activities of the Rigoberto López Pérez column, and reconfirmed its long-standing reformist positions, Fonseca Amador was prepared for a definitive break with the PSN. This break came in 1960 following Fonseca Amador's final attempt to influence the PSN's youth group, Patriotic Youth, to adopt a revolutionary, armed struggle stance. As he was arriving clandestinely, the PSN decided to combat his efforts by announcing in its social column the arrival of "that brave young student leader Carlos Fonseca" (Borge 1984, p. 30). Aided by this information, the Nicaraguan authorities captured and expelled him to Guatemala. After this betrayal, Fonseca Amador moved to consolidate a revolutionary alternative to the reformist PSN.

In July 1961 the Sandinista National Liberation Front was formally launched in Tegucigalpa, Honduras, at a meeting attended by Borge, Fonseca Amador, Mayorga, and Noel Guerrero. The latter left the organization almost immediately, and as a result is generally not considered one of the "founders." The FSLN consisted of just twelve militants including Colonel Santos López, a veteran of the struggle against the U.S. Marines in the late 1920s, and Victor Tirado López, later one of the nine members of the FSLN's National Directorate, along with Tómas Borge. According to Borge's prison writings (ibid., p. 30), the name of the organization and its clear link to Sandino was suggested and fought for by Fonseca Amador. It is clear that there was not unanimity on the question of the name of the organization, which points to the fact that Sandino was not the only root of the new revolutionary struggle. However, this is not to say that his influence was small. On the contrary, the figure of Sandino was and continued to be a significant factor in shaping the political philosophy of the FSLN.

The new generation of Sandinistas began a movement that was the continuation of the popular struggle of Augusto César Sandino's guerrilla army and efforts by the Nicaraguan masses to assert their control. Drawing heavily on the Cuban revolutionary experience and the writings of Ché Guevara and Fidel Castro, the Sandinistas had to reinterpret Sandino's original struggle in light of historic and ideological developments since his death. Even during his guerrilla war, Sandino had concluded that the Liberal and Conservative politicians were traitors and cowards and must be replaced by worker and peasant leaders (in Ramírez 1982, p. 12). By studying their own fight for national identity and liberation in light of similar struggles in Cuba, Vietnam, and elsewhere, the Sandinistas were able to build on Sandino's tactics and infuse their movement with a coherent ideology.

At the urging of Fonseca Amador, FSLN militants began to study Sandino's writings and tactics as they prepared for their first guerrilla actions in 1963. Colonel Santos López joined the FSLN and offered valuable military advice. Stimulated by the Cuban example, the Sandinistas believed that the only road to power was through armed struggle. However, like other young Fidelistas throughout Latin America, they felt that launching rural guerrilla warfare was all that was necessary to convince the popular masses (beginning with the peasantry) to take up arms and join the guerrillas. In Nicaragua, as elsewhere in the region, this was a fundamental and very costly error. The FSLN's first attempts at guerrilla warfare (Río Coco and Río Bocay, 1963, see Map 2.1) met with tragic defeat. The new Sandinistas had failed to do what their namesake had done so well—mobilize the local populace on the side of the guerrillas through well-planned political and organizational activity coordinated with and part of the armed struggle. Tómas Borge (in Waksman Schinca 1979, p. 21) would later explain: "We committed the error of moving into the zone without first undertaking preparatory political work, without knowing the terrain, and without creating supply lines." Even basic communication with the people was a problem. Many of the local inhabitants in the area of the first fronts spoke only indigenous languages like Miskito (ibid.).

Retiring from their guerrilla adventures in the inhospitable mountainous jungle of northern Nicaragua, most of the remaining Sandinistas began to engage in semilegal political work in urban areas, in uneasy cooperation with the Nicaraguan Socialist Party. However, a few Sandinistas, like Rigoberto Cruz (Pablo Ubeda), did remain in some rural areas to initiate important political work with the peasants.

Tomás Borge (only surviving founding member of the FSLN)

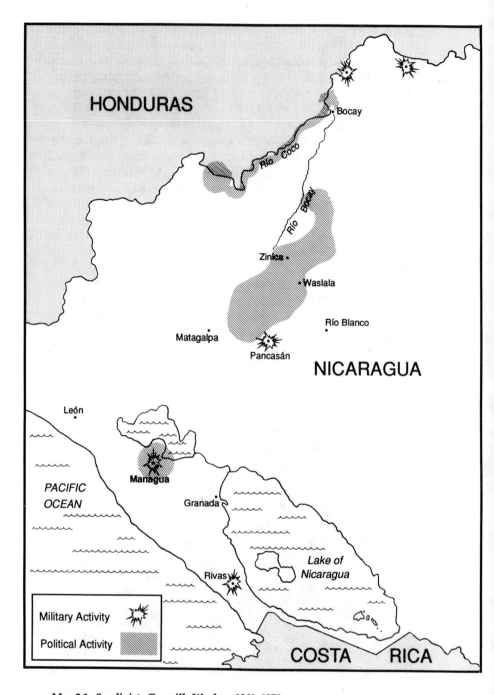

Map 2.1   Sandinista Guerrilla Warfare, 1961–1970

The absurdity of the electoral farce that was developing for 1967 and the antirevolutionary political opportunism of the PSN soon convinced the FSLN that returning to armed guerrilla struggle in the countryside was the only effective means of defeating the Somoza dictatorship and returning the country to the people. Stimulated by Fonseca Amador's leadership and the intensive study of Sandino's tactics and writings he advocated, the Sandinistas gradually began to understand that more political and organizational work was necessary to ensure mass participation in the struggle against the dictatorship.[10] However, before the vital importance of this lesson was completely clear, the second wave of FSLN guerrillas were already engaging the National Guard in combat in the region of the Darien Mountains in the Department of Matagalpa. The FSLN's early operations, like those carried out in other parts of Latin America using the foco theory,[11] were largely failures and resulted in a loss of many of the original cadres of the movement.

In his prison notebooks Borge denies that the early operations were carried out in the pursuit of the foco theory, arguing that, simultaneous with the Río Bocay and Río Coco campaigns, the FSLN was also organizing in factories, neighborhoods, and the university. Borge (1984, pp. 42–43) cites as proof of his position that the FSLN survived 1963 while other Latin American guerrilla groups disappeared almost immediately after suffering their military defeats. An alternate explanation would be that the FSLN learned more quickly than other groups the limitation of the focoist approach because, right after its military defeats and retreat into Honduras, the FSLN concentrated its efforts in the poor neighborhoods of Managua and other cities. Reflecting old ties, the urban work was carried out in collaboration with the PSN and helped to develop deep roots for the party. In hindsight, the leaders of the FSLN believe that they overreacted to the 1963 military defeats and fell victim to a degree of reformism (ibid.). Once again, the FSLN proved incapable of resisting the superior military power of the National Guard. They had not yet fully assimilated the lessons to be learned from the popular struggles for national liberation led by Sandino, Mao, Ho Chi Minh, or Castro.

Tragically, some of the FSLN's best cadres became isolated and surrounded at Pancasán in mid-1967. Although they offered heroic resistance, most were killed as the National Guard closed their trap on the guerrillas. Like the Fidelista guerrilla currents all over Latin America (Ché for instance, was killed in Bolivia the same year), they suffered a disastrous military setback. Things were even worse in the cities. The traditional opposition forces continued to demonstrate their ineptitude. One of the most notorious examples occurred in Managua in January 1967. Here, the Conservative leader Fernando Aguero took advantage of a large peaceful demonstration against the dictatorship to attempt an ill-planned and unorganized putsch against Somoza. This resulted in the massacre of over one hundred unarmed demonstrators and a further loss of prestige for the bourgeois politicians. In contrast, the tenacity of the resistance waged by the FSLN focused national attention on their struggle, and helped to turn a military defeat into a political victory. Beginning with the peasants and university students, the process of merging the vanguard and the mobilized masses into a unified fighting force was slowly getting underway. As Henry Ruíz (1980, p. 10) put it, "Pancasán reverberated in the popular conscience; its echo was felt in the bosom of the Nicaraguan people and the name Frente Sandinista began to spread to the most remote corners of the nation." The masses were beginning to stir for the first time since Sandino—a national reawakening was finally beginning. But there was still much to learn before they could be fully mobilized.

Unlike many other guerrilla movements in Latin America, the Sandinistas were able to learn from the mistakes they made in Río Bocay and Pancasán. They demonstrated a great capacity for self-criticism and were thus able to transcend their initial error of isolating themselves from the masses (Tirado López 1979, p. 7). Through painful trial and error and through an increasingly astute study of Sandino's thought and tactics, and those of other revolutionary movements throughout the world, they were able to fashion a strategy that would eventually unleash the full power of the Nicaraguan people against the dictatorship.

In the period after Pancasán and the 1967 elections, the FSLN's increased prestige brought many new recruits, especially from among students and youth in the cities. At this time the organization focused mainly on developing a base among the campesinos in the north central part of the country, in the mountains around Zinica. It was there that the urban recruits were sent. The work bore fruit and became the axis of the "prolonged people's war" concept that dominated Sandinista thinking at that time. Commander Henry Ruíz (1980, p. 14) subsequently explained:

> . . . in the balance sheet drawn up on Pancasán, prolonged people's war was mentioned. . . . That idea took shape from studying a little of the Vietnamese and the Chinese experience. Without leaning toward the Cuban experience (that of a guerrilla movement that would generate activity toward total war), we involved ourselves in the question at the same time we did organizational work in the countryside.

While the Zinica front was the focus of the FSLN's armed activity following Pancasán, increased attention was being paid to urban work that was necessarily clandestine. The FSLN began to establish what it called "intermediate organizations." Indeed (in Waksman Schinca 1979, p. 21), intermediate organizations made up the umbilical cord to [the masses]. We had student organizations, worker organizations, neighborhood committees, Christian movements, artistic groups, and so on. . . . We led these intermediate organizations ourselves, through compañeros who followed the orientation of the Front.

The success the Sandinistas were having in winning campesinos to their cause in the mountains alarmed Somoza and the U.S. embassy. Large-scale, brutal counterinsurgency operations were launched. Peasants suspected of collaborating with the FSLN "disappeared," were tortured, hurled out of helicopters or otherwise murdered. What amounted to concentration camps were set up in Waslala and Río Blanco at the northern and southern extremities of the area where the Frente was operating. The counterrevolutionary terror became so intense that the guerrillas were forced further and further back into the mountains and progressively separated from the inhabited areas where they had been gaining support. The "Prolonged People's War" strategy that demanded a secure rural base area was reaching an impasse. The dictatorship's political and economic crisis was maturing, but it was still in a position to deal heavy military blows to the Sandinistas.

While the Sandinistas evolved their theory of mass struggle, progressive sectors within the Catholic church became more and more concerned with the conditions of the masses. Motivated by this concern and the growing "liberation theology" movement, they began to intervene actively in the process of social change. Following the Vatican II conference in the early 1960s and the Latin American bishops meeting at Medellín, Colombia, in 1968, a section of the Latin American church began to become involved in the struggle for social change. In Nicaragua the key institution was the Institute for Human Advancement (INPRHU) that began to organize using the methodology that Paulo Freire developed in *Pedagogy of the Oppressed.* Numerous Christian popular organizations emerged in the 1970s as the struggle against Somoza deepened. Eventually, an important unity was struck between the FSLN and these forces when prominent church figures like Ernesto and Fernando Cardenal and Miguel D'Escoto became part of the FSLN. Such unity was not easily achieved because for a long period Christians and the Marxist-oriented leaders of the FSLN were wary of each other (Carrión in Harnecker 1986). The Christian forces perceived an antireligious orientation in traditional Marxist movements, while the mainstream of the FSLN questioned the revolutionary credentials of the Christian forces.

What is most significant about the Nicaraguan case and the FSLN is that this historic gulf between Marxist and Christian forces was bridged not simply through a brief tactical alliance but through the integration of progressive Christians into the revolutionary party. The result of this unity was that the political philosophy of the FSLN, and in particular its attitude toward Christianity, was virtually unique among revolutionary parties with Marxist origins (Girardi 1987). The popular empowerment of the masses and the mobilization of grass-roots participants through Christian base communities and the growing popular church also interjected strong democratizing tendencies and helped to introduce ideas of direct democracy and less centralist views of governance into the Sandinista movement.

Luis Carrión was a crucial figure in helping to forge the eventual unity between progressive Christians and the FSLN. He was one of the prime leaders of the Christian university movement, which first made contact with the FSLN in 1972. Initially Carrión sought a strategic alliance between the Revolutionary Student Organization (FER) and the FSLN while remaining independent. Later he was convinced to join the FSLN directly. Once in the FSLN, Carrión and others who came from the Christian organizations convinced the FSLN leadership, including Fonseca Amador, that political work among progressive Christians was particularly important in overwhelmingly Catholic Nicaragua. At the universities in Managua and León during the 1970s, the University Christian Movement was an important recruiting ground for the FSLN. Reflecting on this period, Luis Carrión (in Harnecker 1986) has said

> The Frente never fell to the temptation to design a political program for the Christians and another for the rest of the people. This would have been sectarianism. The Christian University Movement was a place where young people realized their revolutionary work on their way to higher levels of consciousness and integration into the FSLN.

Carrión has also spoken frankly about discrimination and prejudice that occurred against Christians in other Latin American revolutionary parties. This discrimination makes the FSLN's record particularly important. As Carrión stated (ibid.):

> Revolutionary leaders in Latin America must facilitate the incorporation of the extraordinary potential of Christians. Religion is a strong ideological force that can hinder or accelerate the coming to consciousness of the people. The overcoming of sectarianism requires on the part of the revolutionaries a recognition that the principles of Christianity positively interpreted are a moral base that can bring men to the struggle against oppression and injustice. This is an historic fact.

Carrión goes on to say that he became involved with the revolutionary process through his religious convictions and only later discovered Marxism. His own development and conviction that there did not have to be a contradiction between being a Christian and being a member of the revolutionary vanguard party obviously contributed to the open door policy of the FSLN to active, believing Christians. In a similar vein, José Carlos Mariátegui did not see a contradiction between religion and Marxism and thought that the inspirational nature of religion was similar to the revolutionary myth that was such an important force in mobilizing the masses.[12] Although but one example of the flexibility of the FSLN as a revolutionary organization, this is nonetheless an important contribution to the theory and practice of revolutionary organizations throughout the world.

Between Pancasán and late 1974, the FSLN carried on what it termed "accumulation of forces in silence." "Our work in that entire period took place through intermediate organizations, in ways that any theorist or dogmatist might have criticized. Everything from sending our militants to build latrines, teaching adults to read and write, treating the sick, or organizing festivals for the youth in order to introduce them to a process of political life, to the formation of organizations with revolutionary content" (Arce 1980, p. 24). The "silence" was broken in a spectacular way with the December 27, 1974 seizure of the home of a wealthy and prominent Somocista during a gala party for the U.S. ambassador. An FSLN commando unit held more than a dozen foreign diplomats and top Somocistas for several days, finally forcing Somoza to release Sandinista political prisoners, pay a large sum of money, and broadcast and publish FSLN communiques.

Developments subsequent to December 1974 were contradictory. On the one hand the FSLN's spectacular feat earned it further prestige and belied Somoza's repeated claims that the guerrillas had been wiped out. But the state of siege the dictatorship imposed and the repression launched against the trade unions and other expressions of urban opposition—as well as the rural terror described above—caused the mass movement to undergo an abrupt downturn after the increasing struggles that had taken place in 1973–1974.

Discussions concerning strategy intensified among the Sandinistas. Mass political work had to have its own objectives, not simply support for the organized guerrilla groups in the countryside. While this recognition of the need for a multi-faceted strategy can be seen in the writings of Fonseca Amador in the 1960s, the question of the relative weight of different areas of political work would seriously divide the FSLN before its ultimate triumph in 1979.

Three tendencies emerged during a period of great difficulty for the FSLN. For example, from 1970 to 1975, the National Directorate of the Party did not hold a single meeting. Separated groups carried out their political work in isolation from the others, and many cadres were in prison during that time. By the time the National Directorate met in Cuba in

1975, the division of the organization into three factions was clear, and membership in the Directorate was adjusted to reflect those divisions. The three tendencies were called Prolonged People's War, Proletarian, and the Insurrectionalist or Tercerista.

The Prolonged People's War group, which included Ricardo Morales and Tomás Borge, was basically Maoist in orientation. Their strategy and concrete political work emphasized rural guerrilla warfare. They had advanced beyond the focoist theories of the 1960s but still downplayed political work in the cities except as a recruiting ground for guerrilla fighters. As the decade of the 1970s developed, this tendency was probably the slowest to arrive at the judgment that a revolutionary situation was at hand. That this group would be slow to recognize the potential for Somoza's overthrow is not surprising because of their relative isolation from the growing discontent in the cities, their general strategy of slow accumulation of cadres, and caution in committing their forces to a direct confrontation with the authorities. In spite of their caution, the Prolonged People's War tendency may have been the weakest by 1977–1978, with many of its key cadres, including Morales, killed or imprisoned.

The Proletarian tendency, which included Luis Carrión and Jaime Wheelock, based itself in large measure on dependency theory[13] and the traditional Marxist-Leninist emphasis on the industrial working class. This tendency saw the Nicaraguan revolution as unfolding along more traditional lines as a confrontation between the bourgeoisie and the proletariat. As a result, Nicaragua's urban working class, small as it was, was seen as the main motor force of a coming revolution. Political work in the cities was emphasized, and this group also built a base among students.

The Insurrectionalist tendency, which included Daniel and Humberto Ortega, was the last one to emerge. In reality it did not represent an entirely new approach; rather it served primarily as a mediator between the two existing tendencies. The Terceristas (or third force) did not draw a sharp distinction between a rural and urban emphasis, seeing the need for action in both arenas. Its main and most controversial contribution was its alliance strategy. While the Insurrectionalists were not the first in the FSLN to propose or carry out an alliance strategy (Fonseca Amador had been a major proponent of this tactic), they were the first in the era of Somoza's decline to place it at the center of political work. There was also ample historic precedent for it in the strategy of both Sandino and the 26th of July Movement in Cuba. Both movements incorporated heterogeneous elements while maintaining a revolutionary position. Maintenance of the revolutionary position was crucial because, while pursuing an alliance strategy, the FSLN never compromised its fundamental revolutionary position that a basic reconstruction of Nicaraguan society was essential, not just the removal of Anastasio Somoza. While the exact form of that reconstruction, particularly its overtly socialist content, may have been unclear, the desire of the Sandinistas to make a clean sweep of the old order was clear. The Insurrectionalists also strongly believed that it was necessary to mobilize a broad mass-based coalition to overthrow the dictatorship.

The FSLN's consciousness of the need to mobilize the masses was already apparent in Fonseca Amador's landmark article of 1968, *Nicaragua: hora cero* (1984c, pp. 32–34). Drawing a balance sheet on the Pancasán period, he wrote that: "Organized mass work (student, peasant, worker) was paralyzed. On the one hand the quantity of cadres necessary for this work was lacking, and on the other, the importance this activity could have in the course of the development of the armed struggle was underrated." To overcome this weakness, he pointed to the need "to pay attention to the habits the capitalist parties and their hangers-on have imposed on the mass of the people. . . ." Many, he said, sympathized with the armed struggle but did not show this in action. "This leads to considering the need to properly train a broad number of individuals from among the people so that they will be capable of supporting the armed struggle. To seek the people is not enough—-they must be trained to participate in the revolutionary war."

The separation into tendencies did not mean the disintegration of the FSLN. Each current pursued the struggle according to its own lights, and as the crisis of the dictatorship deepened, all achieved successes. Efforts by the leaders to reestablish unity did not cease, although they were hampered by the imprisonment of key figures such as Borge and by the National Guard's murder of Fonseca Amador in November 1976.

The three tendencies finally converged around the fresh tactical and strategic questions brought to the fore by the upsurge of mass struggle that opened in late 1977 and as the urban masses moved into action after Pedro Joaquín Chamorro's murder in early 1978. After the first serious confrontation between the urban masses and the National Guard—the uprising in the Indian community of Monimbó in February 1978—the Insurrectionalist tendency adjusted its policy as follows: "After the insurrection in Monimbó . . . we decided to dismantle the guerrilla column we had on the Carlos Fonseca Amador Northern Front and all the cadres that were in those columns. . . . The columns had been victorious; nonetheless, the mass movement in the cities demanded immediate leadership from the vanguard of the movement. So we decided to dismantle those guerrilla columns and send all the cadres to lead the mass struggle" (Ortega 1980b, p. 30).

Disagreements over the question of alliances had led the Insurrectionalists to participate in the Broad Opposition Front (FAO) through their supporters in the "Group of Twelve," while the GPP (Prolonged People's War) and the Proletarian tendency was concentrating on building what was to become the United People's Movement (MPU). The political capitulation of the bourgeois opposition elements in the FAO to the U.S.-sponsored "mediation" in October 1978 quickly led the Insurrectionalists to adjust their policy and withdraw from the FAO, denouncing the imperialist maneuvers. All three tendencies then collaborated to establish the National Patriotic Front (FPN), which had the MPU as its axis. The FPN took on the character of an anti-imperialist united front, drawing in the trade unions, two of the three factions of the old PSN, student groups, and petty bourgeois formations such as the Popular Social Christian and Independent Liberal parties—all under FSLN hegemony.

Finally, the experience of the September 1978 attempt at insurrection—which the Insurrectionalist tendency spearheaded most enthusiastically—taught the need for better organization and preparation. The cumulative effect of these lessons, and the massive organized mobilization that resulted, paid off in June 1979 as the FSLN coordinated a massive popular insurrection.

The mid-1970s division of the FSLN reflected different approaches and partial answers to the complex problem of taking political power and smashing the dictatorship. This problem was resolved as all three tendencies brought the best of their particular experiences and approaches to the final struggle. This process was facilitated through their mature handling of unification and their willingness to learn from each other and work together even before the achievement of full unity in March 1979. All had success in mobilizing and empowering segments of the people. The old divisions were then superseded by the historic victory of July 19, 1979. Commander Humberto Ortega summed this up in this way:

> The leaders of the three tendencies were concerned with the problems of the revolution. The problem was that each one wanted to lead the process, wanted to be the one that stood out the most, but that was overcome in the course of the struggle itself and everybody realized the importance of everybody else's work. . . . The whole Sandinista movement agreed on a single policy which upheld the insurrectional nature of the struggle, called for a flexible policy on alliances and the need for a broad-based program, etc. This programmatic political and ideological foundation made it possible for us to coordinate our efforts with increasing effectiveness and pave the way for our regrouping.[14]

If the history of a people is one of the struggle to improve their lives and gain freedom and independence, then "the history of Nicaragua is a history full of struggles and heroic acts by its people, from the time of the Indians who resisted Spanish colonialism, passing through Sandino's heroic actions to the war of national liberation . . ." (Ortega 1980c, p. 5).

The ideology of the Nicaraguan Revolution was at once the recuperation of a long history of popular national struggle and the specific Nicaraguan manifestation of the new wave of revolution that was sweeping the Third World. As such, it shared some beliefs with sister nations like Cuba, while others were uniquely Nicaraguan. As in the past, the way in which Sandinist ideology was applied depended in large part on evolving national conditions. Thus the specific nature of Nicaraguan social formations have, according to one Sandinist theorist, allowed the youth and certain segments of the middle class to play a much more revolutionary role than in past revolutions (Núñez Soto 1982, 1980).[15] Likewise, the role of members of the church in the revolutionary process has allowed them (and liberation theology) to occupy a unique position in the new society. Indeed, the genius of FSLN ideological development has been its consistent popular mobilization and its practical application of Sandino's thought and Marxist concepts and methodology to the Nicaraguan reality. Through it, the people were involved in a process of liberation and inspired to become participants in their own governance.

Notes

1. Ortega (1980c).
2. See also Fonseca Amador (1984a) for the same essay. By August 1983, Sandino noted that "It is with great pleasure that our Army awaits the coming world conflagration to begin to develop its humanitarian plan in favor of the world proletariat" (in Ramírez 1979, p. 233).
3. Sandino's earlier biographer Gregorio Selser (1981) emphasizes the importance of the Tampico experience but does not give as much detail as does Hodges (1986, pp. 3–7).
4. Vanden interview of Pavletich, Lima, February 13, 1974.
5. Macaulay (1967, p. 113) mentions, for instance, the support work done on Sandino's behalf by the Chilean poet Gabriela Mistral, by the Costa Rican writer Joaquín García Monge, and by the Peruvian writer José Carlos Mariátegui.
6. Macaulay (1967) underlines the close ties that Sandino's guerrilla fighters had with the local populace and notes that Sandino's tactics "essentially were the same as the tactics of the People's Liberation Army in China, the National Liberation Front in Algeria, the 26th of July Movement in Cuba, and the Viet Minh and Viet Cong in Vietnam" (p. 10). All these struggles were premised on mass involvement in the armed struggle and looked to well-developed political awareness and very close organizational ties to the masses as essential ways of achieving popular involvement and participation. Nor did others miss the importance of the nature of Sandino's struggle—Ché Guevara "discerned the reasons for Sandino's success in resisting the Marines: the inspirational quality of his leadership and his guerrilla tactics (ibid., p. 262). Colonel Alberto Bayo, the Spanish Republican guerrilla who later trained Castro's original forces in Mexico, was also much impressed by the military tactics that Sandino's army employed (ibid.).
7. This book is generally believed to have been ghost written for Somoza. For a better understanding of the role of Sandino in the development of national con-

sciousness, see Frazier (1956).

8. The "Generation of '44" refers to a younger group of militants who emerged from labor and student demonstrations against the dictatorship in 1944.

9. For a fuller treatment of the ideas of José Carlos Mariátegui, see Vanden (1986).

10. Fonseca Amador assembled pithy quotations from Sandino in pamphlet form (1984a) and began to circulate short studies of his thought and tactics (1984d).

11. The foco theory of guerrilla warfare was developed by Ché Guevara and Fidel Castro in Cuba. It maintains that the guerrillas concentrate their activities on a focused area (foco) to achieve a critical mass and then spread out to other focos as they achieve success.

12. Mariátegui's thought in this regard was instrumental in providing an intellectual basis for the development of liberation theology. Gustavo Gutiérez knew the Mariátegui family and attended school with the Peruvian Marxist's youngest son, Javier. Gutiérez used and cited Mariátegui in his ground-breaking work *Theology of Liberation.* Tomás Borge befriended Gutiérez when he was exiled in Peru. See also Vanden (1986).

13. Dependency theory views the development of Third World countries like Nicaragua as being conditioned and controlled by the economic needs of advanced industrial countries like the United States.

14. Humberto Ortega Saavedra, interview by Martha Harnecker. The English translation was originally published in *Bohemia* (Havana), No. 52, December 28, 1979, p. 4. It then appeared in *Granma Weekly Review* (Havana), January 27, 1980.

15. "La tercera fuerza social en los movimientos de liberación nacional," a paper presented at the IV Central American Congress of Sociology (Managua, July 1980), was written to "demonstrate the significant presence of the petite urban bourgeoisie, united to the proletariat and peasantry, during the revolutionary taking and exercising of power in the formation of a process different from that of capitalism" (p. 1).

❖ THREE ❖
Democracy and the Development of Mass Organizations

Like many successful revolutions in the Third World, the 1979 Sandinista revolution promised democracy for the Nicaraguan people. Even before the triumph, the "Historic Program of the FSLN" (1969) had committed the revolutionaries to political structures "that will permit the full participation of all of the people at the national as well as the local level" (FSLN 1981, sec. I). Further, as an ever wider coalition of forces joined the revolutionary movement in 1978 and 1979, the prospects for Nicaraguan democracy seemed to grow with the inscription of each new political group, many of which had ties with traditional parties, were strongly committed to Western representative democracy, or had already experienced the participatory democracy of the popular Christian movement (Booth 1985a). Indeed, it could be argued that the particular forms that democracy took in Nicaragua were related to the specific (and very diverse) nature of the class coalition that overthrew the Somoza dictatorship and to the way in which the FSLN's political leadership conceived and interpreted those classes and their role in the continuing revolutionary process. Likewise, external pressures from the United States and other actors would also condition the ways in which democracy would develop during Sandinista rule.

Responding to traditional Nicaraguan conceptions of what constituted democracy, elections for a National Assembly were promised ("to the extent that the conditions of national construction permit it" ["Program," 1979]) as the new regime came to power in 1979.

In that the triumphant coalition of forces (and classes) became very broad indeed, the invocation of democracy by the new government at the time of the triumph was less of a commitment to a specific program to institutionalize democratic participation than a general commitment to democratic ideals similar to that first invoked by Bolívar at the time of independence. On the practical plane, each group might define democracy very differently and look to very different structures to ensure that the

49

demos would indeed be able to actively engage in the process of governance. Perhaps the most fundamental point of agreement was that very little democracy existed under Somoza and that the realization of the ongoing practice of democracy would represent a radical break with Nicaragua's past. If the new regime's commitment to pluralism acknowledged a diversity of political groupings ranging from traditional parties to ultra-left movements, it also tacitly acknowledged several different conceptions about exactly what democracy was, or more specifically, which structures maximized its realization. Thus members of the two traditional parties, the Liberals and the Conservatives, wanted Western-style elections and representative government, as did most of the bourgeoisie and quite a few in the middle class. Members of the popular classes, who had mobilized for the revolution or who had participated in local community or church organizations, wanted to make sure that their direct participation would continue and would be given effect. Rural and urban workers and peasants wanted more power over where they labored as well as in national affairs. Sandinistas wanted to ensure the predominant position of the Sandinista movement and to make sure that the lower classes would be enfranchised for participation that would guarantee ongoing, effective participation in decisionmaking *and* economic justice for the toiling masses. And many Sandinista militants wanted to ensure the hegemonic position of a vanguard party in which democratic centralism would be practiced.[1]

The plurality of political groupings and democratic conceptions was reflected in the initial Junta and structure of government. The Governing Junta of National Reconstruction (JGRN) was composed of three Sandinista leaders—Daniel Ortega, Sergio Ramírez, and Moisés Hassán; Violeta Barrios de Chamorro, the widow of Conservative party leader and strident Somoza critic Pedro Joaquín Chamorro; and Alfonso Robelo Callejas, a businessman from the Nicaraguan Democratic Movement, a political grouping formed by middle- and upper-class leaders and politicians to help precipitate Somoza's ouster. The three Sandinistas wanted to maximize popular participation in economic and political processes, while the latter two clearly were wedded to more traditional forms of Western-style representative democracy. The former, like most of the Sandinista leadership, were very much aware that liberal democracy had had its drawbacks in Latin America and that in countries like Bolivia and Mexico it seemed to have helped derail the revolution (Walker 1982, p. 9). Thus they were skeptical of a narrow, bourgeois definition of democracy that minimized direct popular participation and did not include a social and economic dimension. They also wanted to make sure that the democracy that was implemented did not block necessary social and economic restructuring and did not facilitate foreign manipulation.

"Democracy neither begins nor ends with elections. . . . Effective democracy, like we intend to practice in Nicaragua, consists of ample popular participation; a permanent dynamic of the people's participation in a variety of political and social tasks . . ." (Ortega and Ramírez in Ruchwarger 1987, pp. 3–4).

What they did envision was a popular democracy that would not just allow participation by the few (or domination by the upper classes), but would build democracy from below through the construction of neighborhood, gender, or functional grass-roots, mass organizations (Walker 1982, pp. 9–10). These new mass organizations were to become the primary mechanism for popular empowerment and for the political education and guidance that the masses would need from the FSLN until they fully understood the importance and complexity of their political role and were ready to assume their dominant class position in the revolutionary process (had achieved full political consciousness). These organizations were also to be the direct communication link between the masses and the political leadership. They would inform the people of new political directions and channel popular demands through the party to the National Directorate (see Gilbert 1988, esp. chap. 3). To hold the victorious coalition together and transform society, some form of political representation was needed that would allow the participation of anti-Somoza elements from the upper and middle classes but would facilitate direct representation from the lower classes and the Sandinistas.

Rather than an elected assembly, an appointed assembly became the first representative institution in the new Nicaraguan state. The Council of State was to a certain degree a compromise between the representative and participatory conceptions of democracy. Different political and functional groups would directly designate their own representatives to a national council. It guaranteed that traditional parties would be represented and even included representatives of private-sector organizations in the eventual fifty-one seats. But the mass organizations and the FSLN were even more heavily represented. Each of the seven other parties had one seat while the FSLN had six. The neighborhood-based Sandinista Defense Committees (CDSs) had nine representatives, the Sandinista Workers' Central (CST) had three, and the Sandinista-linked Rural Workers Association (ATC) had two. Legislative powers were shared with the Junta, but much of the policy direction and initiative actually originated with the nine-man Sandinista National Directorate (Booth 1985b, pp. 35–36). While some central control was exercised by the leadership of the FSLN, the mass organizations were not only engaged in grass-roots democracy at the lowest level, but also had direct representation in the national policymaking process. The fact that the traditional parties and upper classes had only minimal representation in the evolving governmental structure, through the Council of State, occasioned some criticism from their leaders and was a precipitating factor in the resignation of Alfonso Robelo from the Junta (ibid., p. 32). Representative democracy existed but was infused with a form of popular democracy that provided for direct national representation. Also in place was a form of democratic centralism that guaranteed the National Directorate of the FSLN dominance in the party and a great deal of influence in governmental decisions.

Clearly the most vibrant form of democracy in Nicaragua from July 1979 to the mid-1980s was that practiced by the mass organizations. Indeed the new political leadership was seeking a daily democracy, not just one that took place every four years. And effective democracy consisted of ample popular participation. For the new leaders, democracy was "not merely a formal model, but a continual process capable of giving the people that elect and participate in it the real possibility of transforming their living conditions, a democracy which establish[ed] justice and end[ed] exploitation" (Ramírez in Ruchwarger 1987, p. 4).

Like the Parisians who formed the Paris Commune in 1871, the Nicaraguan masses had taken to the barricades and driven out the remnants of the *ancien régime.* They were, in the words of Augustín Lara, a Sandinista observer, "architects of their history" because they had demonstrated that they were "the principal agents in the revolutionary transformation" and had been "active and conscious agents of the revolution" (in ibid., p. 139). Having felt the exhilaration and power that resulted from their direct involvement in this process, they were ready for a meaningful say in governing the nation. The theoretical inspiration for their empowerment could be found in the testimony of Karl Marx who, upon witnessing the Paris Commune, was so enthralled by the possibilities of liberation and actual rule by the demos that he wrote *The Civil War in France.* It could also be found in the direct democracy practiced in Paris almost a century later in 1968. In Nicaragua, the toiling masses—if not the people generally—had been mobilized to overthrow the tyrant. But unlike Paris in 1871 and 1968, it was a *national* (and not just local) revolution and *national* political organizations led by the FSLN that led the revolt and made sure that the masses would continue to exercise their newly found political power. And it would be necessary for the national political leadership to deal with these new organizations in which the revolutionary process had awakened a new consciousness. For the members of the mass organizations in particular it was the "beginning of a revolution that they felt was very much their own" (Núñez 1980, p. 10). The construction of these participatory organizations proved to be an excellent way of integrating thousands of isolated citizens into large collective structures (Lobel 1988, pp. 879–880). By the mid-1980s, membership in all these mass organizations had increased dramatically.

Inside and outside the FSLN, most of the organizations that did exist had been constructed from the ground up in the late 1970s and the Nicaraguan revolution had triumphed because the people had organized and fought not only at the national level, but at the neighborhood or *barrio* level. Indeed, it was the uprising in the mostly Indian neighborhood of Monimbó in February 1978 that set off the first phase of the national uprising that later spread through much of the country in 1978 and was rekindled in 1979.[2] Some of the fiercest fighting occurred at the barrio level as the people mobilized against the dictatorship. After the victory, revolutionary neighborhood organizations that had grown up all over the country during the struggle soon coalesced into neighborhood Sandinista Defense Committees. Other Sandinista-affiliated political organizations became mass organizations like the Sandinista Workers' Central (CST), the Rural Workers' Association (ATC), the Nicaraguan Association of Women Luisa Amanda Espinosa (AMNLAE), the National Union of (Small) Farmers and Ranchers (UNAG), and Sandinista Youth (Juventud Sandinista). The political mobilization that had guaranteed victory was now channeled into ongoing participation through these organizations.

By structuring participation in such a way that the common people could participate meaningfully at the local level and be represented directly at the national level, the Sandinistas had broken new ground. They had come the closest to realizing the vision of democracy that Marx glimpsed in the Paris Commune and that the most radical of the American revolutionaries had contemplated. And there were few precedents for this in Marxist or Western democratic regimes. Although some mass organizations did exist in Eastern Europe, they were almost universally completely subordinate to the Communist parties and lacked any substantial autonomy. In Eastern Europe only the workers' self-management movement in Yugoslavia could offer any basis for popular empowerment, and here it was limited to the workplace. As suggested in chapter 1, socialism had been weak in turning over power to the demos. The popular power movement in Cuba came close to granting power to the common citizens, but even there its successses were exclusively at the local level, and most observers believed that the central party apparatus still exercised a control function in regard to neighborhood democracy and especially popular organizations. In the West, there were few participatory town meetings (New England town meetings) or other structures of popular empowerment (block meetings) that functioned regularly and effectively, although there were scattered examples of vibrant local democracy and the stirrings of a growing movement in some countries for grass-roots democracy, such as the Greens.

Neither of the superpowers seemed to have been able to evolve meaningful structures for participatory democracy or to provide viable structures that allowed the people to take power from centralized institutions. Undaunted, the Nicaraguan leadership would try to accomplish what neither the Soviet Union nor the United States had been able to achieve.

A confluence of factors made this possible. From early 1978 on, the revolution was in large part a series of insurrections all over the country. The mass organizations and the people themselves were the backbone of these and sometimes fought with little or no direction from the FSLN. Prior to the February 1978 uprising in Monimbó, the FSLN had only a few hundred full-time fighters. Building on Sandino, however, they did realize that they would prevail only if the people mobilized against the dictatorship. Their organizational work in the barrios set the stage for the insurrection.

As suggested in the previous two chapters, the Marxism that guided the FSLN was far from the bureaucratic Stalinism of traditional Communist parties. It was not only very Nicaraguan, but was influenced by the voluntaristic interpretations that the Cubans championed and by the example of *poder popular* (popular power) in Cuba. It was also open to the participatory democracy that had captured the imagination of much of the new Left in Europe and North America and was not adverse to worker control in factory or field.

Few of the masses knew of the vision of popular democracy represented in Karl Marx's writings about the Paris Commune, but they were clear in their desire to take matters into their own hands and forge their own destiny. Supporting this impulse for democratic empowerment, the Sandinista leadership hoped to lend sufficient support—while exercising some guidance and direction—to the empowerment of the masses until the *people* acquired the political consciousness necessary to realize their full potential.[3]

Because the new government was credited with ridding the country of Somoza and because it represented such a broad base at the time of the victory, it initially received considerable support from many of the Latin American Western-style democracies as well as from Cuba, Panama, and Western Europe, and even limited support from the United States, while Jimmy Carter was in office. As the revolution was perceived as being more socialist and as it was attacked by the United States, Cuba, the Soviet Union, and other Eastern European countries increased their aid and support. Until 1987 or 1988, Nicaraguan foreign policy was able to maintain good—and useful—ties with the Nonaligned Movement and to use the United Nations and the World Court to stop direct invasion and minimize the degree of intervention (Vanden 1991). These two factors allowed the Sandinista experiment some breathing space to develop and some of the material assistance necessary to do so.

There were, however, several tensions inherent in this project. Given the multiclass composition of the victorious coalition that the Sandinistas headed, decisions that might be necessary to induce cooperative members of the bourgeoisie to remain part of the coalition—or even to just continue to produce—might work directly against the short-term economic interests of the Nicaraguan toiling masses who (in Sandino's words and in contrast to the bourgeoisie of then and now) might be the only ones to "go all the way."

Also, the form that Leninism had assumed in the FSLN (in part because of elitist vanguardism and in part because of the influence of Russian/Soviet authoritarianism) often mitigated against democracy—participatory or representative—and for centralized decisionmaking. The establishment of representative democracy might work against the development of participatory democratic structures, in that representative democracy generally favors elites who are or become well-entrenched, while participatory democracy favors broader, mass-based participation.

In addition, in Nicaragua there were relatively few resources to use or distribute—particularly when the economy was under attack—and this meant that there were insufficient resources to satisfy the perceived economic needs of all classes. Trying to do so would risk alienating a large portion of all classes, including the popular classes who would be the natural political base for the Sandinistas in difficult times.

Last, although committed to the people and their rule (democracy), many Sandinista and governmental leaders were from elite families and all had been exposed to the highly authoritarian political history and resultant authoritarian political culture that predominated in Nicaragua. Thus their experience with and expectations for actual popular rule might not have been as full as some expected.

The project for mass organizations was in part informed by the way Italian Marxist Antonio Gramsci thought socialism would be constructed. He believed it would be achieved by a broad alliance of people from all subordinated sectors of the population (see Cunningham 1987, p. 281). The mass organizations would give voice and power to the peasants and small farmers, urban workers, rural laborers, women, and youth. They would enable these hitherto disenfranchised groups to actively and effectively participate in the policymaking process in the new government so that they—and not the traditional elites—could decide their future. As with other visions of democracy, participation would be the guarantee that the people were actually ruling, actually exercising their power (Pateman 1970, p. 20). But in Nicaragua the people had been marginalized from the political system and badly undereducated (in 1979 the national literacy rate was barely above 50 percent and much lower for the popular classes). Nor had they been given opportunites for political participation or organization, or even to run their own enterprises before the revolution.

Socialists have traditionally looked to the working class to lead the people in building socialism. This would prove difficult in Nicaragua. In 1975 the urban working class was only 16 to 18 percent of the economically active population and was mostly scattered in small productive units of less than one hundred workers (Ruchwarger 1987, p. 43). Nor was it well organized—only 10 percent of the labor force was unionized, and they were scattered among five different federations, one of which was controlled by Somoza (ibid.). If rural unions were also taken into account, there were still only 27,000 union members in the entire country in July 1979 (1 percent of the population; Pérez Flores 1989, p. 15). "At the time of the triumph, the FSLN found a union movement that was disorganized, weak, and poorly developed qualitatively or quantitatively, and was eminently economic in character" (ibid., p. 13).

In order to empower and mobilize the urban working class, the FSLN helped develop the Sandinista Workers' Central (CST), which would serve as a sympathetic national labor federation as well as a mass organization for urban workers. Given the dearth of organizational experience and organizers, FSLN militants were often placed in key positions to ensure that the organization functioned well and pursued an enlightened political path. A similar strategy was followed in the development of the Rural Workers' Association (ATC).

These emerging national organizations were to provide the masses with the proper tools for assuming their place in the construction of the new Nicaraguan nation. Eventually the masses were to achieve the necessary political wisdom and maturity to realize their full potential. Education was an important component of this process. Two weeks after the victory, the Sandinista newspaper, *Barricada,* called on Nicaraguans to "mobilize yourselves politically, educate yourselves *to overcome your political and cultural deficiencies,* and cultivate revolutionary values" (in Gilbert 1988, p. 37; emphasis added). Months later, *Barricada* declared that the purpose of the educational system was "to strip the system naked before the eyes of the exploited and give them an instrument that will convert them into active subjects of their own history" (ibid.).

The mass organizations, like the educational system, would contribute to the development of a new political consciousness. Once achieved, the control and guidance that the FSLN believed were necessary in an initial (less politically conscious) phase could be relaxed. Until the masses had their consciousness fully developed, the Sandinista leadership would, however, have to be very wary of how the masses were being manipulated by other political forces. They continued to be quite concerned that the bourgeoisie would gain control of the revolutionary process and drastically limit its scope to little more than the removal of Somoza (ibid.).

Given the political history of Nicaragua (if not Central America generally), it would be easy for Nicaragua to slip into a process of Western-style representative democracy where the elite competed for political office and the participation of the masses was limited to selecting among elitist candidates every few years. As in James Madison's view of government, the demos itself would not participate directly in government, rather others—who were more capable—would decide for them. Thomas Cronin (1989, p. 8) suggests that this view of government stems directly from (elitist) opposition to "widespread and public participation in the conduct of government." Such broad participation was precisely the long-term goal of the Sandinistas, who were informed by a belief in the common people found in Sandino, Marx, and Jefferson and traceable back to Rousseau's benevolent view of human nature.

Although they might express some trepidation (and even exhibit some Madisonian tendencies) in the short run and exert too much control at times, the long-term participatory goals were consistent with the most radical forms of democracy and socialism. As noted by Dennis Gilbert (1988, p. 77) there was, however, a certain tension between the FSLN's desire to liberate and empower the oppressed masses and yet control and transform them at the same time. He also goes on to suggest that the mass organizations might be used to mobilize their members behind a program prescribed from above rather than one of their own making.[4]

A contrasting view is expressed by the Sandinista leader Carlos Núñez (1980, p. 21) who argues that as the mass organizations became part of the revolutionary process, if they were not being heard they had the right to make use of everything "from internal criticism, public criticism, the utilization of all the communication media, and even mobilization to take the steps necessary to guarantee that their proposals are listened to."

Neighborhood Organization:
The Sandinista Defense Committees

Although these occurred throughout the nation, the effect of their involvement is best seen in an individual case. Georgino Andrade, a poor neighborhood on the outskirts of Managua, came into being in 1981 when poor families from other overcrowded Managua neighborhoods decided to build homes on the unoccupied land. The first residents soon formed a Sandinista Defense Committee (CDS), and others followed as more families arrived. Eventually there were thirty-five CDSs and a Sandinista Barrio Committee to coordinate them (Ruchwarger 1987, p. 181). They were confronted by a variety of problems, such as the need to reorganize the layout of streets and to construct community buildings. "After numerous CDS meetings, the block coordinators and the barrio's executive committee worked out the problems of restructuring their community. . . . There was a high level of participation in the entire process. Long discussions took place during the block-level and the barrio-level meetings concerning new building materials, loans for families that had to rebuild their houses, and plans for building a new community center to complete the restructuring" (ibid.).

Although the barrio was young, the residents of Georgino Andrade utilized the CDSs to express their needs and frustrations and to organize around specific tasks such as better local organization, obtaining electricity and sanitation, and the eventual construction of a preschool, an elementary school, and a community church. They resolved problems and enlisted the aid of the city government and even outside agencies through a vigorous process of discussion and concrete actions initiated by the people themselves, who clearly felt they had gone a long way toward taking charge of their future (despite the frustrations caused by interpersonal difficulties, slow action from the government, and inflation and other economic difficulties).[5] Similar events were occurring in neighborhoods and villages throughout Nicaragua.

Though not without their problems, the CDSs continued to grow. By 1984 they were engaging some 600,000 Nicaraguans (40 percent of the adult population) in direct grass-roots democracy (ibid., p. 161). This meant that some 15,000 CDSs had been organized at the block or rural community level (Serra 1985, Mondragón and Decker Molina 1986). Throughout the country, masses of people had become vitally involved in the everyday decisions that affected their lives.

Women's Organization: AMNLAE

Women had traditionally been passive in Nicaragua and had often been hesitant to engage in public affairs. This began to change with the incorporation of more and more women in the Sandinista ranks. Section seven of the 1969 Historic Program of the FSLN guaranteed the emancipation of women, the end of discrimination, and political and economic equality. By the time of the triumph, some one third of the Sandinistas were female and many, like Dora María Téllez and Mónica Baltodano, occupied important leadership positions.

A women's organization (AMPRONAC) had been founded in 1977 and continued to grow through July 1979. After the victory it was renamed the Association of Nicaraguan Women Luisa Amanda Espinosa (AMNLAE), after the first Sandinista woman killed in the revolution, and became one of the most successful of the mass organizations. By April of

1980, the AMNLAE already had 17,000 members and by later that year 25,000 women were participating in 420 rural and 380 urban chapters (Ramírez-Horton 1982, p. 115). Chapters encouraged participation from women of all classes around issues of consciousness raising and concrete tasks such as reproductive rights, the legal status of women, and equal representation in political structures. Women were also quite active—and often dominant—in local CDSs and any labor or productive organization to which they might belong. Indeed, they, like the men who were mobilized, often felt pulled in several directions. Should they participate in AMNLAE, in the CDS, in their union? Unlike the men, they still had primary (and often total or near total) responsibility for child rearing and housekeeping. Thus the possibility of a triple day (productive, reproductive/domestic, and political/participatory) served to diminish women's involvement in some political activities (*Envio* 1987, pp. 22–23). Nonetheless, the organization's membership continued to grow and included 85,000 card-carrying members by 1984 (Molyneux 1985a, p. 247).

Further, and unlike most trade unions in the Central Sandinista de Trabajadores (which was often controlled by the FSLN), AMNLAE frequently displayed a healthy degree of autonomy, staked out independent positions, and was not afraid to pursue them vigorously in the policymaking process even if that meant challenging positions advocated by the government or the FSLN. The organization's early successes included the passage of a 1979 equal rights law that mandated equal pay for equal work and guaranteed maternity leave. Although support was mobi-

Mural Formerly in Front of the AMNLAE Headquarters

lized on other issues, the results were mixed. For instance, by 1982 the FSLN and AMNLAE formally disagreed on women's military participation. Female participation in the military was diminished and the initial version of the 1983 draft law would have excluded women from conscription even though so many had fought (and died) in the insurrection. At the end of the debate in the Council of State the law was amended to allow women to volunteer, but even this compromise took some time to implement.

Attention was also focused on other issues such as abortion (previously a taboo issue in public because of the strong position of the Catholic church and traditional values). This led to a vigorous and highly publicized roundtable discussion in the FSLN newspaper *Barricada* in 1985 but did not lead to a specific freedom of choice provision in the draft constitution.[6] This and such related issues as family planning, divorce, and child care were vigorously discussed in June 1986 *cabildos abiertos* (open forums) to consider the draft of the new constitution. This meeting was organized by AMNLAE, was held in Managua, and was specifically for women. Many women activists saw the highly charged meeting as an important demonstration of women's participation in the revolutionary process (*Envio* 1987, p. 29). However, in the final version of the new constitution (promulgated in January 1987) only some—and certainly not all—women's issues were addressed.[7] Complete equality was guaranteed (Article 27), and Article 73 stated that

> Family relations rest on respect, solidarity and absolute equality of rights and responsibilities between the man and the woman. Parents must work together to maintain the home and provide for the integral development of their children, with equal rights and responsibilities.

Although these measures did not satisfy the more militant feminists, they did set the stage for more equitable relations inside and outside the home. However, by 1990 many Nicaraguan women felt the promise of more equitable relations was left unfulfilled.

Through mass participation, AMNLAE had been able to involve thousands of women in the process of demand articulation and had significantly raised their consciousness and awareness of their ability to have an impact on the political process. The contradiction was, however, that many of the demands had not been met, thus raising the question of just how much effective democracy actually took place.

In her seminal article on women in Nicaragua, Maxine Molyneux (1985a) provides an important perspective. She argues that the realization of goals, such as the basis for more equitable family and conjugal relations and major strides in education, health, and child care, are concrete results of the general revolutionary process. These policies have an impact directly and positively on the lives of the vast majority of Nicaraguan women and suggest that the revolutionary process provides benefits that would not have been achieved otherwise. Further, she takes issue with the view that "women's interests have been denied representation or have been deliberately marginalized through the operations of 'patriarchy'" (p. 247). However, AMNLAE did not experience the growing political influence that most Nicaraguan women and many European and North American feminists had hoped for. Often the women's organization "would only voice limited demands while waiting for more favorable circumstances to develop when the 'general interest' will no longer clash with the particular interest" (Coraggio 1985, p. 70). In defense of their gradualist strategy, many AMNLAE leaders have suggested that their immediate task was the defense of the revolution, since that, as one leader put it, was a "necessary condition for the subsequent struggle for women's liberation" (ibid., p. 69). By the mid-1980s women did constitute 22 percent of the membership in the FSLN (down from a high of 33 percent at the time of the victory) and 37 percent of the party's leadership positions. They also comprised 50 percent of the militia (Molyneux 1985a, p. 247). Likewise, the FSLN has been the only party to seriously analyze women's issues and take them into consideration in the formation of its policies and plans. In the 1984 elections, thirteen women (all FSLN candidates) were elected to the National Assembly.

AMNLAE was not able to achieve all policy objectives, and from 1987 on participation and interest began to decline as more time had to be invested in economic survival in the midst of a deteriorating economy. Even amidst the adversity, mobilized women continued to take advantage of participation opportunities offered by the mass organizations and the new structures of representative government. Though many felt that AMNLAE was being caught in the general decline in support for and interest in the mass organizations, it continued to advocate for women's issues. Thus in April 1988, the National Assembly finally passed a no-fault divorce law that allowed *either partner* to unilaterally end a marriage. This was a radical break with the old law in Nicaragua and current practice in most of Latin America (*Update* 1988). Either partner could seek a divorce and was not required to accuse the other of misconduct. The entire process took only from five to twenty-four days. As the head of AMNLAE carefully explained, this was a terribly important issue for large numbers of Nicaraguan women who now had an effective and economical way of ending unsuitable (and often physically abusive) relationships (ibid., p. 1).

Although this law did not satisfy the church hierarchy or many of the more conservative sectors of society, it did suggest that AMNLAE had achieved a great deal through providing a structure in which women could participate meaningfully. The organization brought considerable pressure to bear around key issues such as the divorce law and led one Sandinista leader, who had also occupied an important position in AMNLAE, to suggest that the role of women and their organization in Nicaragua could help bridge the gap between the way women were often asked to subordinate their concerns to general political needs in socialist countries and the way specific feminist demands caused a very narrow focus in some Western countries.[8]

Nonetheless, by 1990, AMNLAE was undergoing a major reorganization that diminished its national organization and reduced the effectiveness of its national leadership.[9] This further accelerated the declining involvement by significant numbers of women and suggested that even the once-vibrant women's organization could not escape the decline in participation engendered by the economic crisis and diminishing national support for participatory democratic organization.

National Union of Farmers and Ranchers: UNAG

After breaking away from the Rural Workers' Association (begun in 1978), the National Union of Farmers and Ranchers (UNAG) was formed in 1981. It was primarily composed of peasants and medium-size farmers and became one of the most successful of the mass organizations. By 1982 it already had 42,000 members and was organized on a local, regional, and national level (Luciak 1987, p. 42). By 1984 the organization had been strengthened and membership had reached 75,000 (Serra 1985, p. 67). The local assemblies were particularly vibrant. They became mechanisms of direct democracy where local concerns were discussed and solutions considered, and where the local organizational leaders, government officials, and FSLN leaders reported and were held accountable.

> In early 1984, for example, they began in Region VI (Matagalpa and Jinotega), with assemblies in different zones that mobilized over 5,000 producers, and ended with a Regional Assembly in which the results of earlier assemblies were summarized in a 'Plan of Struggle' containing the small farmers' various demands of the state and their commitment in terms of developing the economy and improving the rural standard of living. In the same assembly each member of the Regional Board of Directors of the UNAG was ratified by applause. This same process was carried out in other regions, culminating on July 9 in a National Assembly that drafted a 'national plan of struggle' and chose the National Board of Directors of UNAG (ibid., pp. 79–80).

UNAG became a bottom-up organization that based its strength on the hundreds of local assemblies that met each year (see Figure 3.1). It

Figure 3.1 Structure of the National Union of Farmers and Ranchers and the Sandinista Defense Committees

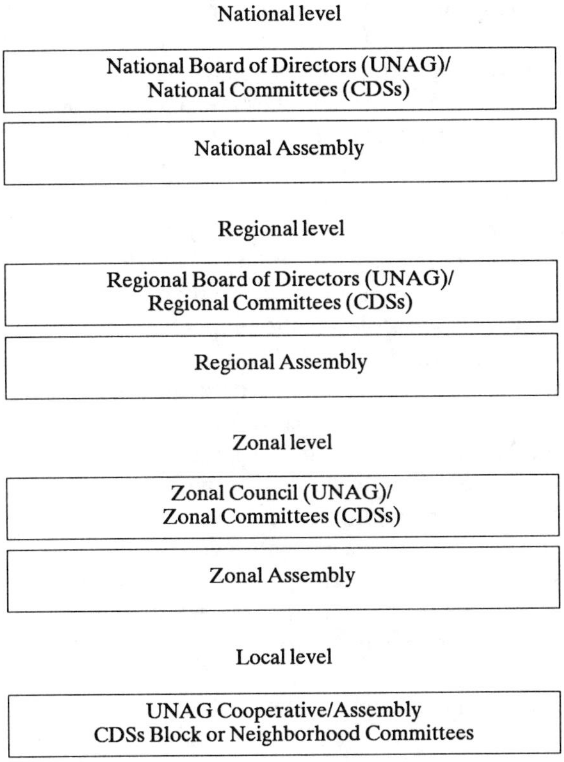

National level

National Board of Directors (UNAG)/ National Committees (CDSs)

National Assembly

Regional level

Regional Board of Directors (UNAG)/ Regional Committees (CDSs)

Regional Assembly

Zonal level

Zonal Council (UNAG)/ Zonal Committees (CDSs)

Zonal Assembly

Local level

UNAG Cooperative/Assembly CDSs Block or Neighborhood Committees

continued to grow in autonomy, organization, and militancy. Its membership also continued to increase and had reached some 124,000 by 1985 (Luciak 1987, pp. 46–47).

UNAG was also buttressed by the fact that rural cooperatives were the most common organizational unit at the lowest (base) level. These worker/owner-run organizations were examples of both economic and participatory democracy. Cooperatives accounted for 21 percent of the total farm land, 35 percent of food production for internal consumption, and 21 percent for exportation (*Barricada,* Dec. 21, 1987, p. 3). As was the case in the Gamez-Garmendia Cooperative near Estelí, the structure, organization, and functioning of the cooperatives promoted economic democracy at the base level (Estrada 1989). The extent to which they significantly increased the feeling of political capacity and ability to influence one's destiny is suggested by the testimony of the member of another co-op: "For us democracy means that we can all be leaders. Thus the Assembly of all members of the cooperative is our highest authority and we want all the members to work on the Board of Directors of the Cooperative, so we can rotate each year" (in Serra 1985, p. 81).

As it grew, the organization was able to influence agrarian policy in such key areas as credit policy and the way in which land was distributed to the peasants and landless laborers (Deere et al. 1985, p. 103). Responding to a widespread feeling among its members that land should be distributed to individuals as well as through the creation of cooperatives, UNAG challenged an accepted belief among government officials (Ministry of Agriculture officials in particular) that to do so would be counter-productive to the long-term goals of the revolution (ibid., pp. 90–91). UNAG argued that to consolidate the support of the rural population for the revolution the land had to be distributed directly to the peasants. After considerable discussion and some peasant recruitment by coun-terrevolutionaries (*contras*) in the countryside, this issue was resolved in favor of UNAG in 1986 when the initial agrarian reform law was modified to provide land directly to peasants as individual producers. After 1986, phase two of the agrarian reform substantially increased the amount of land distributed to individuals and the speed at which it was done. This process was seen as a major victory for UNAG and suggests that it had developed a high degree of autonomy. The organization also managed to have nine of its members elected to the National Assembly in the 1984 elections.

As with the other mass organizations, UNAG also had a well-developed structure for participation. At all levels (national, regional, municipal or zonal, and local) there was an assembly that was the ultimate decisionmak-ing body. Its representatives were chosen by the level below it (the members themselves at the local level) and they, in turn, chose the representatives to the assembly above it. They also selected a council (which met periodically) and a permanent executive committee, which held executive power (Serra 1985). The leaders could be ratified or rejected (but usually by a show of hands or voice vote) by the assemblies at each level and were at least theoretically subject to recall (Ruchwarger 1987, p. 129).

Labor Organizations: CST and ATC

As suggested earlier in this chapter, the workers' movement was not well developed in Nicaragua at the time of the revolution. It was hoped that the new Sandinista Workers' Central (CST) would develop a high degree of autonomy and act as an efficient channel to transmit specific demands and represent the interests of the working class. But by the time economic conditions began to deteriorate and interest in the mass organizations was declining (1987), the CST was often subordinating the immediate economic interests of its working-class members to the national government's austere economic policy and to its defense stance in the contra war. Directives for voluntary labor, more participation in defense, and austerity in wage demands were passed from the party to the CST. Generally these directives were taken up by the union leadership. This, combined with a verticalist decisionmaking style and the semiabandonment of political-ideological work, caused many workers to see the CST as representing the interests of the state and the party rather than their own (Pérez Flores 1989, pp. 17–19). Although less severe, similar processes were occurring in the Rural Workers' Association (ATC).

The official discourse of these two main union movements (CST and ATC) developed in such a way that it was often indistinguishable from that of the government or party. By following party directives and supporting government policy as it developed after 1985, the two labor federations seem actually to have contributed to the deterioration of living conditions for the wage laborers because the organizations did not push for wage increases to keep up with rising inflation. These mass organizations were not able to find their own voice to represent the specific interests of their members. Democracy had clearly broken down in the organizations that had been designed to empower the labor movement (ibid., p. 22). In 1987 a rival labor federation, the CPT, emerged, and nonsanctioned wildcat strikes became common by the late 1980s.

The labor organizations had focused on economic reactivation, vigilance over the decapitalization of enterprises, and defense. This was not because of mass pressure (the rank and file were much more concerned with stopping the deterioration in their real wages and living conditions), but because they were following the policy directions supplied by the FSLN, which was focused on consolidating the revolution and winning the war. The FSLN-affiliated leadership demonstrated a great deal of loyalty to the party and was able to use vertical-style decisionmaking to make sure that the unions adopted party policy even though such policies might not be those favored by the rank and file. This in turn led to a decrease in participation and growing apathy among many workers. The Sandinista worker federations had not always directed specific demands or generalized feedback to government and party decisionmakers (ibid., pp. 38–39; Serra 1985). Part of this abdication of democracy may have resulted from poor union socialization or lack of experience, or from insufficient political preparation. However, it also resulted from the authoritarian tendencies, centralized decisionmaking, and perhaps excessive vanguardism sometimes displayed by key Sandinista officials in the government and the party as they related to the mass organizations and the society.

Religious Organization: The Popular Church

There were many democratic and participatory currents in Nicaragua. Indeed, the most authoritarian of institutions in Nicaraguan society was experiencing an infusion of democracy and mass-based participation. Progressives within the Catholic church were calling for more participation and autonomy at the parish level. The popular church, as it came to be called, had for some time been generating a radical form of participatory democracy in many Christian base communities and parishes throughout Nicaragua. Further, through such church-affiliated groups as the Instituto de Promoción Humana (INPRHU), radicalized Christians had been encouraging popular participation for better than ten years before the Sandinista victory in 1979.[10] By working with barrio residents and poor peasants, and by interacting dynamically with Sandinistas even before 1979, these Christian advocates of popular democracy not only helped to encourage the establishment of popular organizations, but (relying on the critical educational methods pioneered by Paulo Freire) began to condition all with whom they came in contact to think differently about traditional authority and centralized power. This anti-authoritarian approach to decisionmaking served to buttress democratization considerably. Perhaps even more significantly, it began to change the ways people thought about authority and their approach to it and thus combined with other trends in Nicaraguan society to stimulate the growth of a participatory (and strongly democratic) political culture.

By 1984 the more successful mass organizations were experiencing high levels of democracy at the grass-roots level. They encouraged several types of participation and allowed for significant input in the decisionmaking process at the local, zonal, regional, and national levels. This was consistent with the original Sandinista focus on participatory democracy. Borge (1987, p. 92) thus suggests that the involvement of the people in the revolutionary process in Nicaragua was none other than the people in action, and that "without popular participation all our efforts run the risk of losing the social context that ensures that such efforts will be truly revolutionary." But by 1987 participation and enthusiasm generally began to decline as the struggle for economic survival siphoned off energy that previously had been invested in political participation.

Democracy often comes slowly, and authoritarian tendencies can persist, even in the midst of revolutionary change. Thus many noted that important decisionmaking positions in the mass organizations were often occupied by Sandinista leaders or militants and that they felt that their real role was to explain Sandinista policy and encourage the organization to adopt it. Some believed that this diminished their ability to carry the messages and demands of the mass organizations back to the party and pressure for policy decisions that were consistent with them. Frank Cunningham (1987, p. 280) notes that under socialism, party members who are also members of other movements or groups are often expected to carry out party policy no matter what the opinions of members of the group itself. In this context, party loyalty can be placed above group loyalty.

This tension was never totally resolved in Sandinista practice. On the one hand, the party as the vanguard was supposed to guide the mass organizations, and the mass organizations were to pass on and explain party policy. On the other, the mass organizations were expected to channel demands and information from the masses up to the party and advocate for the specific interests of the organization (see Gilbert 1988, p. 77; Serra 1985).

In fact, the internal functioning of the Sandinista party appears to have been authoritarian and centralized. Cultural tendencies and the influence of Sovieticized Leninism were intensified initially by the guerrilla origins of the party and subsequently by the contra war and the generalized, low-intensity conflict waged by the United States. The nine-man National Directorate was predominant (one observer even suggested it was the vanguard within the vanguard) (Gilbert 1988, p. 77). Although a 104-member Sandinista Assembly acted as a permanent *advisory* body, its function was to "support the National Directorate in making the Revolution's most important decisions." Further, "it was not elected directly or indirectly, rather its members were representative cadres named by the National Directorate" (*The FSLN* 1986). There were also base, zonal, and regional committees. But here, too, important positions were usually filled by appointments from above, and the agenda for discussion was generally handed down. As suggested by a political slogan often voiced by Sandinista militants—"the National Directorate orders"— political values seemed less democratic within the party and it remains to be seen if it managed to free itself from the centralized, bureaucratic approach that had characterized many parties in the socialist world. Indeed, the lack of democratic experience in Nicaragua may have facilitated centralized decisionmaking structures and verticalism. This not only meant that the party did not function democratically, but that this same style of decisionmaking was sometimes projected onto the mass organizations and was at times employed in the relationship between them and the party and between the party and the society.

One could conclude that different forms and philosophies of democracy clearly existed simultaneously in postrevolutionary Nicaragua. Both participatory and mass-based democracy advanced in the first five years of Sandinista rule, before deteriorating economic conditions began to diminish participation. But democracy did not grow in the same ways within the FSLN. Likewise, centralized decisionmaking and authoritarianism remained not only in the party, but in some of the mass organizations as well. As will be explored further in the final chapter, the continuation of the contra war and the worsening of economic conditions in the late 1980s combined with authoritarian tendencies to decrease participation and participatory democracy.

As the party grows and matures in opposition, careful scrutiny of its structure and decisionmaking process will be necessary to see if it, too, undergoes a certain amount of restructuring as more and more of the cadres increase in theoretical and practical understanding. The 1990 Assembly and the 1991 Congress began a process of critical assessment and adjustment. In the meantime, however, it should be noted that "there [was] more democracy in Sandinista Nicaragua than any other state in transition to socialism" (Lowy 1986, p. 278). This not only suggests that the demos were, in fact, heavily involved in the process of decisionmaking in Nicaragua (that real democracy of several kinds existed) and that the small Central American country was far from the totalitarian state some have claimed, but that the participatory forms of democracy that Jefferson at his most radical might have championed can in fact grow within a state that is guided by Marxism.

Notes

1. Interviews by Vanden with Salvador Porras (CIERA), Managua, August 1980 and July 1982, and other Sandinista militants—Managua, Masaya, Estelí, and Granada—1980, 1982, 1984, 1987.

2. In February 1978, this tightly knit, lower-class and mostly Indian community on the outskirts of Masaya took over the neighborhood and held off the National Guard for more than a week. They had few weapons that they did not make themselves and had only some Sandinista support several days into the uprising. Interviews by Vanden with several Monimbó families, July 1980.

3. The term "people" (*el pueblo* or *demos*) is the term frequently used because it connotes the multiclass entity of all Nicaraguans who by class and/or consciousness could grasp the historic opportunity the nation had to realize its potential.

4. There is clearly a duality in Sandinista thinking on this issue. We believe, however, that it results from the low level of educational and political preparation of a substantial part of the masses, rather than from simply a somewhat dogmatic adherence to the Marxist-Leninist concept of the vanguard. As we argued in chapters 1 and 2, Sandinismo was far from the Stalinist Marxism that predominated in Eastern Europe. Comparing the mass organizations in Nicaragua with those few that existed in the Soviet Union and Eastern Europe, one finds that

those in Nicaragua were larger, more numerous, more vigorous, and much more autonomous.

5. Interviews with Compañera Yedira and her extended family, and informal discussions with other barrio residents by Vanden, December 11, 1987; conversations with Gary Ruchwarger, Managua, December 11, 1987; see also Ruchwarger (1987, chap. 7).

6. Vanden found, in conversations with many politically conscious women in Nicaragua, that not all female Sandinista militants were in favor of abortion. Specific conditions in Nicaragua made for a very different political culture, as compared to that held by most feminists in North America and Western Europe.

7. For a thorough discussion of women's rights in the 1987 constitution, see Morgan (1990).

8. Interview with Magda Enríquez, former AMNLAE leader and then Head, North American Section, Department of International Relations, FSLN, conducted by Vanden, Managua, December 15, 1987.

9. Conversations with national AMNLAE staff, Managua, February 27, 1990. See also Chuchryk (1991, esp. p. 156).

10. Interview with Reinaldo Antonio Téfel by Vanden, Managua, September 1, 1980, and Instituto de Promoción Humana (1977). See also Dodson and O'Shaughnessy (1985).

❖ FOUR ❖

The 1984 Elections and the Evolution of Nicaraguan Governmental Structures

On February 25, 1990, the people of Nicaragua went to the polls for the second time since 1979 and in a surprising turn of events elected Violeta Barrios de Chamorro president of Nicaragua. These election results were seen in the United States and elsewhere as a stunning repudiation of the eleven-year-old Sandinista revolution. Two months later on April 25, Chamorro assumed office in the first electoral transition of power in Nicaragua. The purpose of this chapter will be to place these recent developments within a historical context. It will focus (1) on Nicaragua's governmental structures both before and after the July 1979 revolution, with primary emphasis on the postrevolutionary period; and (2) on one aspect of Nicaragua's democratization in the 1980s—the construction of a representative democratic system within the framework of a broader social revolution.

A serious analysis of Nicaraguan history shows that prior to 1979 Nicaragua had no history of democratic government or even constitutional rule (Close 1988, p. 107). Suzanne Jonas and Nancy Stein (1990, pp. 16–17) have argued that elections in Nicaragua in the twentieth century have been connected to the oligarchic state, foreign intervention, and the Somoza dictatorship. Nicaragua's closest brush with constitutional rule may have occurred during the increasingly dictatorial reign of José Santos Zelaya (1893–1909). But any possibility that Zelaya's rule may have evolved into constitutional or democratic government was ended when the Conservatives seized power by force with U.S. support in 1909. The Conservative administrations that followed can hardly be called democratic as they governed largely through money and arms from Washington. Following the resolute struggle of Sandino between 1926 and 1933, the Somoza dynasty was imposed on Nicaragua for the next forty-five years. While the Somozas ruled Nicaragua like a family business, numerous elections were held (1936, 1946, 1951, 1957, 1963, 1967, and 1974). The political opposition dutifully attempted to use them to remove the

Somozas, but they failed totally because the elections were openly fraud-
ulent or rigged in favor of the Somoza family's wishes. Any political forces
that challenged the established political processes were forcibly repressed
by the National Guard, Somoza's private army (see Millett 1977). The
entire apparatus of the government—legislature, courts, and public administration—existed to serve the needs of the Somozas. In the words of
David Close (1988, p. 107), "the family became the state."

The arrival in power of the Sandinistas and their allies in July 1979
brought the first possibility of real constitutional government to Nicaragua
because the revolutionary forces were bound to the principle of political
pluralism supported by popular participation. However, the Sandinista
commitment to political pluralism was a complex one and was not based
primarily on the concept as it is articulated in liberal democratic ideology
(this divergence is fully developed in chapter 5). Nevertheless, one aspect
of the Sandinista concept of pluralism was the construction in Nicaragua
of a governmental system based on constitutional principles and the rule
of law.

Until an elected government assumed power in 1985, Nicaragua was
governed by a provisional system that was established immediately after
the triumph. As would be expected in an immediate postrevolutionary
period, government power was concentrated in the executive branch, the
Governing Junta of National Reconstruction (JGRN). Initial governmental changes after the revolution were based on the Fundamental Statute
of August 22, 1979, which set aside the Somoza constitution and established the JGRN and the Council of State.

The most important body was the JGRN, which carried out all executive functions of government and shared legislative responsibility with
the Council of State. From the beginning, the JGRN represented the
diversity of the coalition that had come to power. Three of its members
were Sandinistas—Moisés Hassán, Daniel Ortega, and Sergio Ramírez.
Both Hassán and Ortega had been combatants in the civil war and both
were long-time FSLN militants. Ramírez was a recognized author who had
been a key member of the Group of Twelve, a Sandinista-organized body
of establishment figures who had called for Somoza's ouster. The two
non-Sandinistas were businessman Alfonso Robelo and Violeta Chamorro, widow of the slain newspaper editor Pedro Joaquín Chamorro. They
resigned from the Junta in June 1980 following sharp differences over the
composition of the Council of State. The Council was originally to have
thirty-three seats based on the pre–July 1979 opposition, but the JGRN
under Sandinista leadership added fourteen seats prior to its first meeting
in May 1980. These seats were assigned primarily to Sandinista-led mass
organizations. In hindsight it can probably be said that Robelo and Chamorro left the Junta when it became obvious that they were clearly in the

minority and unable to block the revolutionary direction of the transformation. Some analysts have suggested that Robelo and Chamorro may have initially falsely seen Ortega and Ramírez as social democratic moderates who could be won to their perspective (Gorman 1981, pp. 133–149; Close 1988, p. 121).

Robelo and Chamorro were replaced on the Junta by Rafael Córdoba Rivas, a lawyer affiliated with the Democratic Conservative Party, and Arturo Cruz, a former official of the Interamerican Development Bank. The Junta was pared down to three in 1981 and Ortega, Ramírez, and Córdoba Rivas served until January 1985 when Ortega and Ramírez were inaugurated as elected president and vice-president. The Junta legislated by decree from July 1979 to May 1980, when the Council of State began operation. During its first ten months, the JGRN emitted over 700 decrees that established the basic structures, personnel, laws, and procedures of the revolutionary order.

The Council of State began to function in May 1980, ending the brief period of total authority for the Junta. The Council was a unique political power and reflected closely the revolutionary perspective of the Sandinistas. The composition of the body was its most interesting aspect. The Junta designated which organizations were to be represented and by how many people, but the choice of the actual representatives was determined by the organizations themselves. Political parties, private-sector groups, labor organizations, mass organizations, and social organizations were represented. The actual groups ranged from the long-standing opposition parties, such as the Democratic Conservatives and Independent Liberals, to the new Sandinista mass organizations, such as the Nicaraguan Women's Association (AMNLAE) and Sandinista Youth, 19th of July (JS-19J).

The Council continued to function until it was replaced by the elected National Assembly in 1985. The Council had a number of specific powers though many were limited by the ultimate decisionmaking authority of the Junta. The Council approved or amended laws submitted to it by the JGRN, submitted its own legislation to the JGRN for approval, prepared an elections act upon request of the JGRN, and ratified treaties. Major limitations on its power were the lack of budgetary review and the fact that veto power was held by the Junta.

While the FSLN always held between 60 and 75 percent of the seats, the Council nonetheless was an important arena of debate and compromise for the Nicaraguan political system. Decrees of the Junta became law after ten days, if not challenged by the Council. If challenged, the Council's recommendations went back to the Junta, which could accept or reject them. According to John Booth's analysis (1985b, pp. 33–39), in practice the Junta decrees were often modified and by the 1982–1983 legislative session more initiatives were coming from the Council than from the Junta.

In its final year the Council of State was instrumental in formulating key laws that shaped the future of Nicaragua—the military draft laws, the political parties law, and most importantly a law specifying the nature of and conditions for the November 1984 elections. In spite of the dominance of the FSLN in the Council of State, there was considerable debate and compromise within the body. Coalitions were formed along pro- and antirevolutionary lines. The National Patriotic Front (FP), for instance, was headed by the FSLN but included also the Popular Social Christians (PPSC), the Independent Liberals (PLI), and the Socialist Party (PSN). The antirevolutionary forces were grouped in the Democratic Coordinating Committee (CD), headed by the Social Christians (PSCN) and the Social Democrats (PSD).

Council debates were sharpest in the 1983–1984 session over the electoral and the draft laws. While the FP ultimately got its way on all significant matters, the majority coalition did respond to opposition concerns. For instance, 30 percent of the political parties law approved by the Council in 1985 had been changed substantially from the FSLN's initial draft proposal because of opposition initiative (ibid., p. 39).

The major changes in national governmental institutions were mirrored at the local level. The heads of local governments fled, resigned, or were removed and replaced by Municipal Juntas for Reconstruction (JMRs). These corresponded geographically to the divisions of the country under Somoza, and the actual personnel were mostly people who had no previous experience of working in local government; only about 5 percent of local government employees had worked for the old regime in any capacity (Downs 1985, p. 46). Initially leaders of the JMRs were selected by local FSLN leaders on the basis of charisma and trustworthiness, but as the revolution began to become institutionalized, the local officials came to be selected by the mass organizations, particularly the Sandinista Defense Committees (CDSs). Unlike the national governmental institutions, which were elected after 1984, the municipal governments continued to be appointed until the 1990 elections. In most instances the FSLN party official at the regional and zonal level also served as the representative of the national government. It should also be noted that throughout the post-1979 period the power and importance of the JMRs were limited because they had few resources with which to respond to local problems and priorities.

Democratic Elections

Even before ousting Somoza, the FSLN had promised electoral democracy. In August 1980 the FSLN scheduled the first elections for 1985, citing the need to give first priority to improving social conditions, especially education. Preparation for elections in Nicaragua was not an insignificant task. Prior to the overthrow of the Somozas there had never been truly democratic elections in Nicaragua. Elections in the pre-Somoza period were carried out with strictly limited suffrage; during the Somoza era intimidation and ballot stuffing became the norm.

The Sandinistas prepared for their first elections in a systematic way, and even sent delegations to various Western democracies to study their election laws. Ironically, the Sandinista delegation scheduled to visit the United States was denied entry visas. Another important part of the election preparations was the formulation and passage in the Council of State of a Law of Political Parties. The law, unique in Nicaraguan history, was hammered out in negotiations between the Sandinistas and the major opposition parties of both the Left and the Right. The Council of State also passed an electoral law largely modeled after Western European institutions. The law, similar to those in other Latin American countries, established an independent branch of government to oversee the election. In substance, the electoral law established a unicameral National Assembly based on proportional representation and called for the direct election of the president and vice-president to six-year terms, which was also the electoral term for the National Assembly. Elections were set for November 1984, a year earlier than they had been originally promised.

On November 4, 1984 Nicaragua experienced a unique experiment in democracy. Guided by a nationalist ideology that was Marxist in orientation and a political movement that had incorporated some Leninist elements, the revolutionary government nonetheless held Western-style elections that invited the opposition parties to compete for power through the electoral process and encouraged the world to watch as they did. The result was a rare event in Nicaraguan history—an honest election. Further, it engendered real electoral competition among seven different parties and gave the Nicaraguan people one of their few experiences with democratic competition in this century. It also helped to embed representative democracy in the new governmental structure and diminish the construction of direct, participatory democracy.

The ground rules had been set before the election began. Elections would be held for representative institutions. Suggestions that direct democracy be retained in the form of a second house composed of legislators who were chosen directly by the members of their mass organizations (Yugoslavia had developed such a second house) were not persuasive. Rather, traditional Western representation would be employed through elections for a National Assembly wherein parties would compete for seats. Despite some initial governmental resistance, the opposition parties had been able to achieve a law that defined political parties as "groups of Nicaraguan citizens who have similar ideologies and who have come together, among other reasons, to vie for power with the purpose of carrying out a program responding to the needs of national development."[1] This statute and the pluralist philosophy that engendered it were a far cry from the special status reserved for the vanguard party in Marxist-Leninist states. Article 6 of the 1977 Soviet Constitution, for instance, stated that

> The leading and guiding force of Soviet society and the nucleus of its political system, of all state organizations and public organizations, is the Communist Party of the Soviet Union. . . .
> The Communist party, armed with Marxism-Leninism, determines the general perspectives of the development of society and the course of domestic and foreign policy of U.S.S.R., directs the great constructive work of the Soviet people, and imparts a planned, systematic and theoretically substantiated character to their struggle for the victory of Communism.[2]

The inclusion of the phrase "vie for power" defined the elections as instruments that would determine who would rule, not—as had been the case in traditional Marxist-Leninist states—how the official party would generate obligatory ratification of its policies. It was an example of how Nicaragua had broken out of the traditional East-West mold to forge its own policies and institutions. However, although this allowed for real political competition among parties, it was not consistent with direct popular empowerment of the masses. Nor is it at all clear that this process served as a model for how participatory democracy might be developed.

Unlike Costa Rica, its neighbor to the south, Nicaragua did not have a well-developed democratic tradition. Democratic structures were slow to develop and elections were frequently of questionable validity. In the earlier part of the century the United States had worsened the problem by repeatedly intervening in Nicaraguan politics, often supporting one candidate over another, and had even supervised elections in 1928 and 1932. These actions helped to set the stage for the increasingly undemocratic Somoza years, during which the electoral process is best characterized by manipulation, fraud, and coercion. This reality led the delegation sent to observe the 1984 election by the Latin American Studies Association (1984) to note that before the 1979 revolution, Nicaragua had a "tradition of nondemocratic, militarized politics with rampant human rights violations." Like virtually all the other outside observers, they found the 1984 electoral process to be a far cry from this traditional behavior.

Seven widely different parties and 1.17 million voters (out of a total population of 3 million) participated in what was reported to be Nicaragua's most honest election to date (a wide variety of observer groups attested to the honesty of the process). Other than the CIA-trained and backed counterrevolutionaries (contras), the only group not to participate in the electoral process was the Nicaraguan Democratic Coordinating Committee. Headed by Arturo Cruz and supported by the United States, it consisted of three small parties, the Social Christians (PSC), the Social Democrats (PSD), and the Constitutionalist Liberals (PLC). The Coordinadora, as it was known in Nicaragua, ignored several extended deadlines to register for the elections, claiming that freedom of the press and other necessary conditions for fair elections did not exist. In an effort to foster greater participation and ensure maximum political freedom, the Socialist International, which was then led by West Germany's Willy Brandt, tried on several occasions to mediate between the Sandinista government and the Coordinadora. In early October 1984, an agreement that would guarantee even greater campaign freedom in return for Coordinadora participation was almost worked out at a meeting of the Socialist International in Rio de Janeiro. However, talks collapsed at the last minute and the Sandinista representative Bayardo Arce withdrew. Nor could a subsequent visit to Managua by Brandt resolve the dispute (Kinzer 1984, p. 6).

In retrospect, it would seem that although Arturo Cruz's coalition may have had some legitimate concerns about its ability to freely participate in the electoral process (there had been some tense rock-throwing incidents earlier in the campaign), its unwillingness to join in the election owed more to pressure from the Reagan administration to discredit the process through nonparticipation than to actual internal conditions. Indeed, Cruz now believes that the people who dominated the coalition never intended to go through with the election.[3] He further admitted that he was paid a salary of $6,000 per month by the CIA and added that "Everyone was getting it" (Kinzer 1988). Like the contras, this group eventually called on Nicaraguans to abstain from the voting. This was also the position of the major opposition newspaper *La Prensa,* which, apart from biased and often inaccurate reporting, even refused to run paid party advertisements in its pages and became the principal media conduit for Coordinadora and Reagan administration views.

Direct popular participation as found in the mass organizations had been widely championed by Sandinista leaders. But elections had also been on the agenda ever since the Sandinista victory in 1979. As enunciated by Humberto Ortega in 1980, the FSLN position had been that elections should be held within five years, but that some waiting period was necessary in order to develop election laws and to give the populace time to become accustomed to the new society and the pluralist possibilities it presented. Thus the Council of State (which included representatives of opposition groups including COSEP, the Superior Council of

Private Enterprise) passed the political parties law in August of 1983. In the fall of 1983 the Socialist International joined opposition groups like the Social Christian Party (PSC) in calling on the government to move up elections to 1984. Washington was also able to point to the absence of elections as a verification of their claims that the Sandinistas were indeed totalitarian Marxist-Leninists who, like Fidel Castro, would not hold elections as promised. These events prompted considerable discussion within the FSLN, which once again opted for a pragmatic course. In February 1984, it was announced that elections would be held on November 4th of that year (two days before the U.S. elections).

A draft of an electoral law was introduced in the Council of State during February and, after considerable debate, passed in mid-March. Ironically, the debate in the Council of State was periodically boycotted by some opposition members who in the end reversed their previous calls for an earlier election by claiming that the accelerated calendar did not allow them adequate preparation time. The PSC, the Social Democratic Party, COSEP, and other parties that followed this path eventually joined the Coordinadora and abstained from the election. This led many critics to claim that their actual intent was never to participate in elections but rather, like the Reagan administration in Washington, to use any pretext to embarrass the Sandinistas and discredit the electoral process. Further credence was lent to this view when, under opposition criticism, the Sandinistas lifted the declared state of emergency in July, only to be confronted with yet other reasons why the opposition would not participate in the election.

Though some press censorship persisted, it was mostly limited to military matters. Adequate media access was guaranteed to each of the seven participating parties. The government allocated each party thirty minutes of state television time and forty-five minutes of state radio time each week. Further, each party received 9 million córdobas (U.S. $900,000 at the official exchange rate) in order to buy additional TV and radio time and to purchase other campaign materials.

The election in Nicaragua was very different from the 1984 election in El Salvador. There were no death squads operating, and none of the candidates or party leaders had to fear for their lives from the government. Several election officials were, however, killed by contra groups. Ray Hooker, a Sandinista candidate from the Atlantic Coast, was shot and held captive by a contra band for some weeks and was only released after the election. At the beginning of the campaign, there were some minor incidents at opposition rallies. These seem to have resulted from the overzealousness of some younger Sandinista militants and a general lack of familiarity with the give and take of democratic campaigning on both sides. Careful political education by the Sandinistas and strict police vigilance soon remedied these problems.

There was vigorous campaigning throughout the country; even days after the election one could see numerous posters and slogans on walls, trees, and utility poles. The populace was very much involved in the electoral process. Participating parties included the following:

1. FSLN. The government party developed from the Sandinista National Liberation Front. Daniel Ortega and Sergio Ramírez were the candidates for president and vice-president.

2. PLI. The Independent Liberal Party was formed in 1944 to challenge Somoza dominance in the traditional Liberal Party. The party's presidential candidate, Dr. Virgilio Godoy, had served as Labor Minister in the Sandinista government, and the party had supported the government until shortly before the election campaign. Constantino Pereira was the party's vice-presidential candidate.

3. PDC. The Democratic Conservative Party developed from the Conservative Party in Nicaragua. The party's leader, Rafael Córdoba Rivas, had been a member of the three-person ruling Junta. The party, however, urged negotiations with the contras and the separation of the FSLN Party from the state apparatus. Clemente Guido ran as the Conservative presidential candidate; Mercedes Rodríguez ran for vice-president.

4. PSN. The Nicaraguan Socialist Party was the traditional Marxist-Leninist Party and followed a Soviet orientation on most issues. It was critical of Sandino and the Sandinistas at different times in its history and only supported the FSLN in the final stages of the revolution. Domingo Sánchez ran as the party's presidential candidate and Adolfo Everetz filled the vice-presidential slot.

5. PPSC. The Popular Social Christian Party was inspired by a progressive Christian Democratic philosophy. It initially supported the Sandinista government and advocated more participatory, decentralized decisionmaking. Its presidential and vice-presidential candidates were Mauricio Díaz and Guillermo Mejía.

6. PCdeN. The Communist Party of Nicaragua came into being when a left-wing faction of the Nicaraguan Socialist Party broke away in 1971 to form a separate group. Taking a more traditional Marxist-Leninist line, it considered the FSLN a petty-bourgeois reformist party and was quite critical of government policies. Allan Zambrana and Manuel Pérez Estrada were the PCdeN's presidential and vice-presidential candidates.

7. MAP-ML. The Marxist-Leninist Popular Action Movement was a small far-Left group that actively opposed government policy, particularly in the fields of economics and labor. It ran Isidoro Téllez and Juan Alberto

Henríquez as its presidential and vice-presidential candidates.

For the purpose of electing candidates to the National Assembly, the country was divided into nine territorial districts, and proportional representation was used to award seats from party lists in each of these. In addition, a seat was awarded to each of the six presidential candidates who did not win. All the ninety-six new members would serve six-year terms. The Assembly's first task was to act as a constituent assembly to determine the exact organizational structure for the new government. This task was begun in early 1985.

Any doubts about how well the FSLN would do were set aside by the party's tumultuous election-eve rally in Carlos Fonseca Plaza. Although the rally began slowly, after the first couple of hours thousands of enthusiastic FSLN supporters surged into the plaza. The throng eventually included 300,000 of Managua's 850,000 residents. The festivities continued into the night amidst a general feeling of joy (Reding 1984, pp. 488–489). Increased contra attacks in outlying regions did, however, convince many to stay away from the polls.

A general calm prevailed on election day. Despite rightist efforts, contra threats, and U.S. pressure not to vote, participation was extremely high. Almost 40 percent of the total population voted in the election. All citizens sixteen years or older were able to vote, and 93.7 percent of those eligible registered. Of these, 75 percent cast ballots on election day. The big winners were the Sandinistas, who garnered 62.9 percent of the votes for president and vice-president and 62.3 percent of the National Assembly votes. The six opposition parties divided 33 percent of the vote, while blank or invalid ballots accounted for a little more than 6 percent of the votes cast. Election results were usually reported as a percentage of the valid votes cast for each office (see Table 4.1). War conditions forced sixteen of the 3,892 national polling places to remain closed on election day. The war, inadequate transport, and abstentionist calls combined to account for the 25 percent of registered voters who did not cast ballots. While registration was obligatory, voting was not, and voter registration cards were marked and entrusted to election judges to make sure that the lack of a stamped voting card would not trigger government harassment as had occurred in El Salvador in 1984.

The entire election process was carefully administered by the Supreme Electoral Council, which was aided by Swedish election officials. A multitude of outside observers closely monitored the actual voting and were virtually unanimous in their praise for how the election was administered. José Figueres, the widely respected political leader and ex-president of Costa Rica, was very favorably impressed by the order and propriety of the election. He was quoted in *El Nuevo Diario* the next day

Table 4.1 1984 Election Results

Party	Percent for president and vice-president[*]	Percent for assembly[*]	Number of seats in assembly
FSLN	67	67	61
PCDN	14	14	14
PLI	9.6	9.7	9
PPSC	5.6	5.6	6
PCdeN	1.5	1.5	2
PSN	1.3	1.4	2
MAP-ML	1	1	2

[*]Percent of valid votes cast for each. These figures are exclusive of blank or defaced ballots, which made up 6 percent of the total vote. Of the total votes cast, the FSLN got 62.9 percent for president and 62.3 percent for the National Assembly.

as not knowing what "those who had predicted otherwise were going to say." The only incident that marred the process happened a few days before the election when Dr. Virgilio Godoy, the presidential candidate for the Independent Liberal Party, attempted to withdraw his party from the ballot and join the abstentionist forces. In that the ballots had already been printed and distributed, the Supreme Electoral Council ruled that the deadline for withdrawing was past and that the party would appear on the ballot. Godoy's initial decision had been made shortly after conferring with the Coordinadora leadership and a conversation with the U.S. am-

Billboard Announcing Election Results

bassador. This prompted Liberal vice-presidential candidate Constantino Pereira to claim a half-hour slot of previously reserved national television time to urge that all party supporters participate in the election. Most seem to have heeded his call, for the Liberals culled close to 10 percent in the voting.

Judged against Nicaragua's historically authoritarian tradition, the 1984 elections were an immense success. Although political conditions prior to the election were not perfect, the voting itself did not see the type of corruption and vote fraud that had been so common in countries like Nicaragua, Guatemala, and El Salvador. The opposition was allowed to run and to win a third of the seats in the National Assembly. The government and its policies were openly criticized during the campaign. This was a major accomplishment for a country like Nicaragua and was despite the best efforts of the Reagan administration that (according to a National Security Council document leaked to the *Washington Post* on November 6, 1984 [Guillermoprieto 1984]) had actively campaigned to convince the North American public that the elections were a farce. Subsequent developments suggest that Reagan had pressured the Coordinadora not to participate in the elections and tried to do the same with elements of the Independent Liberal Party. It is also interesting to note that just as information about the success of the election was starting to hit the U.S. press, the White House leaked a story to the media about MiG fighters en route to Nicaragua. Thus the American public heard about (nonexistent) MiGs in or on their way to Nicaragua and not the elections (*Latin America Weekly Report* 1984).

The Nicaraguan election marked a significant expansion of the political horizon for Marxist-oriented regimes, if not a turning point in the evolution of Marxism. It was the first historic case in which a Marxist movement that had come to power by revolution was willing to allow opposition groups to challenge it in an open balloting process and to actually share power with these groups in an elected assembly. In retrospect, this process proved to be a precursor for many similar elections in Eastern Europe. As also was the case in Eastern Europe, while this type of election and the representative institutions that resulted were a major concession to Western-style representative democracy, it seemed to contradict earlier pledges to enact a democratic system that more fully empowered the masses.

It is by no means fully established that such representative institutions best serve popular democracy or are optimum for ensuring governmental responsiveness to popular need. In a 1986 paper on the real nature of democracy, the well-known Mexican political scientist Pablo González Casanova (in Jonas and Stein 1990, p. 15) notes that democracy is only meaningful if real popular power lies below the form of representative democracy. Indeed, he asks "What democracy are we speaking about, and whom does it serve?" As the organization of the new legislative assembly was debated in the Council of State prior to the 1984 elections, the opposition parties were able to successfully remove any structures that would give the mass organizations a role in the new assembly. When the newly elected National Assembly first convened, the mass organizations no longer had their own direct representatives. This ended the strong direct participation of these popular organizations in the legislature and thus in the governmental structure as a whole (Lobel 1988, p. 868).[4] George Vickers (1990, p. 23) argues that the actual 1984 election and "more importantly, the decision to replace the Council of State with a National Assembly constituted by political party representatives, drastically undermined the role of mass organizations in shaping the course of the revolution." He further suggests that this represented the beginning of a movement away from the initial Sandinista conception of revolutionary (direct) participatory democracy to "the more traditional notion of democracy based on political parties and representative elections" (ibid.). In his seminal article on representative and participatory democracy in Nicaragua under the new (1987) constitution, Jules Lobel (1988, p. 868) noted that "the attempt to develop representative institutions in the context of a dominant role for participatory democracy [presented] several important contradictions" (see also Mijeski 1991, chap. 8). He further argues that such representative government acted as a brake on the political demands that flowed from the mass movement. The new political institutions facilitated and became increasingly responsive to middle- and upper-class mobilization as manifest in the opposition parties that had gained seats in the National Assembly, and retarded and became increasingly less responsive to the lower-class constituency of the mass organizations, which no longer had seats in the new legislative body.

Constitution Making

There was one last attempt to involve the masses directly. As a means of continuing popular participation in the governmental process, a series of open forums (*cabildos abiertos*) were scheduled after the National Assembly; acting as a constituent assembly, they fashioned a draft for a new constitution. Begun in May 1985, the process itself had been laborious. The delegations had visited a wide variety of different nations whose legal systems were examined (Reding 1987, pp. 259–260). The assembly (primarily functioning through its Constitutional Commission, which included representatives of all parties in the assembly) had considered twenty-four constitutional proposals submitted by different political parties and other groups.

The initial drafting of the constitution was the responsibility of a Special Constitutional Commission appointed in April 1985 by the National Assembly. The Commission generally reflected the results of the November 1984 election, but the opposition parties were purposely over-represented to induce them to participate fully in drafting the new constitution. Of the twenty-two members, twelve were from the FSLN and the remaining ten were divided among the six opposition parties that competed in the 1984 elections. As had occurred prior to the elections, several delegations visited Eastern Europe, Western Europe, and Latin America to explore a variety of alternative constitutional experiences. In the spring of 1986, a Nicaraguan constitutional delegation gained entry into the United States and participated in a review of the developing Nicaraguan constitution at Rutgers University in New Jersey.

The first draft of the new constitution was completed in February 1986. In an effort to harmonize representative and participatory democracy, the draft obligated the state to remove obstacles that effectively impeded the equality of Nicaraguans and their participation in the political, social, and economic life of the country. Consistent with that intent, 150,000 copies of the draft were distributed and twelve televised debates were held between representatives of opposing parties. Thereafter, a series of seventy-three cabildos abiertos were held across the country. Two thousand five hundred Nicaraguan citizens made presentations and 100,000 attended (Reding 1986, p. 435). Several of the more conservative, middle-class parties, like the Democratic Conservative Party and the Independent Liberal Party, refused to participate in the cabildos on the grounds that since the population had already elected its representatives to draft a constitution, there was no need for further popular participation (Lobel 1988, pp. 868–869). Quite a few provisions were challenged in these meetings and many were changed. Of particular note were the spirited attacks led by the national women's association (AMNLAE) on the concept of *patria potestas* (Article 102), which referred back to Roman law and the dominant position of the *pater familias* in the household (see Morgan 1990).

Another demand that came out of several cabildos was a proposal for a permanent legislative chamber for popular organizations. Such an institution would give direct representation to the mass organizations and again incorporate them into the mechanism of the state. However, when this measure was debated in the National Assembly, it was strongly resisted by the traditional middle-class and bourgeois parties. Although some aspects of the constitution such as the patria potestas were deleted and others were added, the proposal for direct representation for the mass organizations was not included.

While the constitutional process was quite open, it was marred by important abstentions. Most of the opposition parties on the constitutional commission boycotted the open forums on the grounds that they were being manipulated by the Sandinistas. In addition, the Coordinadora, a U.S.-supported right-wing coalition of three political parties, two labor unions, and the Superior Council of Private Enterprise (COSEP) that boycotted the 1984 elections, extended its abstention to the constitutional process.

In the view of Andrew Reding (1987, p. 262), a key observer of the process, what emerged was "a document that combines the Western emphasis on civil and political rights with a Marxist stress on social and economic rights." The constitution established a separation of powers among four branches of government: executive, legislative, judicial, and electoral. The Supreme Electoral Council broke a certain amount of new ground while the other principles of presidential government, proportional representation, and an independent judiciary drew heavily from existing Western European models.

A special feature of the Nicaraguan constitution is the direct incorporation of two international human rights declarations (the Universal Declaration of Human Rights and the American Declaration of the Rights and Duties of Man) and three human rights treaties (the International Covenant on Economic, Social, and Cultural Rights; the International Covenant on Civil and Political Rights; and the American Convention on Human Rights). It should be noted that the treaties are included in a section of the constitution entitled "Rights, Duties, and Guarantees of the Nicaraguan People" and cannot be suspended even in "national emergencies." The inclusion of these treaties is significant because few other Latin American countries have done so and because key leaders of the FSLN were initially opposed to their inclusion. According to Reding (ibid.), strong support from the revolutionary Christian wing of the FSLN eventually convinced other FSLN deputies to support their inclusion.

Another significant provision is the explicit banning of the death penalty in Article 23. This provision extended the prohibition made at the time of the revolutionary triumph in 1979. Nicaragua was the first social revolution to abolish the death penalty and joined just a handful of countries who have done so. The constitution also specifically limits the terms of imprisonment to a maximum of thirty years.

Not surprisingly, the Nicaraguan constitution places a high priority on economic, social, and cultural rights. In this arena the Sandinistas sought to emulate the revolutionary experience of Cuba. Rights explicitly listed in the constitution include the right to be protected from hunger, the right to decent housing, social security, health, education, and a healthy environment. On the whole, the constitution mandates that the government must step in to guarantee basic needs when normal market forces do not succeed in providing them.

The Nicaraguan constitution also bars discrimination on the basis of race, color, sex, religion, or national origin. The document is definitive in its defense of women's rights and includes general equal protection provisions, sexual equality provisions, equality in marriage and the family, equality in employment, and equality in civil, political, economic, and social affairs. It should be noted that the initial draft of the constitution was not so progressive. The Special Constitutional Commission of twenty men and two women came under heavy attack from AMNLAE for its emphasis solely on the family and its use of sexist terminology. The final document reflected many of the concerns of Nicaraguan women but fell short in the eyes of many by not guaranteeing access to abortion and birth control.[5]

The New Governmental Structure

The constitution reaffirmed the basic structure of government codified in the 1984 electoral law and strengthened the power of the National Assembly and the judiciary. Government leaders sought to create a system that gave substantial authority to the executive and legislative branches to confront the country's serious socioeconomic problems while retaining sufficient checks on governmental power to prevent abuses of individual rights. According to Reding (1987, p. 280), each branch was assigned a particular task. The strong, elected presidency was charged with making the necessary structural changes to further the revolutionary process. The legislature shared the role of transformation with the presidency, but with broader participation. During the era of a Sandinista majority, that meant involvement of the opposition parties in the revolutionary process. The independent judiciary, appointed by the legislature, was charged with enforcing human rights and guarding against abuses of authority. The independent electoral branch, also appointed by the legislature, was given authority to conduct all elections and referenda.

During the Sandinista period the presidency was a powerful office. Constitutionally, the president was empowered to enforce the constitution and laws, conduct foreign relations, declare war, and appoint ambassadors, government ministers, and regional administrators. Also, to curb the power of the legislative branch, the president had line-item veto authority over budgetary matters. He also nominated the comptroller general and the magistrates of the Supreme Court and Supreme Electoral Council. However, the Nicaraguan reality during the Sandinista era also served to increase executive power. Because Nicaragua was at war with the contras for much of this period, the president, as commander-in-chief of the armed forces, assumed even greater power. From Ortega's inauguration in Jan-

The National Assembly in Session

uary 1985 until 1989, Nicaragua was officially in a "state of emergency." As a result, he assumed more and more power, also reflected in the creation in 1985 of a five-person Executive Committee of the Directorate of the FSLN; four of the five were key members of Ortega's cabinet.

The judiciary is headed by the Supreme Court of Justice whose magistrates serve six-year terms. In addition to the customary power of judicial review of the constitutionality of laws, the Supreme Court is assigned the power of *amparo* in defense of the constitutional rights of individuals. Amparo, which means "protection," is unique to Latin America, and extends the protection of the court to all rights, including political and economic rights. It should be noted that during the state of emergency, President Ortega suspended recourse to amparo. The Sandinista-appointed Supreme Court objected to the suspension but this remained an unresolved constitutional question when the state of emergency was ended in 1989. During the Sandinista period, questions were also raised about two courts that existed independently of the regular court system: the Agrarian Reform tribunals and the People's Anti-Somocista tribunals. Both were presided over by three judges, two of whom were selected by Sandinista mass organizations. The decisions of these courts were not appealable through the regular court system and did become the source of abuses (Americas Watch 1982, pp. 27–29).

Like most progressive Latin American countries, the Nicaraguan political system has an independent electoral authority, the Supreme Electoral Council. Unlike many other countries that have such a body, Nicaragua's is given formal status as a fourth branch of government. The council's five members are selected by the National Assembly for six-year

terms from nominees submitted by the president. The effective independence of this particular organ was demonstrated in the 1990 elections won
by the United Nicaraguan Opposition (UNO). These elections were
closely scrutinized by international observers and the commission was
credited with overseeing fair elections in which the ruling party was
defeated—the ultimate test of electoral fairness (Latin American Studies
Association 1990).

During the years of Sandinista power a wholly new government
structure was established in order to remove the Somoza apparatus completely and to provide a governmental base for the social and economic
transformation of Nicaraguan society. The Sandinistas sought to combine
what they viewed to be the best aspects of both participatory and representative democracy. However, the 1984 elections and the resultant constitutional structure suggest that great care must be taken to nourish direct
participation lest it be subordinated to traditional representative institutions. Under strong international pressure the Sandinistas did not take
care to protect the participatory process and as a result the impact of the
mass organizations was greatly diminished as representative institutions
gained an unprecedented hold on the Nicaraguan political process.

Notes

1. See the political parties law passed by the Nicaraguan Council of State in
February 1984 after considerable debate by the opposition parties and some
redrafting. See also the Nicaraguan electoral law, passed by the Council of State
on March 15, 1984.
2. With the restructuring and democraticization of the Soviet Union, this
article was subsequently changed to reflect new Soviet realities.
3. Arturo Cruz admitted that he was pressured by the United States to stop
his organization from participating in the elections; see Kinzer (1988).
4. It should be noted, however, that the FSLN did include mass organization
members on its slate of candidates, even though some of them were not themselves
FSLN members. Several of these candidates were so elected, but became part of
the FSLN bloc rather than direct delegates of the mass organizations. Some
believed that this further subordinated the mass organizations to the FSLN.
5. Interview by Prevost with Bertha Argüello, AMNLAE representative,
January 1987.

❖ FIVE ❖
Sandinista Thought and Action

For eleven years the Sandinista National Liberation Front (FSLN) held state power in Nicaragua and undertook a profound program of political, economic, and social change. The Sandinistas relinquished government power in April 1990 to the United Nicaraguan Opposition (UNO) coalition that had triumphed in national elections two months earlier. The years of Sandinista rule left an indelible mark on Nicaraguan society. This chapter analyzes the years of Sandinista power by focusing on the evolution of the political philosophy of the FSLN as reflected in its political practice as a ruling party. Specific Sandinista political practice in the arenas of state construction, the economy, and foreign policy will receive the greatest attention. This chapter will also analyze to what degree there has been an evolution in the political philosophy of the FSLN since 1979 and how that evolution, if any, is to be explained.

Principles of FSLN Political Philosophy

How would the political philosophy of the FSLN be characterized at the time the movement took power in 1979, and to what degree was there a shift in perspective by the FSLN during its eleven years in power? By late 1979, the FSLN could be described as a vanguard, political-military organization supported by three pillars: Marxism (as interpreted by Lenin, Mao, Ho Chi Minh, and Fonseca Amador), the revolutionary and class-conscious ideas and practice of Augusto César Sandino, and the inspiration of the successful Cuban Revolution led by Fidel Castro and Ché Guevara. Numerous studies of the Sandinista movement generally agree on the importance of these three primary factors plus several secondary ones, particularly liberation theology (see Vilas 1986, pp. 13–48; Booth 1985a, pp. 272–273; Walker 1985, pp. 22–24; Gilbert 1988, pp. 19–40; Hodges 1986). While these studies often seek to place relative weights on

89

the three pillars, such attempts fail largely because of the complicated interaction of the three. For tactical political reasons borne of Nicaragua's life-and-death struggle with the United States, Sandinista leaders in their public speeches and official interviews emphasized primarily the connection to Sandino and downplayed the role of Marxism in their development. On the other extreme, firm opponents of the Sandinista revolution placed sole emphasis on the FSLN's connections to the Soviet Union and Cuba and to Marxist-Leninist ideas.[1] A truer assessment of the development of the FSLN's political philosophy would include a significant role for both Sandino and Marxism—to focus on either one exclusively is simply not historically accurate—and adequate attention to the role of liberation theology.

The leaders of the FSLN stated on numerous occasions soon after the defeat of the dictatorship that their philosophy was embodied in three principles—political pluralism, nonalignment, and a mixed economy with a socialist orientation.[2] While the three primary principles of Sandinista rule remained basically intact until the transfer of power, important shifts did occur. A sharp move away from the socialist orientation of the economy was seen under conditions of hardship after 1987. The effort to achieve nonalignment was severely hampered by the intensity of the Cold War and the resulting reliance on military and strategic assistance from the socialist countries. And the achievement of political pluralism was hampered throughout the Sandinista years by the vertical nature of FSLN structures. The basic principles of political pluralism, nonalignment, and a mixed economy can be seen in the historic program of the FSLN, but the specific focus on those three pillars does represent a subtle shift. That shift occurred in the alliance engineered in the last year of the struggle against the dictatorship.

A review of the 1969 program of the FSLN (1980) does not reveal policies that specifically contradict these principles, but its overall thrust is somewhat different. The document challenges at least one key aspect of political pluralism by calling for "the replacement of the constitutional theory of elected representation with a revolutionary government that would promote direct popular participation." Freedom of expression is supported but hedged with the phrase "in the interest of the people." The program also called for "respect for religious beliefs." But as a whole, the document does not have a significant emphasis on political pluralism.

The desire for a mixed economy can be gleaned through the phrase "protection of small and middle-sized proprietors," but the general thrust of the program's economic pronouncements are more anticapitalist and prosocialist. It called for the nationalization of the property of the Somozas and associates of the ruling government, U.S.-based companies, natural resources, and foreign commerce. The rural sector was to be drastically affected with major land expropriations, and compensation was to be paid only to those who had cooperated with FSLN guerrillas. Other socialist recommendations included national economic planning and worker participation in state enterprises.

The nonaligned thrust of the revolution was made most clear by a desire to break free from domination by the United States and a strong identification with other Third World revolutionary movements, particularly in Latin America. There is no mention of the socialist countries within the document.

However, the 1969 document was not the final word on Sandinista philosophy prior to 1979. A later document (in *Latin American Perspectives* 1979), released in 1978 under the influence of the developing revolutionary situation and the domination of the Insurrectionalist (Tercerista) tendency, makes some subtle but significant shifts that are important to this analysis. The 1978 version makes no statement on the type of government that is to be constructed in Nicaragua, but it is more explicit in defending democratic liberties by stating that "everyone will enjoy the right to express his/her opinions as they wish, and no one will be harassed because of his/her ideas." Unlike the 1969 document, no conditions are placed on the exercise of freedoms. The 1978 document is more explicit than the 1969 program as to how the economic face of Nicaragua would be dramatically altered. In addition to projecting the seizing of Somoza-held land and enterprises, the nationalization of the country's natural resources, government control of the banking system, and agrarian reform, the document gives greater detail to reform measures related to unionization, labor laws, price controls, transportation, and electric services. It does not specifically mention the concept of a mixed economy and no guarantees are provided for private property. On economic questions it would be incorrect to label the 1978 document as less revolutionary than the 1969 program.

In the foreign policy realm, the 1978 version is more explicit in its profession of nonalignment, though the term is not used. Rather it states, "Nicaragua is going to have relations with all countries of the world, depending on whatever agrees with the country's development interests." The main difference is that all direct references to the United States have been removed; gone are references to "the expulsion of the U.S. military mission, the Peace Corps, and other instruments of Yankee intervention." The section calling for abolition of the Chamorro-Bryan canal treaty is also removed, as are references to the cultural penetration of "Yankee imperialism" in society and the university. Unlike the 1969 document, there is no reference to "support for national liberation movements in neighboring states" or "solidarity with Third World anti-imperialists and North American blacks." The softer tone toward the United States is the greatest change and seems to reflect an effort by the FSLN leaders to remain open to accommodation with the Carter administration. The moderate stance toward the United States also reflected the more pro–United States stance of the liberal, nonrevolutionary opposition that was being courted by the Tercerista strategy. However, it is also important to repeat that the fundamentally radical political and economic program of the 1969 statement was not significantly compromised, and therefore the FSLN organization that gained power in 1979 was not fundamentally different in political philosophy from the revolutionary guerrilla organization that articulated its full program for the first time a decade earlier. The leadership of the FSLN made important tactical alliances with non-revolutionary forces in the months prior to the defeat of Somoza, but the basic principles of the Sandinista movement were not altered.

Political Pluralism

The political system envisioned for Nicaragua in the Historic Program of the FSLN is not simply a classic liberal democratic model but rather one that combines representative democracy, participatory democracy, and the protection of broadly defined individual rights. This system is categorized in Sandinista pronouncements as political pluralism. The use of this term, usually associated with Western liberal democracies, seems to represent an attempt by the FSLN leadership to accommodate their broad political coalition and to promote their project in North America and Western Europe. Whatever the motivations behind the use of the term, it does represent a standard by which the Nicaraguan political process can be judged.

A key aspect of Nicaragua's political pluralism is the existence of more than twenty-five legally registered parties that function in the public arena and put forward candidates in national and local elections. In the February 1990 elections nine parties and one coalition of fourteen parties offered candidates for president, vice-president, National Assembly, and local offices.[3] The fourteen-party coalition, the United Nicaraguan Opposition (UNO), won 55 percent of the vote and gained control of the presidency, National Assembly, and a majority of municipal governments. In a most significant test of Sandinista commitment to political pluralism, the transfer of political power to UNO occurred virtually without incident in April 1990.

However, it is important to note that political pluralism did not begin with the 1990 elections, as some U.S. government spokespeople have suggested. In the 1984 elections, seven political parties competed; opponents of the Sandinistas gained approximately one third of the popular vote and more than one third of the representation in the National Assembly. If the first election had been conducted on a single-member constituency basis, the Sandinistas would likely have won all the seats. Instead, the six opposition parties that participated each won at least two seats in the National Assembly, which was elected on the basis of proportional representation. While only UNO, the FSLN, and two other parties—the Social Christians and the Movement for Revolutionary Unity—gained seats in the new Assembly, pluralism was virtually guaranteed by the heterogeneous character of the UNO bloc. Minority currents representing as little as 1 percent of the voters are represented in the Assembly. In all other countries with proportional representation, the threshold is higher: 2 percent in Denmark, 4 percent in Sweden, and 5 percent in Germany. The Nicaraguan electoral law also provides for a seat in the National Assembly for any defeated presidential candidate who gains at least 1 percent of the vote.

It can also be argued that the political pluralism of the Nicaraguan system is demonstrated in the practice of the National Assembly and in the Nicaraguan constitution that was drafted by the Assembly and put into place in 1987. In the National Assembly between 1984 and 1990, the FSLN carried out a certain degree of power sharing in spite of its overwhelming numerical advantage. The Assembly elected a Governing Council consisting of a president, three vice-presidents, and three secretaries. The late Carlos Núñez, former member of the National Directorate of the FSLN, was the president. The vice-presidents, who took over the president's functions in his absence, were from the FSLN and two opposition parties: the Democratic Conservatives and the Popular Social Christians. The secretaries, who were responsible for communication within the Assembly and with other government agencies, were from the FSLN and the Socialist party. The Assembly had twelve permanent commissions dealing with policy areas such as health, education, justice, human rights, and defense. Opposition parties were represented on all the commissions, and if a consensus was not reached on proposed legislation, then minority and majority reports were presented to the whole Assembly (see Reding 1985, pp. 269–277).

Another indicator of the prominent role of the opposition was in the drafting of the constitution. The Constitutional Commission had twenty-two members, of whom twelve represented the FSLN; the other ten were from the six opposition parties. Thus the opposition was accorded a greater weight in the Commission than it achieved in the elections. Further, four members of the FSLN delegation were not members of the FSLN. They were drawn from among the seventeen members of the FSLN parliamentary group who were not members of the FSLN party. While these representatives usually voted with the FSLN party line, they held dissenting views and cast opposing votes on numerous occasions. These nonparty members included some highly prominent figures with considerable influence in the country. One was Sixto Ulloa, a vice-president of the Baptist Convention and committed pacifist, who sought to bring the principles of mainstream liberation theology into the revolutionary process. Others represented the sector of the private entrepreneurs that supported the Sandinistas.

Further, the Nicaraguan constitution, drafted by the Commission and later ratified by the Assembly, embodies political pluralism. It is a document that combines a capitalist emphasis on civil and political rights with the socialist stress on social and economic rights. The constitution draws from the progressive Latin American tradition of presidential government with proportional representation and an independent judiciary. A centerpiece of the constitution is its incorporation of international human rights treaties, a feature that divided the Sandinistas on the Constitutional Commission.[4] On the question of human rights, the constitution also codifies an important Nicaraguan law that was adopted in 1979: abolition of the death penalty. Regardless of the crime, no Nicaraguan can be imprisoned for more than thirty years. The abolition of the death penalty places Nicaragua in a select group of countries worldwide and is particularly significant in the wake of the repression of the Somoza era. No earlier social revolutions have ever taken such a step. It has been suggested by many that the charitable stance taken by the Sandinistas toward the former guardsmen is a reflection of the Christian influence on Sandinista philosophy.

The willingness of the Sandinistas to allow a vigorous opposition press even in time of war, and a good measure of their tolerance, was demonstrated by the fact that the opposition paper *La Prensa* functioned openly until June 1986 and was then reopened in early 1988 even before a complete cease-fire agreement was negotiated between the contras and the Sandinistas (opposition newspapers have not existed in war-torn El Salvador for a decade). Before June 1986 and since its reopening, *La Prensa* served as a voice for the leadership of the contras and was widely reported to have accepted funds from sources tied to the U.S. government (Nichols 1988). Media freedom was not limited to *La Prensa*. Throughout the 1980s numerous opposition radio stations operated largely unimpeded; they consistently broadcast views sharply critical of the government and gave implied support to the armed counterrevolution.

Another important aspect of the FSLN's concept of political pluralism was the involvement of mass organizations in the political process. The legitimacy of FSLN rule came not only from the parliamentary electoral process, but to a greater extent from its leadership of a thoroughgoing transformation of Nicaraguan society (see, for example, Jonas and Stein 1990). Well before the construction of formal representative institutions, the mass organizations (described in detail in chapter 3) were democratizing the Nicaraguan political process. Sandinista-led organizations, such as the Sandinista Defense Committees (CDSs), the Rural Workers' Association (ATC), and the Nicaraguan Women's Association (AMNLAE), were crucial both to the transformation of society and democratic participation. The mass organizations had direct governmental representation on the governing Council of State until it was superseded after the 1984 elections. Ironically, this aspect of pluralism declined after 1984 due to a variety of factors. As the contra war heated up, the CDSs in particular became an arm of the FSLN and government to enforce ultimately unpopular programs such as food rationing and the military service draft. While problems in the CDSs were recognized as early as 1982 and various attempts were made to reform them, their role as grass-roots participatory institutions has largely failed.

While their problems may not have been as dramatic as the CDSs, other Sandinista mass organizations also experienced the problem of becoming primarily organizations for enforcing FSLN policy rather than fostering grass-roots democracy. For example, the Sandinista Workers' Central (CST) became focused on gaining acceptance for government economic policies rather than on the direct defense of workers' interests. Even as the FSLN carried out austerity measures in 1988 and 1989 that undercut the economic position of the CST members, the union did not mount any significant opposition to the government's plans. The Sandinista-led union movement only began to rebuild itself as a grass-roots force during 1990, in response to the economic and political policies of the UNO government.

The creation of the parliamentary system also served to blunt the importance of the participatory democracy side of Nicaraguan pluralism. In contrast to their direct representation in the Council of State, the mass organizations ultimately found themselves shut out of real political power in the new constitutional arrangements. Initially the FSLN had hoped to retain some formal role for the mass organizations in the parliamentary system, but the intense opposition to this by the conservative parties convinced the FSLN to compromise on this point. The compromise was justified on the grounds of emulating the Western model as closely as possible. The mass organizations were promised that their representation would continue through the vehicle of the FSLN party. The failure to provide that representation is symptomatic of another shortcoming in the full achievement of political pluralism in the Nicaraguan political process.

Due to the domination of Nicaraguan politics by the FSLN, pluralism and democracy within the organization becomes a crucial variable. Chapter 6 provides a detailed analysis of the party and its processes that reveals some significant flaws. While it is definitely true that ideological diversity and flexibility existed in the FSLN throughout this period, the lack of democratic party structures prevented the Sandinista mass organizations from fully playing their democratic and grass-roots role. The concentration of power in the hands of the National Directorate and its staff and the lack of available forums for democratic decisionmaking inevitably flawed the pluralistic process. While the centralization of power can be understood to a degree in the context of Nicaraguan political culture, the FSLN's history, and the pressures of the contra war, it is now generally recognized by both the leadership and ranks of the party that the move to democratize party structures was long overdue.

The 1990 national elections were a crucial test of political pluralism in Nicaragua. In spite of the factors discussed previously, many actors, headed by the government of the United States, doubted that the Sandinistas would oversee a fair election and transfer power to the opposition. The U.S. perspective was summed up in a U.S. Department of State bulletin (1984) that depicted Nicaragua as a totalitarian state, the antithesis of political pluralism. The primary thrust of the U.S. policy of backing the contras was based on the judgment that the Sandinistas would never relinquish power unless forced to do so by an armed opposition. Even as the Nicaraguan government began to plan the 1990 elections within the framework of the Nicaraguan constitution and the Central American peace process, the United States cast doubt on the commitment of the Sandinistas to political pluralism and withheld its full support of the electoral process until after the voting results were announced.

While maintaining a commitment to political pluralism expressed in the electoral process, the constitution, and the defense of individual rights, the FSLN did not until recently expect that that commitment would extend to the relinquishing of political power. For many years the Sandinista leadership simply scoffed at the idea that there could be any effective challenge to their position. By transferring power as they did, the Sandinistas became the first revolutionary government that had achieved power by armed struggle to relinquish power through an electoral process to a nonrevolutionary opposition. Some observers may place the Nicaraguan action in the context of reforms occurring in Eastern Europe. While this analysis is tempting, it is not ultimately accurate. The events in Eastern Europe have had an impact in Nicaragua through a reduction of Soviet assistance, but the FSLN's commitment to political pluralism easily predates glasnost and perestroika in the Soviet Union. Well before Gorbachev came to power in 1985, the pluralistic character of Nicaragua's revolution had been clearly evident.

In summary, the commitment of the FSLN leadership to a revolutionary definition of political pluralism was carried out to a significant degree. Ironically it was in the arena of more traditionally defined political pluralism (elections, constitutional rights, alternation of political power) that the FSLN was most successful. The effort to expand political pluralism to fully integrate grass-roots organizations and the vanguard political party are projects that at this time remain unfulfilled.

Mixed Economy

In analyzing the nature of the Nicaraguan economy under Sandinista rule, it is essential to look at its historic character (see Harris 1985, Spalding 1986). Like most small, underdeveloped countries, Nicaragua's economic development has been based on agroexports, primarily cotton, beef, and coffee. The overspecialization in agroexports also retarded and deformed the industrialization of the economy. The light industry that was developed was based on imported inputs and few indigenous resources. Ownership of both the agroexport sector and the weak manufacturing sector was largely, though not exclusively, in the hands of large and medium producers, which contributed heavily to the high concentration of the nation's wealth in the hands of a relative few prior to the revolution. In addition to the inequities, the economy that the Sandinistas inherited was also weak, highly vulnerable to the prices of both exportable agricultural goods and manufacturing imports. The revolutionary government that took power in 1979 had the task of both rebuilding the damage done during the insurrection and establishing a new economic system that would reverse the historic poverty and dependency. The government made no attempt to socialize the entire productive process or definitively eliminate private capital. From the beginning, it pursued the strategy of a mixed economy with a socialist orientation.

"Mixed economy" was a description of the heterogeneous character of the Nicaraguan economy and a recognition that it would continue to have a significant private sector well into the foreseeable future. Commandante Bayardo Arce outlined the Sandinista perspective in a 1987 interview:

> Looking at Nicaragua's experience, our economic and social configuration, and knowing the experience of other countries, we decided that a completely state-run economy wouldn't work for us. Given our circumstances—a developing country, without technology or the economic resources to exploit our natural riches—we could not make the state the administrator of everything.[5]

Based on this logic, the leaders of the FSLN said that they had made a strategic adoption of the mixed economy, not a tactical one (Borge 1985, p. 178). How is this statement to be interpreted? It meant that while they were not opposed to socialism in principle, it was their judgment that fully implemented socialism was impractical in Nicaragua at that time. Their acceptance of a private sector in Nicaragua's economy did not mean they embraced capitalism. Jaime Wheelock, Minister of Agrarian Reform, said that he believed "that all revolutions must choose a path that is not capitalist. Socialism naturally follows capitalism, as capitalism followed feudalism" (in Invernizzi et al. 1986). Tomás Borge (1985, pp. 177–178) explained the mixed economy in another way:

> The mixed economy in Nicaragua is not the same as elsewhere in Latin America. This is a mixed economy within the revolution. In other words, a mixed economy in the service of the workers. In other countries, it is a mixed economy in service of the bourgeoisie.

In an interview, Arce also made clear that he did not see the FSLN as representing the political and economic interests of the landlord class:

> The FSLN defends the owners of this country's greatest wealth and it represents them in terms of the nation. But in terms of the popular and class struggle, we cannot represent them because we have made the decision to base ourselves in the worker-campesino alliance (*Barricada International*, July 16, 1987, p. 10).

While acknowledging that more than half of the economy remained in private hands, it must be noted that percentages do not tell the whole story. The Nicaraguan economy was state run in a number of ways. The government had total control over import-export, which forced all private owners to sell their products to the state at a price determined by the state. Also, the private sector could import luxury goods only under significant government regulation. However, it was generally not these restrictions on the private sector that most distressed its adherents. The private sector generally did well economically in spite of government restrictions, the war, and the state of the economy. They retained their wealth and privilege to a large degree, but they were concerned about the future direction of the economy, and they feared that they did not have the political power to stop the Sandinistas from nationalizing their holdings and moving to a fully socialist economy. These fears were significantly reduced by the election of Chamorro, and today it is the Sandinistas who fear for the erosion of the system of socialist orientation that they fostered in eleven years of rule.

Two other arenas—agrarian reform and the war-time economy—demonstrated the mixed character of the Nicaraguan economy and the flexibility of the Sandinista leadership. In the early years of the revolution, the land reform program concentrated on the expropriation of Somoza-held land, the creation of a state-owned agriculture sector, and the promotion of cooperatives. The Agrarian Reform Law of 1981 went beyond the initial expropriation of Somoza land to provide mechanisms for the

expropriation of unused or underutilized land. At that point the Nicaraguan agrarian reform program seemed to be following definitively radical
lines, surpassed in Latin America only by Cuba. However, in 1985 the
direction of the program changed as the government implemented phase
two of the agrarian reform and began to distribute a significant number
of individual land titles. This was undertaken because the movement
toward cooperatives was slow and in many cases resisted by the rural poor.
The move to provide individual private ownership was, at least in part, to
win the loyalty of the rural people in the contra war. Much of the political
pressure to reorient the agrarian reform program came from within a mass
organization created by the FSLN, the National Union of Farmers and
Ranchers (UNAG). The 1981 law permitting expropriations had actually
been used quite sparingly in spite of considerable pressure for its more
systematic use from those without land. In July 1988 the Nicaraguan
government did nationalize the San Antonio sugar mill, one of
Nicaragua's largest private businesses, but this came only after significantly decreased production and constant pressure from some of its
employees for government action. It was not followed by similar actions
against other private enterprises.

In many ways the socialist orientation of the mixed economy was
significantly gutted by the economic policies carried out in the last two
years of Sandinista rule. Prior to June 1988 all economic measures, including the drastic actions of February 1988 (such as the reduction of subsidies)
had significantly cushioned Nicaragua's poorest people (Central America
Historical Institute 1988). The FSLN leaders seemed to keep in mind
Borge's notion of a "mixed economy in service of the workers." However,
the June 1988 measures and other reforms that followed in 1989 affected
all elements of the society, lifting price controls on almost all goods and
services, and removing almost all of the remaining subsidies to consumers.
As a result, transportation and food prices rose sharply. Nicaragua's
poorest people were hit the hardest, and problems of malnutrition that
had largely been eliminated began to resurface. Reprivatization of some
parts of the health care system also exacerbated the situation, and the
infant mortality rate increased.

In contrast to the hard-hit poorer sectors, the Sandinista economic
reforms gave significant benefit to the private, agroexport sector. Believing that hyperinflation could only be controlled by a significant increase
in production, the government increased subsidies to large private farmers. The nature of the June 1988 reform was evidenced by the relatively
warm reception it received from the anti-Sandinista business sector. By
1989 subsidies to the private sector were accounting for 65 percent of the
total government budget (Cooper 1989). The FSLN continued to pursue
this strategy in spite of no significant increase in productivity and growing

evidence that the subsidies were largely being squandered or sent to bank accounts in the United States (ibid.).

While the elimination of many subsidies may have been necessitated by the near economic collapse brought on by the years of war, the FSLN leaders went well beyond short-term belt-tightening arguments to justify the changes. In a two-part interview in *Barricada* on March 15, 1989, Borge provided theoretical justification for this policy course, arguing that market mechanisms are an expression of "objective relations" and "general economic laws" that transcend capitalism and socialism and can be used to serve "specific class interests." Borge sought to maintain a Marxist framework for his argument by comparing the Sandinista reforms to the New Economic Policy undertaken by the Soviet Union in 1921.

These arguments paralleled those made by Soviet leaders in defense of perestroika, their version of economic reform. However, in the Nicaraguan context of a mixed economy and relatively weak socialist forms, these changes and their justification were more significant. While the retreat from a socialist orientation may have been only temporary had the FSLN retained power, with renewed international economic assistance, that was not likely. A definite shift in FSLN economic thinking was apparently underway, representing the dominance of more social democratic rather than revolutionary socialist ways of thinking. Sandinista leaders increasingly pointed to countries like Sweden as representing their model rather than Cuba. As a further validation of the largely procapitalist direction ultimately pursued by the Sandinistas, one must note that the incoming Chamorro administration made few changes from their predecessors in their overall macroeconomic policies.

Nonalignment

Less than two months after the new government established itself in Managua, the Sandinistas decided that Nicaragua should become a member of the Nonaligned Movement (NAM). A delegation was sent to the Sixth Nonaligned Summit when it convened in Havana in September 1979, and Nicaragua became a full member of the organization. At that meeting, Daniel Ortega delivered a speech explaining Nicaragua's new affiliation by saying that the Nonaligned Movement was "the broadest organization of the Third World states that play an important role and exercise increasing influence in the international arena and in the people's struggle against imperialism, colonialism, and neo-colonialism" (cited by Bendaña 1982, p. 320).

The decision to join the Nonaligned Movement was a natural one for the revolutionary leaders, as it followed from their origins in an anticolonial national liberation struggle. The nationalism of Augusto César Sandino was imbued with solidarity with anticolonial struggles throughout the world. It is important to understand that while the Nonaligned Movement sought to avoid hegemonic domination by any superpower, it was not "neutral" but rather actively supported anticolonial struggles. It was this stance that most appealed to the Sandinistas. Ortega argued (in Vanden and Morales 1985, p. 474) that "in the Sandinista revolution there is not any alignment, but an absolute and consistent support for the aspirations of people who have achieved independence or are struggling to do so. That is why we are nonaligned." Therefore, Nicaragua's subsequent support at the Havana meeting for the Southwest African People's Organization in Namibia, the Palestine Liberation Organization, the Polisario Front in Western Sahara, and Puerto Rican nationalism was understandable.

The Nonaligned Movement also consistently supported the position of the revolutionary forces in Nicaragua both before and after July 1979. Resolutions at New Delhi in 1981 and Havana in 1982 focused global attention on Central America, particularly the growing political and economic pressure against Nicaragua. This support for Nicaragua was underscored by the convening of a special ministerial meeting of the Coordinating Bureau of the Nonaligned Countries of Latin America and the Caribbean in Managua in January 1983. For Nicaragua the meeting and resulting "Managua Communique" succeeded in focusing attention on the growing contra efforts emanating from Honduras. The Managua meeting also provided a preview of the diplomatic defeat that would be received by the United States at the United Nations in March 1983. As a testament to her growing influence as a nonaligned country, Nicaragua had been elected to a nonpermanent seat on the UN Security Council in the fall of 1982. Using her position on the Council during five of its sessions, Nicaragua succeeded in late March 1983 in bringing attention to the growing attacks against her and in isolating the United States in its attempts to portray the conflict as an internal Nicaraguan affair. Indeed, the support for Nicaragua in the Security Council debates by countries such as Mexico, Venezuela, India, Zaire, and Algeria showed that much had changed in the world since the 1950s, when an isolated Guatemalan government had been overthrown by a CIA-backed invasion.

In the following years Nicaragua had continuing success in gaining support for its political positions in both the NAM and the UN. While Nicaragua was disappointed by its failure to gain the presidency of the Nonaligned Movement, each subsequent Nonaligned Summit significantly addressed Nicaragua's concerns. The 1986 meeting in Harare, Zimbabwe, devoted 15 percent of its discussion to Nicaragua, Contadora, and the Central American peace process and made several condemnations of U.S. intervention.[6] The Ninth Nonaligned Summit meeting in

Belgrade in September 1989 ended with a declaration that supported the Central American Peace Accords and called on governments outside the region—particularly the United States—to respect the decisions taken by the Central American heads of state. The Belgrade resolutions were largely the result of work done by the special Committee of the Nine that had been set up by NAM two years earlier to oversee events in Central America and Nicaragua (*Barricada International* 1989, p. 3).

By 1989 Nicaragua had convened the UN Security Council some fifteen times to consider charges of external aggression. Two resolutions calling for an end to the conflict were passed, and the United States vetoed four others. Nicaragua was also able to use the powers of the General Assembly to obtain the passage of four resolutions condemning the U.S. trade embargo and others that called on the United States to implement the decision on the contra war made in Nicaragua's favor by the International Court of Justice (Torres 1989a, p. 158). The predominance of nonaligned nations in the United Nations (103 out of 159) was crucial to Nicaragua's successes in that organization and also her election to the presidency of the World Parliamentary Union.

One instructive way of analyzing Nicaragua's commitment to nonalignment in practice is to look at her voting patterns in the United Nations. Vanden and Morales (1985, p. 159) have argued that Nicaragua sought a middle ground among the nonaligned countries, accepting neither the "natural ally" thesis of Cuba, which sees the socialist countries as the natural ally of the developing countries, nor the "two imperialisms" thesis of Algeria, which fears domination by either superpower. For instance, on January 14, 1980, the United Nations General Assembly voted 104 in favor, 18 opposed, with 18 abstentions, on a resolution calling for immediate withdrawal of Soviet troops from Afghanistan. Nicaragua, unlike the countries aligned with the socialist bloc such as Angola, Grenada, and Ethiopia, did not vote against the resolution but instead abstained, as did India, Algeria, Cyprus, and Finland. Similarly, in the September 1983 Security Council resolution criticizing the Soviet downing of a Korean airliner, Nicaragua abstained as did China, Guyana, and Zimbabwe.

Nicaragua's concept of herself as a nonaligned nation was not limited to membership in the NAM and courting Third World support at the United Nations. For Nicaragua nonalignment meant having firm relations throughout the world—the socialist countries, including both the USSR and the People's Republic of China; the developed capitalist nations, including the United States; and the rest of the Third World. The Sandinistas sought a sharp break from the Somoza period when Nicaragua maintained relations with only forty-one nations, a product of the dictatorship's anticommunism and close ties to the United States. By 1989 Nicaragua had established diplomatic ties with 117 countries (Torres

1989b, pp. 6, 12). The Sandinista leaders hoped that a variety of foreign relations would allow them to have "diversified dependency," dividing their aid and trade among the United States, Western Europe, socialist countries, and the Third World. By using the term "diversified dependency," the Nicaraguans were acknowledging that as a poor and underdeveloped country they could not survive without outside assistance, but that they hoped they would not be dominated by a single supplier of aid, as they had been for most of the century by the United States.[7] The Sandinista effort to establish four roughly equal poles of trade and aid was only partially successful. In fact, the economic vulnerability of Nicaragua that grew from the failure to replace the lost U.S. aid and trade was a critical factor in the Sandinistas' ultimate downfall in the 1990 elections.

Nicaragua sought to increase its ties to Western Europe significantly and between 1979 and 1981 gained considerable success. Western Europe provided 33 percent of all loans to Nicaragua (Vanden and Morales 1985, p. 159). European aid donations exceeded $61 million between 1979 and 1982. Likewise, 28 percent of Nicaraguan exports were purchased by Europeans, who in turn accounted for 14 percent of Nicaragua's imports (Malley 1985, p. 487). Initially, all but the most conservative European policymakers were receptive to aid for Nicaragua. At the July 1983 European Economic Community meeting in Stuttgart, ten EEC leaders seemed to affirm Nicaragua's position and to criticize the Reagan administration's Central America policies (ibid.).

However, intense diplomatic pressure by the Reagan administration, combined with growing European dissatisfaction with Nicaraguan actions, prompted a reassessment of the European position. Many Western European critics became quite concerned about what they perceived as Nicaragua's growing alignment with the socialist bloc, its enroachments on the private sector, and its limitations on political democracy. Even though generally good economic and political relations continued, European aid to Nicaragua declined. For each year between 1984 and 1987, the EEC countries gave between $40 and $80 million to the Central American region. Nicaragua received the largest amount of aid (30 percent) but the total amount was still lower than the early years and was only a fraction of what Nicaragua needed in the face of the U.S. embargo and the U.S.-inspired loss of international multilateral assistance (*Envio* 1989). In spite of the setbacks, Nicaraguan leaders continued to vigorously pursue European aid; they were generally careful to always include stops in both Eastern and Western European capitals. However, by 1988 only Sweden was increasing its support to Nicaragua. After announcing plans for the February 1990 elections, the FSLN leaders hoped for a strong European aid response at a May 1989 two-day conference on Nicaraguan aid hosted by Sweden. At the end of what came to be called the Stockholm Conference, European nations finally increased their support in recognition of Nicaraguan initiatives and domestic concessions. Sweden, Italy, and Spain each put up $10 million in grants, while $20 million would be forthcoming from Norway, Finland, Denmark, the Netherlands, and the EEC (*Latin American Weekly Report,* May 25, 1989, p. 7). The $50 million pledged fell far short of the $200 million goal that the Nicaraguan government had set for the meeting; the full sum was needed to begin to remedy the desperate economic situation Nicaragua was experiencing.

After the first few years of Sandinista rule, problems with the United States, the contra war, developing economic crisis, and the difficulties engendered in maintaining good relations with Western Europe combined to necessitate a cautious policy of engagement with socialist countries. From 1979 to 1982, only 18.5 percent of loans came to Nicaragua from the socialist countries. During this period, a scant 12 percent of Nicaragua's imports came from socialist countries (as compared to 19 percent from the United States), and only 2 percent of Nicaragua's exports went to socialist countries (Vanden and Morales 1985, p. 159). A review of the Sandinistas' decade of relations with the socialist countries yields an uneven picture. Aid and trade relations between Nicaragua and the Eastern European countries were slow to develop, reached a high point in the middle of the decade, and then went into sharp decline in the final three years of FSLN power. In contrast, Cuba maintained the closest relationship with Nicaragua. Cuban aid and political ties to the Sandinistas were strong even before the end of the dictatorship. Throughout the years of Sandinista rule relations between Managua and Havana remained warm, and Cuba continued to supply substantial amounts of technical support and economic and military aid (Prevost 1990).

The Soviets had no relations with the FSLN except through Cuba prior to July 1979. As suggested in chapter 2, the Soviets' main ally in Nicaragua, the Nicaragua Socialist Party (PSN), was hostile to the FSLN since the future Sandinista leaders had broken from the PSN in the early 1960s. The PSN played almost no role in the revolution and the Soviet Union initially paid little attention to Nicaraguan events even after the Sandinistas had taken power (Blaiser 1987, p. 140). The first economic-technical pacts were not signed until almost two years after the Sandinistas came to power and only after the Reagan administration had begun its punitive economic policies (Schwab and Sims 1985, p. 452). Soviet assistance increased dramatically only after the contra war had begun in earnest in 1982.

Even though Nicaragua wanted to maintain a balance in its economic and diplomatic relations, the military needs of the contra war and the economic needs that resulted from the 1985 U.S. trade embargo forced it to rely more heavily on the socialist nations, which did damage to its own planned strategy of diversification. However, it should be noted that according to the Nicaraguan Ministry of Foreign Cooperation, donated aid from all the socialist countries only totaled $214.6 million for the period 1979 to 1986, whereas the donated aid received from Western countries, private Western organizations, and the United Nations came to $365 million (Barraclough, et al. 1988, app. II).[8] The Soviet Union did dramatically increase its aid during the 1986–1988 period but it was not matched in the trading arena at a time when Nicaragua needed a replacement for markets lost in the U.S. trade embargo (*Latin American Weekly Report,* January 14, 1987, p. 8).[9] While Soviet aid was crucial to Nicaragua's short-term survival, the Soviets also made clear that the Cuban option of a place within the Council of Mutual Economic Assistance (CMEA) and a greater amount of ongoing economic assistance was not going to be made available to Nicaragua. Throughout the period of Sandinista rule, the ideological diversity of the FSLN made the Soviets wonder if the Sandinistas might make a deal that would eliminate Soviet influence entirely.[10] Beyond that, Cuba's position in the CMEA had probably pushed the Soviets to their limits of economic assistance.

Even as Soviet aid increased to its highest levels, a variety of domestic and international forces forced a reevaluation of Soviet and Eastern European support. In June 1987 the USSR announced it intended to limit the amount of crude petroleum that it would supply to Nicaragua. At the Reagan-Gorbachev December 1987 summit, the Soviet leader indicated a willingness to negotiate over Nicaragua (Apple 1987). These remarks followed a November 1987 visit by Daniel Ortega to Moscow where the message of decreasing future aid was given by the Soviets (*Latin American Weekly Report,* November 19, 1987, p. 2). Once the contra war began to scale down during 1988, Soviet arms shipments to Nicaragua fell off sharply, and by February 1990 aid of all types from the socialist countries (except Cuba) was in decline.

Nicaragua tried to turn its strong nonaligned political ties into a significant economic pole, especially in Latin America. Political support remained strong from throughout the hemisphere in spite of U.S. pressure to isolate Nicaragua, but the economic arena never materialized. Nicaraguan–Latin American trade actually fell between 1982 and 1986. This trend was not reversed until 1987 and even then it was much below 1981 levels (International Monetary Fund 1988, p. 302). Reasons for the decline can be seen through the example of Nicaragua's oil trade. Initially Mexico and Venezuela aided Nicaragua with concessionary pricing, but when Nicaragua fell behind in its payments they ceased providing oil, forcing the Nicaraguans to turn to the Soviet Union. There were a few successes for Nicaragua (i.e., financial support from Libya and Iran), but most of Nicaragua's Third World allies were simply too poor to help her with aid or trade.

Nicaragua largely carried out its stated commitment to pursue a nonaligned foreign policy. However, the unrelenting hostility of the United States toward Nicaragua's independent trajectory and the ambivalence of the Western European governments toward the Nicaraguan revolutionary project severely damaged Nicaragua's ability not to be labeled with the socialist camp. When the political and economic crisis in the East began to erode the strength of the socialist countries, the Sandinistas found themselves ultimately forced to submit to the reality of U.S. hegemony in the Western Hemisphere.

The political practice of the FSLN underwent some important changes between 1979 and 1990. Some of these changes were the natural result of a revolutionary party adjusting to the reality of governance, while other changes were definitely forced upon the Sandinistas by an increasingly hostile international environment. When the FSLN came to power in 1979 it did so in the context of an increasingly favorable environment for revolutionary forces. Their success came at the end of a decade marked by the triumph of revolutionaries in Indochina and in Southern Africa. At the same time rebel groups in nearby El Salvador and Guatemala were poised for success. However, the 1980s turned out to be a different story. By the end of the decade, the crisis in the Eastern bloc, the generalized Third World economic crisis, and the aggressive counterrevolutionary polices of the United States had combined to limit revolutionary success throughout the world. The leaders of the Nicaraguan revolution ultimately shifted their program in a more conservative direction in response to these combined pressures. While not fully abandoning their revolutionary principles, the FSLN leaders became very sober about the prospects for achieving socialism in Nicaragua. Obviously the electoral defeat, at least partially a consequence of the worldwide revolutionary retreat, has further reduced the expectations of the Sandinistas. Recently, Daniel Ortega summed up the achievements of the Nicaraguan revolution by saying: "We waged a revolution to open a new democratic space."[11] Given Nicaragua's long history of dictatorship, the achievement of a democratic political process is truly significant but clearly falls well short of Carlos Fonseca Amador's vision of a socialist Nicaragua.

Notes

1. For a detailed but ultimately anti-Communist treatment of the Nicaraguan revolution and the FSLN, see Nolan (1984).

2. For example, see the 1984 electoral platform of the FSLN reprinted in

Marcus (1985, pp. 313–327).

3. For a complete listing of the parties in the 1990 elections, see Table 7.1 on pp. 134–136.

4. Interview by Prevost with FSLN National Assembly member Alejandro Bravo, Managua, January 20, 1987.

5. Interview by Prevost with Bayardo Arce in *Excelsior* (Mexico), June 25, 1986, excerpted in *Barricada International*, July 16, 1987.

6. Interview by Vanden with United Nations diplomat, New York, August 8, 1989. See also UN Document GA S.C., A/41/697, A 18392, 14 October 1986, which contains the proceedings of the meeting.

7. Interview by Prevost with Francisco Campbell, First Secretary of the Nicaraguan Embassy in Washington, D.C., Collegeville, MN, October 31, 1984.

8. Long- and medium-term loans and credits from the socialist countries for this period totaled $1.57 billion.

9. Also, U.S. Department of Defense, "Trends in Soviet Bloc Aid to Nicaragua," provided by U.S. State Department in interview by Vanden, Washington, D.C., August 3, 1989. Deteriorating conditions in Nicaragua prompted the Soviets to increase their overall aid to $200 million for the 1986–1987 period and to supply more and more of Nicaragua's petroleum needs. The socialist countries did continue to supply relatively high levels of military aid to Nicaragua (estimated by the U.S. Department of Defense to run over $500 million annually for 1986–1988).

10. Interview by Prevost with Moscow University international relations specialist, Moscow, January 21, 1986.

11. Ortega, quoted in *Nicaraguan Perspectives* (Fall/Winter 1990), p. 1.

❖ SIX ❖

The Evolving Structure
of the FSLN

The arrival of the FSLN leaders in power in July 1979 came at the end of a brief, rapid rise to prominence. The task they faced was enormous. An entirely new state and military apparatus had to be organized, and the party had probably only about 1,500 members.[1] The FSLN made an important decision. At that time, thousands of Nicaraguans considered themselves to be Sandinistas because they had taken up arms under FSLN leadership. However, the National Directorate of the FSLN decided soon after the triumph to embrace the Leninist concept of a cadre party of limited membership, systematically incorporating only the most committed revolutionary individuals.[2] Throughout the ensuing decade, the FSLN described itself as a vanguard organization. It was difficult to find a party text in which the term was not used, usually in the context of a description of FSLN militants who had led heroic struggles against seemingly insurmountable odds. This flavor was captured in a quote from Dora María Téllez (in Randall 1981, p. 53) soon after the overthrow of the Somoza dynasty:

> Sandinismo is our national identity. And it is more than that. There are a few men and women who at a given moment in history seem to contain within themselves the dignity of all the people. They are examples to all of us. And then, through the struggle the people as a whole reclaim the strength and dignity shown by a few. That's what Sandinismo is to the Nicaraguan people. It is our history, our heroes and heroines, and our people's struggle and victory.

In more definitively Marxist terminology, the National Directorate of the FSLN (1982, p. 40) placed the party in the vanguard or leadership position:

> The Party, by taking a determined class position, a unique political principle, a scientific ideology, correct strategy and tactics, places itself

at the forefront of all society and gathers in its bosom the political and military leadership of the revolutionary forces which struggle and work to bring the revolution towards bigger achievements.

Such a historical stance, taken throughout the long guerrilla war, is entirely consistent with the political-military structure of a primarily guerrilla army. The organization was small, disciplined, and clandestine. It fit quite well with the model articulated in Lenin's *What Is to Be Done?*, the manual on revolutionary party organization written in 1902. There is no doubt that for the first eighteen years of the existence of the FSLN, this was the mode of operation of the organization. But one is led to ask to what degree the FSLN shifted its form of organization after assuming power in July 1979.

The National Directorate

The leading body of the FSLN, the National Directorate, remained dominant throughout the period from the final offensive against Somoza to the party's departure from state power in April 1990. (See Figure 6.1 for the complete party structure.) Its membership of nine was determined in early 1979 when three factions came together to form a united front. There is no official or unofficial account of how the nine commanders of the revolution were selected for their positions. They were Daniel and Humberto Ortega, Victor Tirado (Terceristas); Tomás Borge, Bayardo Arce, Henry Ruíz (Prolonged Popular War); and Jaime Wheelock, Carlos Núñez, and Luis Carrión (Proletarian). There was a great expansion in the membership of the FSLN and much restructuring of the organization at most levels, but the National Directorate was a consistent force throughout the years of Sandinista state power. The balance among the three factions made it difficult to add a female commandante to the group, nor did all of its members have equal weight and prominence over the years. But all remained highly active, and the membership remained unchanged until April 1990. Such a record of stability was not common in revolutionary Third World organizations and was an indicator of the level of both flexibility and unity within the Sandinista Front.[3]

Unfortunately, little can be said about the functioning of the National Directorate. Its meetings, though apparently quite regular, were not often publicly reported. When a decision of the Directorate was reported, only the results were made public. If differences existed within the Directorate, and they most likely did, they were not known to the outside world. However, given the stability of its leadership, it is plausible to speculate that the differences were manageable and pragmatic, not differences of

Figure 6.1   Pre-1990 FSLN National Party Structure

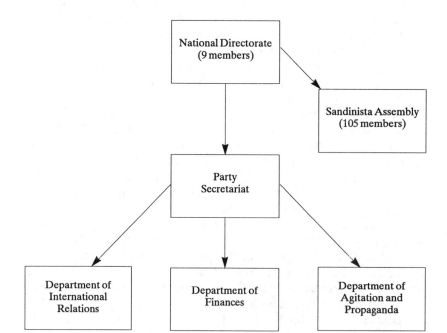

fundamental principles.

What insight we do have on the functioning of the Directorate comes from an interview with Jaime Wheelock (1984) published under the title *Nicaragua—The Great Challenge.* In response to a question on the functioning of the body, Wheelock stated (pp. 12–14):

> We have achieved a collective function in which the National Directorate is the leader and each one of us has more or less the same weight. . . . Similarly, there is no opinion that could be imposed through external conditions, through the weight the opinion might have, but rather the opinion imposes itself through absolute logic. . . . Our opinions are formed as the opinions of a collective. In this way it is harder to be mistaken. . . . The experience that we have from all these years is that with rare exceptions, the National Directorate always arrives at consensus. The system of voting has been an exceptional procedure, and when, in rare opportunities, we reach a vote of five to four, we consider that there is no consensus and we return to discussing the problem.

The National Directorate was officially the highest decisionmaking body of the FSLN. Its decisions were final and authoritative. When the structure of the party was formalized in 1980, an official communique stated: "The National Directorate is the supreme leadership body and central authority of the FSLN and of the Sandinista People's Revolution" (FSLN 1980). It is important to note that in the year after Daniel Ortega was elected president of the country, an FSLN statement (1985) on party organization reiterated the language of the 1980 communique describing the authority of the Directorate.

In keeping with the collegial style of leadership, the Directorate never named a party general secretary. Instead, the members of the Directorate divided responsibilities in the state and party among themselves. For example, Humberto Ortega became Minister of Defense, Tomás Borge became Interior Minister, Jaime Wheelock became head of the agrarian reform program, and Henry Ruíz became Minister of Planning. This arrangement led to what Dennis Gilbert (1988, p. 47) called "rule by a college of caudillos, each with its own minions." Observers have noted that the commandantes in government tended to surround themselves with members of their own pre-1979 party factions. While there is no significant evidence that this form of rule led to major problems, the National Directorate (FSLN 1985) did declare that "overcoming divisiveness and feudalism" was a basis for the 1985 party reorganization. That reorganization created an Executive Committee of the Directorate, made up of five of its members—Daniel and Humberto Ortega, Wheelock, Arce, and Borge; it replaced the smaller Political Commission, which was formed in 1980. In addition to becoming president of Nicaragua, Daniel Ortega was also named coordinator of the newly created body. Its powers were strictly circumscribed; it was declared to be solely an administrative body with "none of the attributes" of the Directorate (ibid.). Bayardo Arce, named vice-coordinator of the body, retained his position as coordinator of the daily activities of the party's central apparatus. In the years since the Executive Committee was formed it does seem that the authority of the full Directorate has been diminished. Nonetheless Daniel Ortega's daily contact with state affairs inevitably increased his weight in decisionmaking though not to the point of significantly reducing the authority of the Directorate.

Departments of the National Directorate

The August 1985 reorganization established seven auxiliary departments of the National Directorate: Office of the Secretary General, Department of Organization, Department of Propaganda and Agitation, Department of Political Education, Department of International Relations, Department of Finances, and Institute for the Study of Sandinism. The Office of the Secretary General was responsible for supervising the work of the other six departments and the regional apparatus of the party.

The Department of Organization was responsible for overseeing the structures of the party at all levels and had the strategic job of determining what political assignments were to be taken by each member of the party.

This department also recruited new members to the organization. The formal position of the FSLN was that it was interested in recruiting the "best workers, best peasants" into the party, provided that they were interested in the party and willing to subject themselves to its discipline and the responsibilities that went with party membership.[4] It was not easy to be a member of the FSLN. The Frente had two types of members, aspiring militants and militants. A person gained candidate stature of an aspiring militant only through recommendation by an FSLN base committee and approval by zonal, regional, and national party offices. Normally, aspiring militants waited between a year and eighteen months before gaining full party membership. During that time the individuals involved assessed whether they were ready for party membership and the party organization did likewise. Full membership was also ratified at all levels of the organization, just like the original nomination to candidate status.

Even among the party militants there were some important distinctions. Special honor was accorded to those FSLN members who died during the long years of struggle against Somoza. This group was called the "First Promotion" under Carlos Fonseca Amador, who was killed in 1975. More important for the ongoing work of party after 1979 was the group called the "Second Promotion." To be a member of this group it was necessary to have been involved in the armed struggle against Somoza, not necessarily as an armed combatant but as a participant in the clandestine movement. The exact number in this category is not known but it was probably no more than one thousand.[5] It was the "Second Promotion" that dominated the life of the FSLN after 1979. Its members made up all of the National Directorate, most of the Sandinista Assembly, and most of the local and regional party leaders. Gaining full membership in the FSLN virtually required recommendation by a member of the "Second Promotion." The leadership of the party recognized the need for new members but clearly sought to bring in recruits who were at least known to the core revolutionaries who led the overthrow of Somoza.

What types of people did the party seek and where did it find them? The primary recruiting ground of the FSLN was in the mass organizations established by the revolution—trade unions, Sandinista Defense Committees (CDSs), Nicaraguan Women's Association (AMNLAE), the National Union of Farmers and Ranchers (UNAG), and the Sandinista Youth organization (JS-19J). Sandinista party members who had active roles in these organizations looked for people who were good organizers and public speakers, and who had respect among their peers. It is not clear which of the mass organizations was most productive for the FSLN, but based on sheer numbers of participation, it was probably the Sandinista Defense Committees. The Sandinista Popular Army (EPS) would likely always be important for the party, but during the time of war it seemed to take on an added importance: from 1983 to 1988 it was apparently the largest area of recruitment for the FSLN.

The overall picture of FSLN recruitment is mixed. In 1979, virtually anyone who had participated in the insurrection—at least tens of thousands of people—considered themselves to be Sandinistas, because up until that time membership in the FSLN had meant participation in the military structure of the organization. However, soon after 1979 the FSLN decided that it would remain a cadre party—an organization of limited and selective membership. Thus, the party acknowledged that the period between 1979 and 1981 would be described as absorption, not recruitment. Many people were brought into the organization without much care or thought. After 1981, the process became more systematized, and the organization grew steadily from 4,000 in 1981 to 12,000 in 1984 to 20,000 in 1987, and 30,000 in 1988.[6]

The actual social composition of the FSLN membership was not easy to validate, though clearly all classes were represented. As with most revolutionary vanguard parties in Third World countries, the upper and middle classes seemed to be overrepresented. Lea Guido, head of the party's Department of Organization in the mid-1980s, estimated that 30 percent of party members were professionals and technical experts (in Gilbert 1988, p. 53). The Sandinista Party always accepted members from all class backgrounds; but in a country where access to education had always been limited to a relative few, the overrepresentation of the elite was inevitable.

The Department of Propaganda and Agitation was headed by Carlos Fernando Chamorro, the editor of *Barricada,* the FSLN newspaper. In addition to being responsible for the publication of the country's largest circulation daily newspaper, this department controlled Sandinista radio and television programming and a wide-ranging publications program. During the period of the confrontation with the United States, this department directed the publication of numerous pamphlets and position papers in English explaining and defending positions of the Nicaraguan government. In that sense it was very much responsible for presenting the Nicaraguan revolution to the outside world.

The Department of Political Education was primarily responsible for the education of members of the party. It organized schools for the cadres and set the curriculum for these schools. Initially the education program was quite centralized and built around six-month courses at a national cadre school, during which students were released from their regular political and work assignments. The cadre schools were open only to full FSLN members, and selection was a high honor. In the early years (1980–1982) the curriculum was largely orthodox Marxism, primarily using texts donated by the Soviet Communist Party to the FSLN.

However, beginning in 1982 the education program was dramatically changed in both content and form. The length of study was significantly shortened, and greater emphasis was placed on courses at the lower levels of the party structure. While the study of Marxism was not abandoned completely, the Soviet textbooks were set aside and greater attention was given to direct readings of Marx, Engels, and Lenin. The writings of Sandino and Nicaraguan history were also studied.[7] The works of Paulo Freire, the Brazilian educator, were widely used. In the ensuing years the curriculum was adjusted to meet changing circumstances. Lenin was apparently a key figure studied in the period before gaining power; while in the mid-1980s, importance was placed on Marx's *The Civil War in France* (1978).[8] The choice of the latter was not surprising since it deals with the Paris Commune and the efforts of French revolutionaries to hold on to power in the face of a strong counterrevolutionary challenge. Throughout the years of state power, education at the local levels of the party concentrated on studying key decisions of the party leadership related to the war and the economy.

The International Relations Department was responsible for dealing with all political parties that chose to have relations with the FSLN. This included a broad spectrum of political parties ranging from Communist to Social Democratic and Christian Democratic. This department also oversaw the work of a nongovernmental organization, the Committee in Solidarity with the People (CNSP), which worked with grass-roots organizations in over fifty countries that provided Nicaragua with humanitarian and technical assistance in a variety of fields.

The Department of Finances managed the financial matters of the organization. The Institute for the Study of Sandinism fostered the study of the life and writings of Augusto César Sandino and the later founders of the FSLN.

The Sandinista Assembly

The closest thing in the FSLN structure to a party congress was the Sandinista Assembly. As delineated in the 1985 reformed structure, the Sandinista Assembly consisted of not more than 105 members. It was given the role of advising the National Directorate, and it was stipulated that it would meet at least once a year. A communication of the National Directorate (FSLN 1985) stated that the Assembly was a "consultative organ of the party which supports the National Directorate in making the most important decisions of the Revolution."

The wording of the description was crucial. Although an important body, it was not intended for day-to-day administration; it was clearly subordinate to the National Directorate, which designated the delegates and called it into session. The Assembly, which had no existence independent of the National Directorate, was intended to be a sounding board and a pulse point. It was comprised of party functionaries and government officials (who were well represented) and also included cultural figures and professionals (ibid.). But, overwhelmingly, the Assembly was made up of FSLN leaders who participated in the guerrilla war against Somoza. It was a body that reflected the commitment of the FSLN to remain strongly linked to its historic past as a clandestine political-military organization.[9]

Regional, Zonal, and Local Organization

In addition to the national level institutions, the FSLN also had three other levels of organization—regional, zonal, and base or local. The regional structure of the FSLN, which corresponded to the governmental division of the country into six regular regions and three special territories in the Atlantic Coast area, was headed by a regional committee made up of no more than ten members. Subordinate to the regional committees were zonal committees, often covering an entire city or part of a large city. Coordinators of the regional and zonal committees, together with their executive committees, were appointed by the party center. In a tight linkage of party and state power, the regional and zonal coordinators almost always served as the governmental representatives appointed by the president.

The FSLN also comprised hundreds of base committees. Each member of the FSLN, except those with national or regional tasks, was a member of a base committee. As with most vanguard parties, these units were usually based in the workplace. In addition to neighborhood organizations, there were base committees in the factories, on state and cooperative farms, in the army, and at the universities. The base committee was led by a political secretary chosen by the zonal committee and met regularly to discuss improving labor productivity at work, recruiting new members, planning political activities, and carrying out educational sessions on the decrees from the higher leadership bodies. In the early years of the revolution it seemed that the neighborhood committees were the norm, but as the revolution was institutionalized, the workplace committees became more common, particularly in the case of workplaces populated by party professionals.[10]

Organizational Changes After 1987

The organizational structure of the party, established in 1979 and modified slightly in 1985, underwent significant changes after 1987. First, three departments—Office of the Secretary General and the departments of organization and political education—were combined into one department simply called the Secretariat. The merger did not result in a significant streamlining of staff; rather it was done to better coordinate the work of the three departments. In the same year the Institute for the Study of Sandinism was transferred out of the party structure and into the government under the wing of the Sandinista army. This move was justified on the grounds that the scope of its inquiry was going well beyond party history to cover numerous examples of popular struggle in Nicaraguan history. The name was changed to the Institute for Nicaraguan History. Outside of the changes in these auxiliary departments, most other institutions of the party remained largely unchanged until after the 1990 elections. The Sandinista Assembly began to meet more regularly in 1988 and 1989, and there were serious discussions about changing its membership and functions, but those changes did not occur before the election defeat. Increasingly there were voices that called for a party congress, but a congress was not convened until July 1991. Figure 6.2 shows the current party structure.

There were also significant changes in the National Directorate. As part of the negotiations with the incoming leadership, Humberto Ortega was retained as head of the Sandinista Army but with the stipulation that he step down from his party leadership positions in the National Directorate and Sandinista Assembly. Ortega's departure from the Directorate in April 1990 marked the first change in the membership of that body since it was reconstituted in the reunification of March 1979. A second change occurred with the sudden death in October 1990 of Carlos Núñez from complications of pancreatic cancer. Former Nicaraguan vice-president, and head of the Sandinista parliamentary group, Sergio Ramírez was elevated to the National Directorate at the first Congress, along with Rene Núñez. The Congress also elected Humberto Ortega to the Directorate, but he declined to serve, citing the transition agreement.

The new political situation also resulted in a significant shift in political responsibilities for each individual member of the Directorate. A new Executive Committee was formed with Daniel Ortega, Carrión, and Ruíz

Figure 6.2 Current FSLN National Party Structure

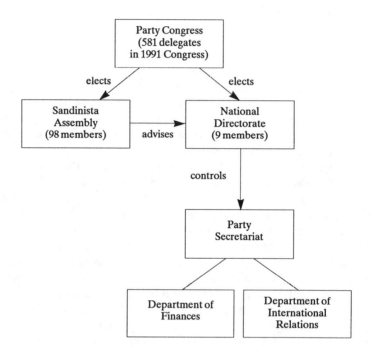

replacing the old body of Daniel Ortega, Borge, Wheelock, and Arce. Daniel Ortega remained as the coordinator of the Executive Committee while Carrión assumed the role of Deputy Coordinator, previously held by Arce.

Since he was no longer head of state, Daniel Ortega's role changed. He became the recognized chief spokesperson for the FSLN in opposition, and emerged as the chief negotiator for the political opposition during the May and July strikes of 1990. He served as the most prominent international spokesperson for the FSLN when he participated in an extended Mideast peace mission in November 1990. Ortega did not supersede the ultimate authority of the National Directorate but he seemed to be considered by both its other members and the rank and file as the maximum leader of the party.[11] This de facto position was then legitimized at the party Congress by his election to the newly created post of Secretary General. It is not yet clear what new formal powers may come from this status.

Luis Carrión was clearly elevated somewhat by the shift in responsibilities. Formerly Minister of Internal Commerce and Transportation, he assumed the position of overseer of all party affairs, a task previously carried out by Arce. As the Deputy Coordinator of the Executive Committee of the National Directorate, he assumed the coordinating role whenever Ortega was outside the country. Given the latter's frequent international travel after leaving the presidency, this task was not insignificant. Henry Ruíz moved from his governmental position of Minister of Foreign Cooperation to the similar party post of head of the Department of International Relations. His elevation to the Executive Committee also signified added prestige and responsibility.

Bayardo Arce became party treasurer, responsible for overseeing party enterprises. His removal from the Executive Committee could be seen as a demotion, but he continued to carry out international assignments for the party and headed the committee that wrote new rules for party membership. Tomás Borge stepped down as Minister of the Interior and became senior statesman in the party with fewer direct responsibilities. In 1990–1991 Borge worked with COPPPAL (Permanent Conference of Political Parties of Latin America), and carried out an extensive Western European speaking tour. As the sole living founding member of the party, Borge remained a strong moral authority in the party with a loyal personal following that rivaled Ortega's.

Former Minister of Agrarian Reform Jaime Wheelock assumed the task of overseeing an important group of Sandinista-inspired research institutes that emerged after the election defeat. Three of the most important are the Institute for the Development of Democracy (IPADE), headed by Vanessa Castro, former head of the FSLN Political Education Department; the Institute for Nicaraguan Studies (IEN), a public opinion data organization headed by former presidential advisor Paul Oquist; and the Center for International Studies (CEI) headed by former FSLN U.S. spokesperson Alejandro Bendaña. These research institutes will likely play a significant role in shaping the policies of the FSLN as a party in opposition. They became an important resource for the party to replace the losses suffered with their departure from the executive branch. As the architect of the Sandinista land reform, Wheelock also remained the overseer of party policies related to the countryside.

The final member of the Directorate, Victor Tirado, works with the National Union of Farmers and Ranchers (UNAG) and is also engaged in a writing project on the years of Sandinista power. The latter is carried out in conjunction with the again-renamed Institute for the Study of Sandinismo (IES), which has been removed from military jurisdiction and reconstituted at the University of Central America (UCA). While no longer a formal member of the Directorate, Humberto Ortega remains in an important consultative role, a position that was not proscribed by the transition agreement.[12]

After the electoral defeat, the National Directorate continued to be the dominant body in the FSLN. It met at least weekly and on an almost daily basis at times of national crisis and important party gatherings.[13] The basic guidelines of the document produced by the June 1990 assembly, drawing the lessons of the election defeat, were drafted in the National Directorate and the decision to postpone the Congress to July 1991 from February 1991 emanated from the same body. However, significant challenges to the authority of the Directorate also first appeared in the aftermath of the election. Some Sandinistas openly called for the election of a new national leadership (Tünnerman 1990, p. 17). The election procedures for the departmental and municipal party committees first proposed by the National Directorate were changed midstream after pressure from the base, and the Sandinista Assembly in June 1990 mandated the creation of a Party Ethics Commission without any prior recommendation by the top leadership.[14] The Congress gave greater formal authority to itself and the Sandinista Assembly but inevitably the National Directorate retains considerable power between sessions of the Congress and the Assembly. It is yet to be seen how the newly ordained powers of the Congress, Assembly, and General Secretary will affect the long-dominant position of the Directorate.

In 1990 the Sandinista Assembly began to assume a more central role in the life of the FSLN. The formal membership remained unchanged from earlier years except for several deaths and the removal of members of the armed forces as part of the transition agreement. However, participation in Assembly sessions was greatly expanded. The June meeting at El Crucero was expanded to include all FSLN National Assembly members, department coordinators, leaders of mass organizations, and representatives of the National Federation of Workers (FNT). The three-day June meeting was longer than any previous Assembly meeting and contained more genuine debate and airing of different political perspectives.[15] However, in the final analysis, the El Crucero meeting did continue the previous Assembly practice of passing the Directorate's recommendations without significant changes. The decision made at the June meeting to move up the Congress from July to February 1991 was later reversed at the September Assembly. The new party structure adopted at the Congress formally strengthened the power of the Assembly. Previously appointed, the new Assembly of 98 representatives was chosen by secret ballot in a hotly contested election. The body is now more representative of the current FSLN with a more than 60 percent turnover from the previous body. According to party statutes, the Assembly will meet at least twice per year and is subordinate only to the party Congress. At least formally, the Assembly is dominant over the National Directorate, a reversal of previous history.

The lower party structures have also seen significant change in the last two years. First, the old regional and zonal committees were changed, beginning in late 1989, to conform to the national governmental structures mandated by the new election law. The nine regions were replaced by seventeen departments, and over 130 municipal units were created. During the election campaign the FSLN reorganized to match these forms, with the exception that in the Atlantic Coast region the FSLN maintained a division between North and South Zeyala that does not exist in the governmental structures. The party is, therefore, divided into eighteen departments and over 130 municipalities.

The other main change at the departmental and municipal level occurred in August-September 1990 with the first-ever direct election of executive committees and coordinators at both levels. These previously appointed positions, close to 600 in all, were selected in a tumultuous and somewhat confusing fashion. Initially the National Directorate mandated that the Departmental Executive Committees be elected by representatives of different sectors in each region (e.g., women through AMNLAE, campesinos through ATC, and workers through the FNT). In the first election in the Chinendega region, the Executive Committee was selected by this process but soon pressure built from the party ranks for a more open and democratic selection process. As a result, in departments such as Chontales and Boaco, both the Executive Committee and Coordinator were chosen by secret ballot of an assembly of all party members. In the case of Chontales, apparently even sympathizers with the party were permitted to participate. The elections in the Managua Department, with the largest party membership (approximately 3,000), came near the end of the process and represented a hybrid of methods used in other departments. Because of membership numbers, the Executive Committee was much larger (thirty-five compared to five to ten in other departments). The members were chosen in three ways: ten representatives were elected at large in a direct secret ballot of all party members in the district from a slate of thirty candidates; ten other delegates were selected by sectorial mass organizations including the FNT and AMNLAE. (A new organization, the Movement of Historic Fighters, representing primarily combatants from the war against Somoza, was also given representation.) Finally, fifteen representatives were selected by the municipal committees that make up the Managua district.[16]

The elections were clearly a step forward in the democratization process of the party since no elections of any kind had occurred at that level before. It also seems that the direct election process that eventually was established did allow for the emergence to leadership positions of persons who would probably not otherwise have been selected. In Managua, for example, Carlos Fonseca Teran, son of the FSLN founder, and Danilo Aguirre, editor of *El Nuevo Diario,* were elected. Both have been outspoken critics of various leadership policies in recent years. Their selection in a competitive election was significant and was followed by their election to the Sandinista Assembly at the party Congress.

In spite of the progress, limitations on full democracy were still quite evident. Because campaigning for the posts was not permitted, the elections tended to focus on personalities and previous work records rather than a clear enunciation of future perspectives for the party. The lack of that political discussion, in the absence of the formal start of the Congress procedure, did flaw the process.[17] Not having a single systematic process in all departments and municipalities was also a significant problem. Some committees were not as representative because of the manner in which they were chosen, and the failure to establish clear membership criteria for who could vote may provide problems in the future.

The aftermath of the election saw the further contraction of the auxiliary departments and the reduction of staff by more than 50 percent. A process of staff reduction that began in 1989 reduced the number of party professionals from 5,000 to 500.[18] The Department of Propaganda and Agitation was eliminated and its personnel integrated into the Sandinista media outlets—*Barricada,* Radio Sandino, and Extravision (the Sandinista news program on government-run television). Under the new situation, leading Sandinista cadres who head those institutions were made directly responsible for their content in consultation with the National Directorate. There has even been some impetus from the staff of *Barricada* to make it an independent newspaper rather than a party organ, but to this time no such change has been made.[19] In the remaining departments—Secretariat, International Relations, and Finance—there were sharp cutbacks. In the Secretariat the number of political officers was cut from forty-five to seven and the staff of the Department of International Relations was cut by 75 percent.[20]

Across the board, the number of full-time staff was reduced. In most departments and municipalities there are now only one or two full-time people. At the local level, most FSLN staff served a dual role in party and government but received their paycheck from the government. Since most lost their government positions in the elections, their loss of full-time work was inevitable. The sharp staff cutback represented a stiff challenge for the FSLN, but it may have been a blessing in disguise. After the election defeat many Sandinistas singled out middle-level party and government professionals as being responsible for the party losing touch with the Nicaraguan people.[21] If the newly elected and streamlined party apparatus becomes more sensitive to the actual political situation in the country, then the party apparatus may actually be strengthened by the cutbacks. The past two years have also seen a resurgence of volunteer party activity that may serve to compensate for the loss of the paid staff.

Dramatic changes have also occurred in the membership of the FSLN. The last membership survey prior to 1990, done in August 1989, had credited the party with 41,000 members, up from 30,000 in August 1988.[22] However, the party Secretariat now considers the 1989 data to have been highly inaccurate and probably inflated due to double-counting of members and failure to remove inactive people.[23] After February 1990, the party moved both to systematize its membership and to begin the process of integrating thousands of new members. The new direction away from a strictly cadre party was signaled in the March 20, 1990, interview in *Barricada* with Victor Tirado, who called for the simultaneous development of a party of both cadres and masses. This movement was codified in the creation of a new official category of membership called "affiliate." The existing categories of "militant" and "aspirant to militancy" were maintained, but the new category was created to bring in those thousands of people who apparently wanted a more formal connection to the FSLN. Party officials also talked of sympathizers, collaborators, and combatants, but these have not been made formal membership designations. These categories are inexact and often overlapping, but they represent people that the party is now looking to involve in its future. In a couple of departments, people from these three categories were even invited to participate in voting for the party leadership bodies.

As of the end of August 1990 the party officially claimed 18,063 militants, 17,286 aspirants, and 60,398 affiliates.[24] The pace of new entry onto the party rolls in 1990 was such that by December the Secretariat claimed to have run out of membership cards and was issuing simple letters as a substitute. However, this apparent party growth has to be analyzed carefully. With probably only about 15,000 full members at the time of the February elections (less than 0.5 percent of the population), the FSLN was artificially small, even as a ruling vanguard party. Obviously a much greater percentage than that identified themselves as Sandinistas and worked to support Sandinista projects in a variety of ways. Because the membership was artificially low there was a considerable margin for growth. The 1990 growth came primarily from relaxing the membership standards.

There were no significant structural or procedural changes at the base committee level, but 1990 was still a year of significant change for rank-and-file Sandinistas. The trend was toward greater participation in neighborhood base committees. A key factor in the shift was the sharp reduction in full-time party employees who had previously participated in a base committee at their workplace. However, in a more important long-term development, thousands of Sandinistas, many of whom had become inactive, returned to activity in their neighborhood base committees. The surprising electoral defeat seemed to convince many Sandinistas that their active involvement in party affairs was once again needed. In many neighborhood base committees local residents who had never held FSLN membership status, but always considered themselves Sandinistas, demanded to participate in political discussions and party elections. It is primarily these people who swelled the ranks of the new "affiliate" membership category.[25]

The FSLN base committees in the workplace remain important, particularly for industrial and agricultural workers, but a definite shift has occurred. No longer are base committees of full-time party workers dominant. The shift will likely enhance the ability of the party to keep abreast of political sentiments in the wider populace, a process that obviously broke down very badly in the period before the February elections.

A crucial aspect of the process of democratization was the decision of the June 1990 Sandinista Assembly to hold the FSLN's first Congress in 1991. After initially being scheduled for February the meeting was held in July, following a year of preparatory activity. The June Assembly established four working commissions that did the groundwork for the Congress. Daniel Ortega headed a five-member committee, which included Borge and Sergio Ramírez, charged with writing the main political report, a historic review of the Sandinista revolutionary experience that included a balance sheet on eleven years of state power. A second commission, headed by Jaime Wheelock and including Victor Tirado, was charged with spelling out the contemporary political program of the FSLN leading toward the 1996 elections. Former head of party affairs Bayardo Arce headed a third commission that was charged with writing new bylaws for the party reflecting its shift to a wider membership base and different categories of membership. A fourth commission, headed by current party affairs chief Luis Carrión, was responsible for overseeing the logistics of the Congress and the discussions and elections leading up to it.[26]

The year-long preparations for the Congress contained several stages. In summer 1990 the FSLN organized over 200 meetings, called Popular Consultations, that provided input for the working commissions. The party prepared a detailed list of close to fifty questions that covered all aspects of Nicaraguan politics and economy, foreign relations, and party structures. The questions were placed before neighborhood assemblies, open to all citizens regardless of party affiliation. The results were by no means clear and definitive, but they did provide the FSLN with detailed feedback on the preoccupations of their political base. A total of approximately 10,000 people participated in the meetings, many of which occurred during or close to the time of the July strike confrontation between the Chamorro government and the FSLN-led unions. In part because of the timing of the meetings, the prearranged party agenda was often discarded, and discussions focused on more immediate concerns rather than on articulating a strategy for the future of the party.[27]

In 1991, according to the report by Luis Carrión at the start of the Congress, 1,374 assemblies of the party were held at the local level to debate the draft statutes and program. Over 47,000 FSLN members and affiliates were reported to have participated in the meetings (less than half of the membership). More than 5,000 motions were made to amend the preliminary documents. A total of 3,558 delegates were elected by the rank-and-file to the eighteen departmental congresses. Ultimately the departmental meetings elected 501 delegates to the conference. These delegates were joined by seventy-three members of the Sandinista Assembly and the seven remaining members of the National Directorate for a total delegate count of 581. Statistical information provided on the delegates revealed some interesting trends. By occupation, 50 percent of the delegates were white-collar workers and 22.5 percent were self-employed. Blue-collar workers and farmers were seriously underrepresented with only 3.5 percent and 10 percent of the delegates. Occupational statistics on the whole party membership were not available but it is highly unlikely that they would break down in proportions similar to the Congress delegates. There was considerable involvement of the rank-and-file in the selection process, but ultimately the party professionals were definitely overrepresented. Not surprisingly 71 percent of the delegates were between twenty-six and forty years of age and the youth representation was only 5.4 percent. Women were also seriously underrepresented.

The FSLN's first Congress and the preparations leading up to it were in many ways a great success for the party and represented a democratization of the organization. There was considerable debate and controversy in the party following the 1990 election debacle. Many questions were raised about the competence of the leadership and the correctness of the FSLN's approach as a revolutionary and anti-imperialist party. Many Sandinistas, like other members of Nicaraguan society, were forced to face the realities of day-to-day survival in a desperate economic situation. These personal crises were particularly acute for many Sandinistas who suddenly lost government or party positions. In spite of these many questions and problems the party emerged united from the July Congress without any significant splintering. This unity was achieved in part because, at least in its formal documents, the FSLN basically reaffirmed its longstanding political orientation as a revolutionary, anti-imperialist party, committed in the long term to the establishment of socialism. The distinctive shift to the right or "social democratization" of the party, which some had anticipated, did not happen, at least at this Congress. The revolutionary orientation of the Congress was demonstrated by the fact that the international guests who received the warmest welcomes were the representatives of the Cuban Communist Party and the FMLN of El Salvador. In contrast, the representative of the social democratic Spanish Socialist Workers Party (PSOE) walked out of the Congress when representatives of the revolutionary Basque nationalists, Herri Batasuna, were seated.[28]

The Congress and discussions that preceded it strengthened the FSLN, but also revealed that important and serious differences lay below the surface unity. The old National Directorate had renounced excessive verticalism at the El Crucero meeting in 1990, but some of its actions in the pre-Congress period fueled the views of those who argued that it had not changed. Two directives from the Directorate in June, just prior to the Managua departmental congress, were particularly controversial. Most importantly, the Directorate decreed that election of the new body would be by slate only, with no voting for individual members. At the same time the Directorate announced that Rene Núñez and Sergio Ramírez were being proposed as additions to the founding seven. This decision angered many rank-and-file members who were pushing the candidacy of Dora Maria Téllez as the Directorate's first woman member. Others objected to the slate concept because they wanted the option of removing certain leaders who had been most connected to the verticalism of the past and the recent collaboration with the Chamorro government.[29] In addition to the announcement of the slate, the Directorate declared that all members of the old Sandinista Assembly would have automatic voice and vote at the Congress. This was seen as an attempt by the leadership to pack the Congress and reduce the impact of the rank-and-file delegates elected in the departmental congresses. It is interesting to note that more than half of the old Sandinista Assembly members were not elected to the new Assembly.

Two other issues highlighted the lack of full democracy prior to the Congress. First, the main report, given by Daniel Ortega, was not made available prior to its presentation. Since no political report was available for discussion at the departmental congresses, the selection of delegates could not take place in the context of precise political positions. Second, the formation of formal tendencies or groupings was not permitted at any point in the congress process.

These limitations, while not decisive in the context of democratic advances, showed that the FSLN leadership has not fully shelved the verticalism that it had previously admitted. That leadership may have recognized its past errors, but it was not prepared to pay for those errors with any loss of leadership positions. The outgoing Directorate recognized that there was widespread discontent within the organization, but ultimately they moved quite skillfully to co-opt some of that opposition and to indicate a strong willingness to learn from their mistakes. Whether that leadership can be as successful with the Nicaraguan population as a whole remains to be seen.

Notes

1. Interview by Prevost with Mireille Vigil, Director of Party Affairs, FSLN Secretariat, Managua, November 22, 1990.

2. Interview by Prevost with Julio Pérez, Political Secretary, FSLN Department of International Relations, Managua, January 23, 1987.

3. In contrast to the unity of the FSLN, the Grenadian revolutionary movement, the New Jewel Party, was destroyed by an intraparty coup in October 1983, led by Bernard Coard, which led to the assassination of Prime Minister Maurice Bishop and the defeat of the New Jewel Movement by a U.S. invasion. Also, the Salvadoran revolutionary movement has been severely divided at many points of its recent history and those divisions led to the assassination of a Salvadoran revolutionary leader in Managua in 1985.

4. Pérez interview, 1987.

5. Interview by Prevost with Patricia Elvir, FSLN Department of International Relations, November 10, 1990.

6. Information provided by FSLN Secretariat, November 1990.

7. Interview by Prevost with Vanessa Castro, Head, Department of Political Education (1982–1989), Managua, January 9, 1991.

8. Interview by Prevost with Alejandro Bravo, member, Nicaraguan National Assembly, Managua, January 20, 1987.

9. Vigil interview, 1990.

10. Ibid.

11. This view of Ortega as the informal party leader was confirmed in numerous interviews with both FSLN leaders and rank and file, in particular, interviews by Prevost with Vigil, Alejandro Martínez (former cabinet member and presidential advisor), and Victor Tirado (member of the National Directorate).

12. Information about the current political responsibilities of individual members of the Directorate came primarily from interviews with Vigil and Martínez. These work assignments are subject to change but are rarely given in public notification.

13. Vigil interview, 1990.

14. Ibid.

15. For a complete text of the resolutions passed at El Crucero, see FSLN (1990).

16. Details of the departmental and municipal election procedures were gained from several sources: "20 mil militantes FSLN en elecciones distritales" (*Barricada,* August 28, 1990); "Dora María al frente de Managua" (*Barricada,* September 3, 1990); Vigil interview, 1990; and interview by Prevost with Salvador Pérez, Director of the Movement of Historic Fighters, November 13, 1990.

17. This shortcoming was cited as significant by several Sandinistas interviewed in November 1990, particularly Pérez.

18. Data provided by FSLN Secretariat, November 1990.

19. Vigil interview, 1990.

20. Information provided by FSLN Secretariat, November 1990.

21. Interview with Carlos Fonseca Teran in *El Nuevo Diario,* August 27, 1990.

22. Information provided by FSLN Secretariat, November 1990.

23. Vigil interview, 1990.

24. Information provided by FSLN Secretariat, November 1990.

25. This observation is based on numerous interviews by Prevost with rank-and-file Sandinistas during November 1990.

26. Details of the structures for the Congress preparation provided in Communicado No. 1, National Directorate Secretariat, Managua, June 1990 (mimeo).

27. Vigil interview, 1990.

28. All statistics concerning the Congress and its preparation are from *Barricada International,* August 1991.

29. For coverage of this issue, including Daniel Ortega's response to the criticisms, see *Barricada International,* July 1991, pp. 20–25.

SEVEN

The 1990 Elections: Capitalism and Western-Style Democracy Stop the Revolution

In chapter 4 we saw how the Sandinista government in Nicaragua held a clean, honest, Western-style election in 1984, which also had the effect of shifting the focus from mass organizations and direct, participatory democracy to indirect, representative democracy. We also saw how the constitutional structure that evolved further buttressed these trends, and that calls for a second legislative chamber, where the mass organizations would be represented directly (as was the case in the bicameral legislature in Yugoslavia), were not implemented. Nor were the anticipated municipal elections held before the time of the 1990 elections.

These actions suggest that the dimensions of participatory and grass-roots democracy that had been initially envisioned as part of the Sandinista program were sidetracked in a rush toward a system of representative democracy that the dominant group in the Sandinista leadership hoped would satisfy the United States and its capitalist allies and thus increase the legitimacy of the Nicaraguan government in their eyes.

Up to 1979 Nicaragua had been one of the most conservative and authoritarian societies in Latin America, with one of the longest family dictatorships in the hemisphere (1936–1979). Indeed, it could be argued that Nicaragua was among the least democratic of the Latin American republics for the longest time and had very little experience with honest elections (even the ultratraditional regime in Paraguay could only date its existence to the early 1950s). One author even suggested that it not only had an authoritarian political culture, but that the factional nature of party interaction suggested a political system characterized by underdevelopment (Vickers 1990, pp. 19–27).

When the FSLN took power on July 19, 1979, the stage was set for a series of changes that included two of the most honest elections in Nicaraguan, if not Latin American, history (1984 and 1990) and an open constitution-making process. But these events were in turn conditioned by a political culture that had been extremely traditional and authoritarian and a political system that had been slow to develop. New values were, however, eventually interjected into the Nicaraguan context. The 1990 election was held after more than a decade of Sandinista rule and after the general outlines of a transformed Nicaraguan society were already in place. In this process many traditional values had been challenged—if not replaced—by more modern values in many sectors of society.

Many external factors were also brought to bear on the electoral process, as the United States was poised to extend its power through the region again and—as became apparent—to project it further into much of the rest of the world. As it turned out, the election occurred in an international and regional context over which the Nicaraguan government had only limited control, despite its often brilliant use of diplomacy and the international legal system. From 1982 on, the United States used military, diplomatic, and economic means to try to impose its will on the Sandinista government. Although it was often unclear whether the Republican administrations would be able to realize their primary objective of overthrowing the Sandinistas, it was clear that they could make sure that the new government would have very difficult going, would have very limited options, and would be hard put to claim itself a model for other Central or Latin American countries (Vanden 1990, 1991; Vanden and Walker 1991).

Nicaragua experienced a contra war that cost 30,000 lives and in excess of twelve billion dollars in economic losses,[1] a total U.S. economic embargo from 1985 on, and the continual threat of direct U.S. invasion. The Nicaraguans found that they were faring even worse than most other Latin American nations, which had also experienced a lost decade of economic growth in the 1980s. Responding to such pressures and the Central American peace process, the government in Nicaragua not only decided to go ahead with the elections previously scheduled for November 1990, it advanced the timetable to February 1990. This was an attempt to accommodate U.S. and Western European pressure for elections so as to show good faith in the Central American peace process and to achieve a peace that would disarm and disband the contras once and for all.[2] The Nicaraguan leadership also hoped to show definitively that Nicaragua could apply the most stringent Western (capitalist) standards for democracy and could hold a squeaky-clean election that would satisfy even its most strident critics. There was also a desire to demonstrate that Western-style democracy could exist within a state guided by a Marxist party.

Committed Nicaraguans had first struggled to change an archaic system and rid the country of a horrid dictator; next came the struggle to establish a government and make a whole nation out of a country torn by civil war. Then, after the Reagan administration was in office, came confrontation with the United States and a contra war that lasted in earnest from 1982 through 1988 and eventually forced the Nicaraguan government to devote huge amounts of material and human resources to defend itself (by 1987, 62 percent of government expenditures were for defense). A further trial began with the economic war whose start coincided with the contra upsurge, was intensified by the 1985 economic embargo imposed by the United States, and lasted until Violeta Chamorro was inaugurated in April 1990.

The Costly Campaign

In the midst of very difficult economic conditions and sporadic contra attacks, Nicaragua underwent a test that would try the patience of the most saintly. For months, the country was absorbed in a hard-fought electoral campaign that featured ten parties (including a major coalition) and the spending of millions of dollars on the campaign and the election itself.

Although the FSLN had been able to maintain unity, most of the other parties had not been able to overcome the proclivity for factionalism and internecine struggle. Only six opposition parties had opposed the FSLN in the 1984 election (encouraged by the United States, the Coordinadora Democrática boycotted the elections); but by the beginning of 1988, there were fourteen opposition parties plus a few opposition political groupings.[3] The Reagan administration had pushed the military side of low-intensity conflict and discouraged parties from participating in 1984. As Bush took office, U.S. policy began to emphasize an electoral challenge to the Sandinistas. With the support of the United States, the opposition parties pushed hard to get modifications in the electoral laws that would ensure maximum political space and maneuverability. In that the Sandinistas were anxious to achieve full participation as one aspect of their policy to legitimize the elections, they made a sufficient number of concessions to achieve widespread party participation. In so doing they seem to have minimized the clear "refusal of sectors of the former ruling classes and the United States government to accept the new structure of Nicaraguan society" and their attempt to overthrow the new structure (Lobel 1988, p. 871).

By July 1989, both the OAS and the UN concluded that the electoral rules were democratic and agreed to send major observer delegations. In August 1989, a marathon negotiating session between the fourteen opposition parties and the government led to the incorporation of thirty-five additional changes proposed by the opposition. These included the suspension of the draft, the reform of internal security laws, free TV airtime for opposition parties, and Supreme Electoral Council (CSE)

Sandinista Leaders Campaigning (From left to right: Vice-President Sergio Ramírez; the poet Rosario Murillo, Daniel Ortega's wife; Daniel Ortega. A portrait of Augusto César Sandino hangs in the background.)

control of one TV channel as well as CSE control over some police at the time of the election.

If traditional factionalism had held sway, there would have been some twenty opposition parties on the ballot. This would have splintered the opposition vote and allowed the FSLN an easy victory. Realizing this, the Bush administration pushed for a unified opposition coalition and strongly encouraged the selection of a fresh opposition candidate who could serve as a symbol around which the opposition could rally. Although lacking political experience, Violeta Chamorro filled this role very well. With U.S. support, she was able to edge out Enrique Bolaños, a traditional political leader and head of COSEP, and become the coalition candidate. By the time of the election, the U.S.-supported unity of the United Nicaraguan Opposition (UNO) had generally held, and their coalition had fourteen parties. (See Table 7.1 for a complete list of these parties.) Included in the new coalition were parties that traced their origins to the old Conservative and Liberal parties as well as Social Democratic parties, Social Christian parties, a party tied to contra leaders, and even two Communist parties— the Nicaraguan Socialist Party (PSN) and the Communist Party of Nicaragua (PCdeN). Figure 7.1 is a sample election ballot showing the choice of parties.

Ignoring just how honest the 1984 elections had been, the United States and other Western nations increasingly called for new—and osten-

Figure 7.1 Ballot for President and Vice-President

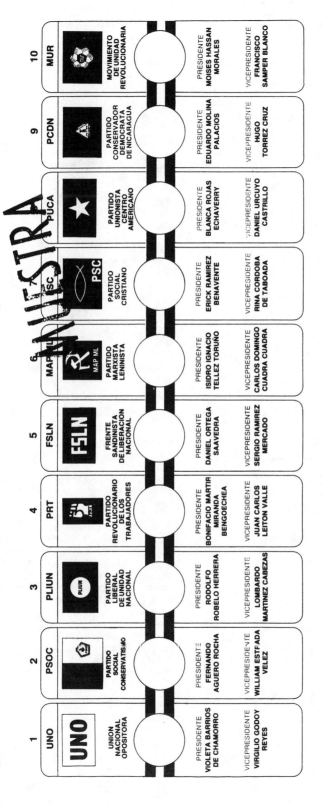

Note: Separate ballots were used for each level of government.

Table 7.1 Parties in the 1990 Election

UNO Coalition
Violeta Chamorro, President
Virgilio Godoy, Vice-President

PNC National Conservative Party	Founded in a 1984 split in the old Democratic Conservative Party (PCDN); most conservative of UNO parties, with contra and U.S. links.
PAPC Popular Conservative Alliance	Initially part of the National Conservative Party (PNC); disagreements prompted a split before the election.
PSD Social Democratic Party	Formed in split from the PCDN after the 1979 revolution; closely tied to *La Prensa*.
PLI Independent Liberal Party	Founded in 1944 in split from Somoza's Nationalist Liberal Party (PLN); became focal point for anti-Somoza forces. Virgilio Godoy led party to right and attempted to remove it from the ballot in the 1984 election.
PLC Liberal Constitutionalist Party	Resulted from a split in Somoza's PLN in 1968; member of the Coordinadora in 1984.
PALI Neo-Liberal Party	Founded in 1985 break with the PLI; incorporated the remains of Somoza's PLN.
PDCN Democratic Party of National Confidence	Formed in 1988 split from the Social Christian Party (PSC).
PAN National Action Party	Founded in 1987 split from the PSC; smallest of Social Christian factions. Strongly anti-Sandinista and pro–United States.
PSN Nicaraguan Socialist Party	Founded in 1944 as orthodox Communist party; remained pro-Moscow. Did not actively support the insurrection until very late. In rift, long-time leader Domingo Sánchez's son Luis Sánchez led successful movement to become Social Democratic Party (1988) and then later join UNO coalition.
PPSC Popular Social Christian Party	See PPSC description on p. 136. A small faction of this party stayed in the UNO coalition after the main faction broke off just before the election.

Table 7.1 continued

PCdeN Communist Party of Nicaragua	Formed in 1966 split from PSN; did not support the insurrection; became anti-Sandinista in stance.
MDN Nicaraguan Democratic Movement	Founded in 1978 by business sectors; headed by one-time Sandinista Junta member Alfonso Robelo (who later left Junta and helped form ARDE contra group with Eden Pastora).*

Government Party

FSLN
Sandinista National Liberation Front

Founded as a nationalistic guerrilla movement in 1961, it led the struggle against the Somoza dictatorship and became a pluralistic socialist party after coming to power in 1979.

Daniel Ortega, President
Sergio Ramírez, Vice-President

Other Opposition Parties

PCDN
Conservative Democratic Party of Nicaragua

Founded in 1956, it emerged in 1979 in a split from the old Conservative Party. It was the only conservative faction to run in the 1984 elections.

Eduardo Molina, President
Hugo Torrez Cruz, Vice-President

PSOC
Social Conservative Party

Formed in 1988 by several contra leaders who returned to Nicaragua.

Fernando Aguero, President
William Estrada, Vice-President

PLIUN
National Unity Liberal Party

Resulted from 1987 split in the PLI.

Rodolfo Robelo, President
Lombardo Martínez, Vice-President

PSC
Social Christian Party

Founded in 1957 as a Christian Democratic Party, it boycotted the 1984 elections and splintered after that. It formed an alliance with the Popular Social Christian Party for the 1990 election.

Eric Ramírez, President
Rina Taboada, Vice-President

Table 7.1 continued

PPSC Popular Social Christian Party	A center-left party that split from the PSC in 1976. Split into two factions shortly before the 1990 election, with the official faction (headed by party leader Mauricio Díaz) leaving UNO to form an alliance with the PSC.
	Eric Ramírez, President Rina Taboada, Vice-President
MAP-ML Marxist-Leninist Popular Action Movement	Formed from split in FSLN in 1972. Claimed FSLN made too many concessions to bourgeoisie.
	Isidoro Téllez, President Carlos Cuadra, Vice-President
PRT Revolutionary Workers Party	Founded in 1971, a small Trotskyist party affiliated with the Fourth International.
	Bonifacio Miranda, President Juan Carlos Leytón, Vice-President
MUR Movement of Revolutionary Unity	Formed in 1988 by dissident elements from the MAP-ML, PCdeN, and FSLN.
	Moisés Hassán, President Francisco Samper, Vice-President
PUCA Central American Unionist Party	Founded in 1920 by Nicaraguan exiles in El Salvador; believes in Central American unification.
	Blanca Rojas, President Daniel Urcuyo, Vice-President

*Parties Not Recognized by the Supreme Electoral Council
(but that supported UNO)

PIAC
Central American Integrationalist Party

PANC
National Conservative Alliance Party

sibly more democratic—elections in Nicaragua. The assumption was that a more Western-style democracy would emerge—one that would be acceptable to the United States and its allies, and, it was further argued, would be more beneficial to the Nicaraguan people by freeing them from authoritarian Sandinista rule. The Sandinistas felt they had already established their democratic credentials but were being asked yet again to prove their worthiness to govern. Ironically, the Bush administration had never promised that it would respect the outcome of a fair election that the Sandinistas won by calling off the remaining contras and ending the economic embargo. As late as February 23, Secretary of State James Baker was questioning whether a fair election could be held. Nor was this point missed by the Nicaraguan electorate. Nonetheless, the Sandinista government agreed to turn the country into a kind of international goldfish bowl by inviting observers from the United Nations, the Organization of American States, (Jimmy Carter's) Council of Freely Elected Heads of State, and a host of other organizations (Ryan 1990). In all, more than 2,500 foreign observers were registered with the Supreme Electoral Council. This made for the most closely observed election to date in Latin America or elsewhere.

The cost of preparing and administering the election was itself enormous. The Supreme Electoral Council, the independent governmental body responsible for overseeing and running the election, spent in excess of $15 million alone.[4] The Sandinista leadership knew that economic conditions were bad, but thought the base could endure a little longer while they employed the human and material resources at their disposal to win the election. They mobilized their followers well and spent $7 million on a fancy campaign that featured not only door-to-door organizing and mass rallies, but give-away FSLN baseball hats, straw hats, t-shirts, back packs, and cigarette lighters.[5] The FSLN used outside media and public relations consultants to develop a slick, rock-star-like presentation for Daniel Ortega. Some use of government resources by the FSLN was also reported (Latin American Studies Association 1990, esp. p. 27). The Sandinistas reasoned that such extravagant spending was necessary to win the election so as to secure their position and legitimize their political system in the eyes of the West. They were playing a high-stakes game. The United States had designated huge sums for the UNO campaign. This was epitomized by the 1989 U.S. congressional authorization of $9 million in overt funding for the opposition to be dispensed through the National Endowment for Democracy. But the Sandinista campaign stood in stark contrast to the austere, impoverished conditions in which most Nicaraguans found themselves (ibid., p. 21). This was clearly a contributing factor to their defeat.

The Economic Realities

Up to the time of the February election it seemed that the Nicaraguan revolution might be able to build on the experiment with socialist democracy that had developed in Chile in the early 1970s. The Sandinistas would give an expanded electorate the opportunity to decide if they wanted to continue in the process of socialist construction or opt for another type of regime. Down to the eve of the election, most opinion polls suggested that the Nicaraguan people would ratify the socialist, mixed-economy experiment and continue with Sandinista democracy. However, the stunning defeat at the hands of the U.S.-sponsored United Nicaraguan Opposition (UNO) suggested that the demos was not entirely satisfied with Sandinista rule or the type of socialist democracy that was developing in Nicaragua.

The real battle for Nicaragua had become economic. As Byrum Weathers (1988, p. 87) observed:

> Despite U.S. backing, the contras' [military] success against the Sandinista regime has been limited. . . . In addition to the threat of insurgency, Nicaragua is faced with a critical economic situation requiring the government to implement severe austerity measures. A serious shortage of foreign exchange exists, and indebtedness to lenders abroad is increasing. Financial stress has been compounded by the U.S. embargo on trade and by a credit freeze on the part of the World Bank. The fight against the contras has absorbed funds that might otherwise have been used for productive economic purposes. Inflation continues to climb at a high rate; living standards are steadily declining . . . wages of the workers are low while the prices of goods and services are high. . . .
>
> The deteriorating economic situation is a major concern to the Sandinistas. . . . That the Marxist government will be able to overcome these formidable obstacles in the near term appears doubtful.

Careful analysis of the facts suggests the low-intensity conflict that the Bush administration was waging against Nicaragua was having disastrous effects on the economy (Vanden and Walker 1991). Nor was the Nicaraguan government well prepared to manage the deteriorating economic conditions. Their own insurgent experience, militant military organization and mobilization, and the excellent technical and material support they eventually received from Cuba, the German Democratic Republic, and the Soviet Union (coupled with the general lack of popular support for the contras and their brutal use of terror) enabled the Sandinista leadership to prevail over the U.S.-backed insurgency. However, when it came to the economic dimension, Managua was ill-prepared.

First, as the Sandinistas came to power, they had little if any substantial training in economics, administration, planning, or management. Second, there were few models of relevant participatory management, planning, or administration with which they had had any experience or on which they could draw; nor was the acquisition of these skills given a high priority. Indeed, the new Nicaraguan government only belatedly got around to setting up its own school of administration and management (INAP) and did not develop any in the public universities. Nor did it

FSLN Campaign Poster on Rudimentary Temporary Dwelling Suggests the FSLN's Increasing Difficulty to Maintain Its Previous Level of Support from the Impoverished Masses

supply sustained, high quality, on-the-job training to those who took over most governmental and party posts (their political training was, however, widely available and of excellent quality). Practically the only in-country training available was through INCAE (Central American Institute of Business Administration), which had been set up in conjunction with the Harvard Business School. It was dominated by the Nicaraguan commercial bourgeoisie, considered a COSEP haven, and thus taught a few upper-level government managers techniques of questionable relevance to socialist revolutionaries who purported to be constructing a popular-based economic system to enhance participation and popular democracy.

Third, Cuba and the socialist nations on whom Nicaragua was increasingly forced to rely for material and technical assistance were ill-prepared to supply the necessary training in these areas. Indeed, subsequent events suggest that the training offered to their own government employees might have been sadly lacking in these areas (Smith 1991).[6] Nor does the Nicaraguan government appear to have availed itself of much of the expertise that could have been acquired through these states or to have sought it from multilateral aid agencies such as the United Nations. The result was that virtually all levels of government and party were not prepared (or predisposed) to deal with the magnitude of the economic problems that befell Nicaragua (because of the war and the embargo) in ways that were consistent with the form of democracy or the model of humane development that the revolution had set as its goals in July 1979 (Albert and Hahnel 1990).[7] In a recent work on participatory development, many of the contributors make the point that such development necessitates a well-founded vision of what is entailed and a clear knowledge of the administrative and technical expertise that is necessary to foster it (Lineberry, 1989). If the first condition was partially satisfied in Nicaragua, the second went completely unmet.

As the United States helped to fashion the program and campaign thrust for UNO, the economy and the claim that the U.S.-supported candidate was the only one who could improve economic conditions (by enlisting U.S. support and stopping the U.S.-backed contras) became increasingly prominent. Only with the election of the U.S.-sponsored candidate, it was suggested, could the Nicaraguans hope to begin to recover from the unbearable economic conditions they were experiencing. In a post-election interview Luis Sánchez, principal spokesperson for the UNO coalition, clearly stated that the economic problem became the primary focus of the UNO campaign.[8] This thrust is equally evident in UNO campaign literature and in Violeta Chamorro's campaign speeches.

By 1988 inflation had reached some 36,000 percent, real wages had fallen to 29 percent of their 1980 value, milk consumption fell by 50 percent, and production reached levels that were abysmally low (Vilas 1990b). In that same year, the deteriorating economy began to have a heavy impact on daily life and increasingly became a subject of intense public concern. The government clearly assigned blame to the U.S. actions. However, the governmental response was an austerity program that was modeled on the "heterodox shock treatments" that Brazil and Argentina had employed in 1985 and 1986 and, as such, fell disproportionately on the poor (Conroy 1990, p. 21). This marked a shift in Sandinista policy, because it was the first time since the insurrection that a program of economic reform did not include efforts to protect the poor from its harshest effects (ibid., p. 22). By the middle of 1988, prices for basic commodities had risen 600 percent, and the government had lifted price controls on the majority of goods and services. The result was that the average individual wage would cover only 48 percent of the minimum "market basket" for a family. Other sources that were normally sympathetic to the government estimated that the average worker's wage would cover as little as 7 percent. Many criticized these policies because they believed they represented a new direction that veered away from the goals of popular consumption and would transfer resources from internal consumption to the export sector, which would ultimately transfer income from workers, peasants, and consumers to those who controlled capital (ibid., pp. 22–24).

As the economic crisis developed in 1988 and after, the government seemed at a loss to find policies or forms of administration that could stem the crisis and protect the lower classes. For instance, the Sandinistas "offered broad economic concessions to large private farmers, while attempting to hold back worker and peasant demand" (Vilas 1990b, p. 12). In April 1989, the government even awarded large cotton producers a subsidy of one million córdobas per manzana of land (1.75 acres), while rejecting the cotton workers' demand for a livable wage that would cover a minimum supply of eight basic foodstuffs (ibid.). Like the Reagan administration in Washington, many members of the bourgeoisie and middle class were unwilling to accept the legitimacy of the societal transformation that the Sandinistas advocated. Yet as the economic crisis got worse, subsidies to middle-class and wealthy entrepreneurs were often financed by "cutting back the consumption, income, and living conditions of the revolution's natural base of support, the workers and the peasants" (ibid.). The government did not seem to know how to organize services or productive functions in ways that were consistent with a state-directed mixed economy and a participatory democratic model. The market increasingly became the primary means of rationing scarce resources— much to the detriment of the popular classes. And when members of the popular organizations tried to take an independent line against this government policy they were dissuaded from it. If they persisted, they were often accused of being unpatriotic, or worse, of being in the service of the United States (Pérez Flores 1989, Vilas 1990).

The austerity measures of 1989 did, however, help to stabilize the economy: inflation slowed, Nicaraguan agriculture exports rose 30 percent in that year, and there were more plentiful consumer goods. The problem was that real wages continued to drop, so that few wage earners could afford to acquire the now more abundant goods (Conroy 1990, pp. 26–28). Some statistics indicated that urban wages had fallen to only 10 percent of 1980 levels. Per-capita income fell virtually every year from 1984 to 1990 (Latin American Studies Association 1990, p. 19). By the late 1980s, the harm had been done, and there was a growing perception that the Sandinistas were not in control or were selling out their poor supporters to gain the economic cooperation of middle- and upper-class commercial interests.[9] It seemed that the only response to the economic crisis that the Sandinista leadership could agree to implement was one that sought to activate traditional commercial groups in the hope that they would lead the recovery. But by the end of 1989 it seemed to many that the economic dimension of the contra war, coupled with internal deficiencies in management and allocation, had caused the Sandinista government to ignore the economic plight of the masses.

In order to diminish any remaining Sandinista support, the Bush administration cranked up the contras again in the summer of 1989. As they rampaged though the countryside they spread political messages for the election: "Only UNO can end the economic crisis"; "There will be no peace under a Sandinista government"; "A Sandinista government means war and a continuation of the military draft. Only UNO can bring peace" (McMichael 1990, p. 166). In all, the United States had invested heavily in supporting opposition forces in Nicaragua—some $26 million in overt and covert aid since the 1984 election (Cook 1989, pp. 2–3). *Newsweek* (Sept. 5, 1989) suggested that $5 million in covert funds had been used for the 1990 election alone. Overt funding for the election was estimated at $12.5 million (Sklar 1989, p. 50). The sophisticated low-intensity conflict campaign was clearly having an effect. By January 1990, 52 percent of those registered voters surveyed believed that the economy was the most important issue for them in deciding how to vote in the coming election.

Closing UNO Rally in Managua

By comparison, 37 percent thought the contra war was the most important issue (Conroy 1990, p. 30).

The Final Outcome

In order to understand why the vote went the way it did, it is necessary to delineate the pressures that were working on the electorate. The economic and human attrition of Washington's economic embargo and the ongoing contra war against the Nicaraguan people finally did wear down popular Nicaraguan resolve to resist foreign pressure and continue their own brand of democracy. Nor was the example of what happened in Panama lost on the Nicaraguan people.[10] Further, as economic conditions deteriorated and political support for the direct, participatory democracy of the mass organizations was diminished by their exclusion from the legislative body after 1984 and their frequent subordination to FSLN control, there were fewer channels through which the masses could effectively communicate the gravity of their plight. Thomas Cronin (1989, p. 10) suggests that when "there is growing suspicion that privileged interests exert far greater influences on the typical politician than does the common voter" there is a demand for more democracy. But neither the official party nor the mass organizations seemed willing or able to provide greater democratic participation. And by lauding the election and the connected Western-style representative democracy, the Sandinistas themselves seemed to be telling the people that this (and not participatory democracy) was the only democratic instrument through which they could express themselves. Meanwhile, the UNO coalition was arguing in its platform that its fundamental objective was to "construct democracy" and that it planned to "profoundly democratize the nation and the society." UNO was the only party on the ballot that had any chance of challenging Sandinista political hegemony. Since Sandinista dominance appeared to many to be ever less responsive to popular democracy, there were very limited options for most voters.

As it turned out, lower-class Nicaraguans were confronted with an awful choice. Vote for the Frente and continue to suffer economically and perhaps risk losing more lives to contras, or vote for the United Nicaraguan Opposition and hope that things would change. Even the week before the election it was not clear how many voters were genuinely enthusiastic about Doña Violeta's administrative or political capacity or the hodgepodge political coalition that UNO represented.[11] In a January 1990 poll, 61 percent thought Violeta Chamorro could reconcile Nicaragua and the United States and 58 percent thought she could end inflation, as compared to 50 and 25 percent, respectively, for the FSLN (see Conroy 1990, pp. 32–33).

If they chose not to vote for UNO, many of the toiling masses were not at all sure of what was in store for them. The incredible inflation rate in 1988 and the lower but continuing inflation in 1989 had greatly reduced confidence in the government. Real wages had plummeted to well below pre-1979 levels and the standard of living of the masses continued to be miserably low. Further, while the government had adopted Sandino's dictum that "only the workers and the peasants will go all the way," it did not seem to have gone all the way with its natural constituency—the very same workers and peasants. As though following the dictates of the International Monetary Fund, an austerity program had been imposed in 1989, ostensibly to curb hyperinflation. As was the case with such programs in other Third World countries, the burden fell disproportionately on the lower classes, who no longer had any monetary or energy reserves left to contribute. After years of Somocismo, the civil war, and then the contra war and the economic embargo, they just did not have anything more to give. Indeed the Sandinista Defense Committees (CDSs) had stopped functioning for all practical purposes for the same reason: *no podían más*—they just couldn't do it anymore (La Ramée and Polakoff 1990).

Many also felt that the Sandinista leaders were isolated from the hardships of the masses and that their political position facilitated access to goods that the poor could no longer afford. Many were angered by what they perceived as increasing bureaucratization in government offices. They saw the formation of a bureaucratic class that was not particularly sympathetic to popular needs and was the beneficiary of a disproportionate share of scarce resources. This created considerable resentment. Thus it seemed to many that the vanguard party had lost contact with the very people it was supposed to represent and consequently was not responding to their needs and feelings (was no longer representing the general will). Rather, they felt the party had become an institution that was ruled from the top down ("the National Directorate commands") and had established a set of interests that was not always the same as those of the people. Nor had many found that party leaders or cadres were always open to criticism or opinions that contradicted those they held; after a while, some Nicaraguans felt they could not express contrary views.

Believing that the results of opinion polls might be transmitted directly to the government, over 20 percent of those surveyed would not even admit to any preference for UNO, but then used the secrecy of the voting booth to support it. As suggested by the discrepancy between the opinion polls and the actual results, Nicaraguans were often unwilling to entrust their political opinion to those they did not know or who might be working for the government. Polls be damned, the people seemed to be saying. As many voters told one of the authors the day before the election, the vote

Lining Up to Vote in Monimbó

is secret and we'll see how well they (the Sandinistas) do.[12]

As the election results trickled in on Sunday night, it soon became apparent that—believing they had been abandoned by the Sandinistas—the residents of many working-class neighborhoods in the capital (Julio Bultrago, Las Brisas, and San Judas among them) had given UNO a majority. And so it went in other urban areas and in much of the countryside as well. UNO got 54.7 percent of the vote while the Sandinistas received only 40.8 percent (most polls had predicted a substantial Sandinista victory; the ABC/*Washington Post* poll predicted 48 percent to 32 percent).[13] In that the FSLN was convinced that it would win big, this was a particularly stunning defeat. To the FSLN's credit, Daniel Ortega announced early Monday morning that the government would abide by the election results and would cooperate in transferring power to the new government. Later statements specified conditions for doing so. Nor could the Sandinistas expect to control the National Assembly (they would control only thirty-nine of the ninety-two seats while the UNO coalition would have fifty-one) or very many municipalities across the country (UNO won 102 of the 131 municipal councils).

It is hard not to feel for the hundreds of thousands of Nicaraguans who stayed with the FSLN through these most bitter of times only to see their dreams shattered by a popular backlash against the economic austerity and the military draft that had been necessary to stem the tide of continuing U.S. economic and military aggression. But equally, one must sympathize with the thousands of workers and peasants who were trying to improve their lot so that they would not have to continue the impossible task of trying to feed and clothe their families on salaries of $20 to $40 a month, who were out of work altogether (the unemployment rate jumped from 24.4 percent in 1987 to 32.7 percent in 1989), or who feared that they or their sons would have to fight in a continuing contra war. Nor did many expect a rapid economic recovery. Domestic production fell 10 percent in 1988 and a further 3 percent in 1989. In the two-year period from December 1987 to December 1989, real wages shrank 40 percent (*Envio* 1990b, p. 15).

Conclusion

A careful analysis of events in Nicaragua suggests that it was the U.S.-induced economic crisis and the ineffective way it was handled that most hurt the Sandinistas in their traditional bastions of working-class support. Ironically, the Frente leadership seemed to have ignored a fundamental aspect of Sandinista doctrine. As repeatedly emphasized by their founding leader and theoretician, Carlos Fonseca Amador, the vanguard must always stay in touch with the masses and must always represent their interests (represent the general will). If one is constructing socialism, it is imperative that the interests of the toiling masses be represented and protected. It would appear, however, that the Sandinista leadership felt that the masses would have to suffer a little longer while they stabilized the economy, increased production, convinced the commercial bourgeoisie to participate more fully, won the election, and played out the Central American peace process. Although thousands of party militants and Frente supporters accepted those terms, the vast majority of middle- and upper-class Nicaraguans were far from doing so (despite the fact that many often received preferential treatment in the late 1980s). And a growing number of lower-class Nicaraguans did not accept these terms at all. Many began to accuse the Sandinistas of arrogance. They thought the revolution had been for them and seemed to feel that continued support for the Sandinistas would only lead to a further reduction of their already miserable standard of living.

By ignoring those aspects of direct, participatory democracy that were part of the initial Sandinista program and by failing to support its mass base (and natural constituency) economically, the FSLN left open only more formal Western-style institutional democracy as an avenue of popular expression. Although complaints about the economy and the war were increasingly vociferous, the masses (in and outside the party) did not find other avenues to communicate the intensity of their suffering effectively to the governmental and party leadership. The mass organizations had lost the direct representation they held in the Council of State when it was abolished in favor of the National Assembly after the 1984 election. And if any leaders of the mass organizations were elected as deputies to the new National Assembly, it was through the Sandinista Party. Thus, as increasingly was the case in the mass organizations themselves, these deputies were susceptible to Sandinista pressure and programs and were not as closely attuned to the immediate needs of the mass base in the organization. Indeed, by the late 1980s, many of the mass organizations were accused of being instruments of the FSLN and not autonomous organizations that represented and articulated the interests of their members. For instance, Sandinista labor unions were repeatedly told not to strike even though the wages of their workers were no longer sufficient even to feed their families. Likewise, those labor leaders and unions that did strike were accused of disloyalty to the revolution if not of playing into the hands of the U.S. imperialists. In those mass organizations that did maintain some degree of autonomy, such as UNAG (the National Union of Farmers and Ranchers) and AMNLAE (the Association of Nicaraguan Women Luisa Amanda Espinosa), leaders with strong party ties often argued that the specific interests of the membership had to be subordinated to general party objectives and that criticism had to be withheld until the revolution was on more firm ground.[14]

Thus, other avenues of criticism and complaint no longer seemed operative. As could readily be seen by interviewing people on the streets from 1987 on, the people were living in increasing misery and the Sandinista leadership was perceived as being impervious to their genuine cries of pain. Further, it should be noted that the democracy practiced in the formal, Western-style structures of institutionalized representative democracy was a far cry from that which was practiced in the heady early days of the revolution when voice and vote counted in mass meetings in the neighborhood, factory, or field, or in the mass organizations themselves. Likewise, notice was taken of the apparent arrogance of the Sandinista leadership (they would be elected simply because they were Sandinistas) and the millions that were spent to orchestrate an election that the government leadership was absolutely positive would be a resounding Sandinista victory and thus an endorsement of their leadership.

Given the desperate plight of the masses, the electoral framework was an imperfect tool for them to express their general support for the objectives of the revolution. But it allowed them to voice their unmitigated opposition to (1) an austerity program that was destroying them economically and forcing many to become sidewalk vendors or to beg for food on the streets, and (2) a war that continued to claim a harsh economic toll and far too many lives (30,000 by 1990). Other, more participatory, mechanisms to articulate their demands for change had been foreclosed or were no longer effective. Nor had the FSLN party been responsive to grass-roots input, nor was it operating in a democratic way. Rather, decisionmaking was from the top down, usually with minimal input from below. It could be said that party structure served more to implement decisions than as a means of including the masses in the decisionmaking process. Indeed, many later said they believed the Sandinistas would win anyway, so they voted for Violeta Chamorro's United Nicaraguan Opposition (UNO) just to let the Sandinista leadership know that their needs were not being met and that they felt they were being ignored. Given the conditions that existed, it is remarkable that the FSLN still garnered even 40.8 percent of the vote. The fact that they did suggests the ambivalence that many of the popular sectors felt about their rule.

Since the Sandinistas won close to 63 percent of the vote (67 percent of the valid vote) in the 1984 election, it would seem that a substantial number of their supporters (or previous supporters), who did not want to vote for UNO, did so without joy, but felt it was the only way to protect their immediate economic interests. After so many brilliant victories, the Sandinista leadership had perhaps overestimated the amount of suffering the masses would endure. With the decrease in popular participation in mass organizations and the delay in the democratization of FSLN party structure, they also seem to have lost access to the nature and magnitude of popular concerns. This was further underscored by the fact that the Frente leaders also seem to have badly underestimated the popular resentment that the continuation of military conscription engendered. In so doing, they left themselves—and the revolution—open to a massive protest vote, which is precisely what elected Violeta Chamorro.

If recent economic policy had better protected popular economic interests, or if the draft had been canceled (as Daniel Ortega was reportedly at the point of doing in the final FSLN rally), the vote might have been different indeed. But opportunities were missed and the FSLN lost. Nonetheless, the 1990 elections in Nicaragua did provide a mechanism, however blunt, for letting the leadership of the ruling Sandinista Party know just how dissatisfied the people were and just how badly they needed a change. It did not, however, enhance the movement to construct a viable participatory democracy that would satisfy the needs of the masses.

It remains to be seen if the initial Sandinista commitment to such participatory democracy can be reinstitutionalized in the party and mass organizations in the future. The electoral defeat sent profound shockwaves through the entire party structure. One of the first responses was to convene a Sandinista Assembly in June 1990 to assess the party's errors and prepare for the future. The 300 delegates (most were elected by party militants) met in the town of El Crucero and passed several lengthy resolutions in which they confronted the party's errors and began to chart a new course. Sections of the document (FSLN 1990) are of particular interest:

> In many cases practices from socialist countries were reproduced which led us to take up a one-party style in the political leadership of society and an excessive emphasis on the control and centralization of public administration, [often] in a coercive and bureaucratic fashion. . . .
>
> Our party should rid itself of attitudes of imposition which tend to reduce or negate the grass roots' initiative and creativity, [of] authoritarianism, lack of sensitivity to the rank and file demands and concerns . . . criticism [and] bureaucratic leadership styles and the imposition of leaders and organizational structures. . . .

Finally, the party was urged to "restructure the FSLN through a democratic process so that grass-roots support can contribute to the solution of the most urgent internal problems" (*Barricada International* 1990; see also *Envio* 1990b, pp. 48–55). In acknowledging its authoritarianism and the autocratic nature of some (Stalinist) socialist influence, the party was setting the stage for its democratic restructuring. The emphasis on the role of grass-roots organization suggested that the initial participatory vision the Sandinistas had when they took power may not have been lost after all.

In the previous chapter, subsequent actions, like the 200 popular meetings (Popular Consultations) that were held in preparation for the July 1991 party Congress and the election of 501 delegates (out of 581) to that Congress, were outlined. Also of note was the expansion of party membership to truly open it to the masses.

The July 1991 party Congress revealed mixed interpretations of democracy and participation. The general delegates were elected through local assemblies, and the National Directorate was elected. However, rather than voting for individual members of the National Directorate, the delegates could only cast their ballots for a preselected slate. In this way the very popular candidacy of Dora María Téllez never came to a vote before the Congress, and the National Directorate continued to be an all-male club. The decision by the National Directorate to automatically include the votes of all members of the old (appointed) Sandinista Assembly also seemed to contradict the general democratization that the party was undergoing. In the meantime, worker and peasant organizations became more radical in their mobilizations against the economic policies of the Chamorro government and made it known that they intended to focus the power of their mobilized constituencies on the problems that affected their daily lives. Unions and newly formed peasant organizations often ignored Sandinista guidance to articulate their demands. The inability of the Chamorro government to solve basic economic problems did little to convince the masses of the ultimate utility of Western-style representative democracy.

New forms of democracy and participation continue to ebb and flow in the wake of the Sandinista revolution. The precise forms they take and the extent to which they become institutionalized will depend on the give and take of the political process in Nicaragua and the extent to which they are supported and practiced by the Sandinista Party.

Notes

1. By the late 1980s, the Nicaraguan government was estimating direct damages from the contras at some $12 billion. As the state of Nicaragua sought damages pursuant to the World Court decision, it also sought monetary compensation for victims of contra attacks and their survivors, and arrived at the figure of $17.8 billion. See Northworthy and Barry (1990, p. 59).

2. For a negative assessment of this action, see Vilas (1990a).

3. Interview by Vanden with Dr. Mariano Fiallos, president, Supreme Electoral Council, Managua, December 15, 1987.

4. Interview by Vanden with Dr. Roberto Estevez, Managua, February 24, 1990. Dr. Mariano Fiallos, president of the Supreme Electoral Council, indicated that it would be difficult to estimate the total cost of running the election, but that his organization had a budget of $18 million; interview, Managua, February 20, 1990.

5. Daniel Ortega, press conference, Managua, February 22, 1990.

6. According to Smith, the Cuban government did not set up a specific administrative school or provide training in participatory administration or economics for its employees. Further, at one point in the 1980s, when it looked as though Cubans might be able to travel to the United States for training, the Cuban government proposed that a group be sent to the Wharton Business School at the University of Pennsylvania to get (business-oriented) training in administration and management.

7. The authors argue that hierarchical production, inegalitarian consumption, central planning, and market allocations are incompatible with "classlessness." They also present an alternative model of democratic workers' and consumers' councils operating in a decentralized, social planning procedure and suggest how egalitarian consumption and job complexes, in which all engage in conceptual as well as executionary labor, can be efficient.

8. Vanden interview with Luis Sánchez, Managua, February 26, 1990. He also stated that the war was the second axis of the UNO campaign and that UNO was firmly committed to the abolition of the draft.

9. These opinions were frequently voiced to one of the authors when he visited Nicaragua in 1987. They were widely discussed on a second visit in early 1990.

10. For an ample, if critical, discussion of these problems, see Vilas (1990b) and Vickers (1990).

11. Vanden was an observer to the 1990 election. His informal survey of people in and around Managua in the days before the voting found many who

showed some inclination for the UNO coalition. Usually, their support for Chamorro and UNO seemed more based on disappointment with economic conditions or the draft or reservations about the way the Sandinistas had been ruling. In few instances did UNO support seem to flow from positive assessments of Chamorro or UNO. See also Conroy (1990, esp. p. 32): "As of mid-January 1990 the opposition candidacy of Violeta Chamorro and the UNO coalition had not convinced a majority of Nicaraguans that they offered a preferable solution to the nation's economic problems."

12. Random conversations by Vanden with people in the street and on public transportation, Managua, February 23–24, 1990.

13. Likewise, Univision's January 1990 poll showed the FSLN with an eighteen-point lead and the final Greenberg-Lake poll gave the Sandinistas a 27 percent lead. See *Envio* (1990a, p. 30).

14. Vanden interview with Magda Enríquez, Managua, December 1987.

❖ APPENDIX ❖
Chronology of the FSLN

1961 FSLN founded in meeting in Tegucigalpa, Honduras

1960s FSLN guerrilla fronts repeatedly destroyed forcing shift to coordinated political and military action

1974 Reemergence of FSLN guerrilla activity with seizure of Somoza associates at a holiday party

1975–77 Carlos Fonseca Amador killed; the FSLN splits into three factions; Insurrectionalists (Tercerista faction) shift strategy from rural guerrilla warfare to urban insurrection and broad alliances

1978 FSLN commandos seize National Palace; September insurrection in major cities defeated by National Guard

1979 Reunification of the FSLN; final offensive defeats Somocista forces and Junta of National Reconstruction takes power on July 19

1980 National Literacy Crusade; Violeta Chamorro and Alfonso Robelo leave JGRN; Council of State, dominated by Sandinista mass organizations, assumes legislative power

1981 U.S. government begins covert financing of the ex–National Guardsmen

1982 Nicaraguan government imposes state of emergency after contra attacks

1983 Visit of Pope John II highlights conflict between official church and revolution; Nicaragua joins Contadora peace process

1984 Elections held; Daniel Ortega elected president and Sandinistas win 63 percent of the seats in the National Assembly elections

1985 Daniel Ortega and Sergio Ramírez are inaugurated as president and vice-president of Nicaragua; United States declares economic embargo against Nicaragua and unilaterally ends the Manzanillo talks

1986 World Court rules that United States is in violation of international law for its support of the contras; National Assembly elaborates new constitution

1987 Constitution approved; National Assembly passes autonomy statute for the regions of the Atlantic Coast

1988 Nicaraguan government institutes harsh austerity measures in the face of declining productivity and 36,000 percent inflation; Sapoa agreement is signed between the contras and the Nicaraguan government; Hurricane Joan devastates the country, particularly the Atlantic Coast region

1989 Central American presidents meeting in El Salvador agree to joint plan for demobilization of the contras; Nicaraguan government moves up the election date to February 1990; economic conditions continue to worsen

1990 Elections are held in Nicaragua, and the final results give 55 percent to UNO and 41 percent to the FSLN; Violeta Chamorro assumes the presidency; the Nicaraguan Workers' Front (FNT) is formed with 200,000 members

1991 The FSLN holds its first party congress

❖ Bibliography ❖

Albert, Michael and Robin Hahnel. 1990. *The Political Economy of Participatory Economics*. Princeton: Princeton University Press.

Americas Watch. 1982. *On Human Rights in Nicaragua*. New York: Americas Watch.

Apple, R.W. 1987. "Contra Issue and the Summit." *New York Times,* December 17, 1987.

Arendt, Hannah. 1958. *The Origins of Totalitarianism.* New York: Meridian Books.

Arce, Bayardo. 1980. *Las fuerzas mortrices antes y después del triunfo.* Managua: Secretaría Nacional de Propaganda y Educación Política del FSLN.

Bachrach, Peter. 1967. *The Theory of Democratic Elitism.* Boston: Little, Brown.

Bachrach, Peter and Morton Baratz. 1962. "Two Faces of Power." *American Political Science Review* 56, no. 4.

———. 1970. *Power and Poverty: Theory and Practice.* New York: Oxford.

Bahro, Rudolf. 1978. *The Alternative in Eastern Europe.* Translated by David Fernbach. London: New Left Books.

Barber, Benjamin. 1984. *Strong Democracy: Participatory Politics for a New Age.* Berkeley: University of California Press.

Barlett, Donald L. and James B. Steele. 1992. *America: What Went Wrong?* Kansas City: Andrews and McMeel.

Barraclough, Solon et al. 1988. *Nicaragua: Desarrollo y supervivencia.* Amsterdam: Transnational Institute.

Barricada International. 1989. "Non-Aligned Movement Supports Peace in Central America." 9, no. 301, September 30.

———. 1990. "Resolution from El Crucero Assembly, June 17, 1990." Barricada Special Document No. 10, July 14.

Bendaña, Alejandro. 1982. "The Foreign Policy of the Nicaraguan Revolution." In Thomas Walker, ed., *Nicaragua in Revolution.* New York: Praeger Press.

Benito Escobar, José. 1979[1980?]. *Ideario sandinista.* Managua: SENAPEP.

Blaiser, Cole. 1987. *The Giant's Rival: The USSR and Latin America.* Pittsburgh: University of Pittsburgh Press.

Blandón, José Miguel. 1980. *Entre Sandino y Fonseca Amador.* Managua: Impresiones y Toqueles.

Bobbio, Norberto. 1976. *Which Socialism? Marxism, Socialism, and Democracy.* Minneapolis: University of Minnesota Press.

Booth, John. 1985a. *The End and the Beginning: The Nicaraguan Revolution,* second ed. Boulder: Westview Press.

———. 1985b. "The National Government System." In Thomas Walker, ed., *Nicaragua: The First Five Years*. New York: Praeger Press.

Borge, Tomás. 1984. *Carlos, the Dawn Is No Longer Beyond Our Reach*. Vancouver: New Star Books.

———. 1985. "This Is a Revolution of Working People." In Bruce Marcus, ed., *Nicaragua: The Sandinista People's Revolution*. New York: Pathfinder Press.

———. 1987. *Christianity and Revolution*. Translated and edited by Andrew Reding. Maryknoll, New York: Orbis.

Bottomore, Tom et al., eds. 1983. *A Dictionary of Marxist Thought*. Cambridge: Harvard University Press.

Caballero, Manuel. 1987. *Latin America and the Comintern, 1919–1943*. New York: Cambridge University Press.

Castro, Vanessa. 1990. *Resultados electorales en el sector rural*. Managua: Instituto para el Desarrollo de la Democracia.

Central America Historical Institute. 1988. "Going All the Way: Economic Reforms in June." *Central America Update*. Washington D.C., July.

Centro de Comunicación Internacional. 1986. *The FSLN: Background and Internal Structure*. Managua: Centro de Comunicación Internacional.

Chuchryk, Patricia M. 1991. "Women in the Revolution." In Thomas Walker, ed., *Revolution and Counterrevolution in Nicaragua*. Boulder: Westview Press.

Close, David. 1988. *Nicaragua*. London: Pinter Publishers.

Coleman, Kenneth M. and George C. Herring, eds. 1991. *Understanding the Central American Crisis*. Wilmington: Scholarly Resources.

Conrad, Edgar, ed. 1990. *Sandino, the Testimony of a Nicaraguan Patriot, 1921–1934*. Princeton: Princeton University Press.

Conroy, M. E. 1990. "The Political Economy of the 1990 Elections." Paper presented at the Coloquio sobre las Crisis Económicas del Siglo XX, Universidad Complutense de Madrid, April.

Cook, Mark. 1989. "Unfit to Print about Nicaragua's Election." *Extra*, October/November.

Cooper, Mark. 1989. "Soaring Prices, Plunging Hopes." *Village Voice*, July 25, 1989.

Coraggio, José Luis. 1985. *Nicaragua: Revolution and Democracy*. London: Allen and Unwin.

Cronin, Thomas. 1989. *Direct Democracy, the Politics of Initiative, Referendum, and Recall*. Cambridge: Harvard University Press.

Cunningham, Frank. 1987. *Democratic Theory and Socialism*. New York: Cambridge University Press.

Dahl, Robert A. 1956. *A Preface to Democratic Theory*. Chicago: University of Chicago Press.

Davis, L. 1964. "The Cost of Realism: Contemporary Restatements of Democracy." *Western Political Quarterly* 17, no. 2.

Deere, Carmen Diana, Peter Marchetti, and Nola Reinhardt. 1985. "The Peasantry and the Development of Sandinista Agrarian Policy, 1979–1984." *Latin American Research Review* 20, no. 3.

Deutscher, Isaac. 1949. *Stalin: A Political Biography*. New York: Oxford University Press.

Dewey, John. 1954 *The Public and Its Problems*. Chicago: Sage Books and Swallow Press; originally published in 1927.

Diamond, Larry and Marc F. Plattner. 1990. "Why the Journal of Democracy." *Journal of Democracy* 1, no. 1, Winter.

Djilas, Milovan. 1957. *The New Class.* New York: Praeger Press.
———. 1962. *Conversations with Stalin.* New York: Harcourt Brace & World.
Dodson, Michael and Laura Nuzzi O'Shaughnessy. 1985. "Religion and Politics." In Thomas Walker, ed., *Nicaragua: The First Five Years.* New York: Praeger Press.
Downs, Charles. 1985. "Local and Regional Government." In Thomas Walker, ed., *Nicaragua: The First Five Years.* New York: Praeger Press.
Eckstein, H. 1966. "A Theory of Stable Democracy" in Appendix B of *Division and Cohesion of Democracy.* Princeton: Princeton University Press.
Envio. 1987. "Becoming Visible in Nicaragua," vol. 7, no. 18, December.
———. 1989. "Nicaragua's Foreign Policy: Ten Years of Principles and Practice: An Interview with Alejandro Bendaña," vol. 7, no. 97
———. 1990a. "After the Poll Wars. Explaining the Upset," vol. 9, no. 104, March-April.
———. 1990b. "After 100 Days: Same Economic Script, New Lead Actors," vol. 9, nos. 109–110, August-September.
Estrada, Daniel M. 1989. "Nicaragua's Worker-Peasant Alliance: A Case Study in Economic Democracy, the Gamez-Garmendia Cooperative, 1979 to 1989." Paper presented at the XV Congress of the Latin American Studies Association, Miami, December 4–6, 1989.
Fagen, Richard. 1986. "The Politics of Transition." In Richard Fagen, Carmen Diana Deere, and José Luis Corragio, eds., *Transition and Development: Problems of Third World Socialism.* New York: Monthly Review, Center for the Study of the Americas.
The Federalist Papers. 1952. Vol. 43, Great Books of the Western World. Chicago: Encyclopedia Britannica.
Fonseca Amador, Carlos. 1984a. *Ideario político de Augusto César Sandino.* Managua: Departamento de Propaganda y Educación Política del FSLN.
———. 1984b. *Long Live Sandino.* Managua: Department of Propaganda and Political Education, FSLN. Also in Spanish, *Viva Sandino.*
———. 1984c. *Nicaragua: hora cero.* Managua: Departamento de Propaganda y Educación Política del FSLN.
———. 1984d. *Sandino, guerrillero proletario.* Managua: Departamento de Propaganda y Educación Política del FSLN.
Frazier, Charles E., Jr. 1956. "The Dawn of Nationalism and Its Consequences in Nicaragua." Ph.D. Dissertation, University of Texas.
Freire, Paulo. 1970. *Pedagogy of the Oppressed.* New York: Herder and Herder.
FSLN. 1980. "Comunicado." *Barricada,* September 10, 1980.
———. 1981. "Programa Histórico del FSLN." Managua: Departamento de Propaganda and Educación Política del FSLN.
———. 1982. *Análisis de la situación.* Managua: National Directorate.
———. 1985. "Comunicado." Secretaría de la Dirección Nacional. *Barricada,* August 4, 1985.
———. 1990. "Resolutions of the FSLN Assembly." *Barricada International,* June 20, 1990.
The FSLN: Background and Internal Structure. 1986. Managua: Centro de Communicacion Internacional.
García Márquez, Gabriel. 1971. *One Hundred Years of Solitude.* New York: Avon Books.
Gilbert, Dennis. 1988. *Sandinistas.* New York: Basil Blackwell.
Girardi, Giulio. 1987. *Sandinismo, Marxismo, Cristianismo: La confluencia.*

Managua: Centro Antonio Valdivieso.

González Casanova, Pablo. "Cuando hablamos de la democracía de qué hablemos." Manuscript.

Goodwyn, Lawrence. 1976. *The Populist Movement in America.* New York: Oxford.

Gorman, Steven. 1981. "Power and Consolidation in the Nicaraguan Revolution." *Journal of Latin American Studies* 13, May.

Greider, William. 1992. *Who Will Tell the People: The Betrayal of American Democracy.* New York: Simon and Schuster.

Guevara, Ché. 1969. *Guerrilla Warfare.* London: Penguin.

Guillermoprieto, Alma and David Hoffman. 1984. "Document Describes How U.S. Blocked a Contadora Treaty." *Washington Post,* November 6.

Gurr, Ted Robert. 1991. "America as a Model for the World? A Skeptical View." *PS: Political Science and Politics,* vol. 24, no. 4, December.

Hahn, Steve. 1983. *The Roots of Southern Populism.* New York: Oxford.

Harnecker, Martha. 1980. *Cuba, Dictatorship or Democracy?* Westport, Conn.: L. Hill, 1980.

————. 1986. "Interview with Luis Carrión." *Nuevo Diario,* Managua, December 26–27, 1986.

Harris, Richard L. 1985. "The Economic Transformation and Industrial Development of Nicaragua." In Richard L. Harris and Carlos M. Vilas, *Nicaragua: A Revolution under Siege.* England: Zed Press.

Harris, Richard L. and Carlos M. Vilas. 1985. *Nicaragua: A Revolution under Siege.* England: Zed Press.

Higgs, Robert. 1987. *Crisis and Leviathan.* New York: Oxford.

Hodges, Donald. 1986. *Intellectual Foundations of the Nicaraguan Revolution.* Austin: University of Texas Press.

Huntington, Samuel. 1989. "The Modest Meaning of Democracy." In Robert Pastor, ed., *Democracy in the Americas.* New York: Holmes & Meir.

Instituto de Promoción Humana. 1977. "Primer Congreso Nacional de Organizaciones Populares." *INPRHU* 1, no. 2, April.

International Monetary Fund. 1988. Direction of Trade Statistics. *Yearbook 1988.* Washington, D.C.: International Monetary Fund.

Invernizzi, Gabriele, et al. 1986. *Sandinistas.* Managua: Editorial Vanguardia.

Jonas, Suzanne and Nancy Stein. 1990. "The Construction of Democracy in Nicaragua." *Democracy in Latin America.* Granby, Mass.: Bergin and Garvey.

Keller, Bill. 1988. "In USSR, a Painful Prying at the Roots of Stalin's Tyranny." *New York Times,* June 11, 1988.

Kinzer, Stephen. 1984. "Brandt Visits Managua but Fails to Settle Dispute." *New York Times,* October 15, 1984.

————. 1988. "Ex-Contra Looks Back, Finding Much to Regret." *New York Times,* January 8, 1988.

Kiss, Arthur. 1982. *Marxism and Democracy. A Contribution to the Marxist Interpretation of Democracy.* Budapest: Akadémiai Kiadó.

La Ramée, Pierre and Erica Polakoff. 1990. "Transforming the CDS and Grassroots Democracy in Nicaragua." *New Political Science,* Fall.

Lasch, Christopher. 1979. *The Culture of Narcissism.* New York: Norton.

————. 1991. *The True and Only Heaven.* New York: Norton.

Latin American Perspectives. 1979. "Why the FSLN Struggles in Unity with the People." Winter.

Latin American Studies Association. 1984. *The Electoral Process in Nicaragua:*

Domestic and International Influences. Austin, Tex.: LASA.

————. 1990. *Electoral Democracy under Pressure: The Report of the Latin American Studies Association to Observe the 1990 Nicaraguan Elections*. Pittsburgh: University of Pittsburgh Press, March 15.

Latin American Weekly Report. 1984. "Invasion Fever Obliterated Memory of Nicaragua's Polls" and "Facts Behind Invasion Scare," November 16, 1984.

Lenin, Vladimir I. 1971. "State and Revolution" and "What Is to Be Done?" In *Selected Works*. New York: International Publishers.

Lineberry, William P. 1989. *Assessing Participatory Development*. Boulder: Westview Press.

Liss, Sheldon B. 1984. *Marxist Thought in Latin America*. Berkeley: University of California Press.

————. 1991. *Radical Thought in Central America*. Latin American Perspective Series, no. 7. Boulder: Westview Press.

Lobel, Jules. 1988. "The Meaning of Democracy: Representative and Participatory Democracy in the New Nicaraguan Constitution." *University of Pittsburgh Law Review*, vol. 49.

Lowy, Michael. 1986. "Mass Organization, Party and the State: Democracy in the Transition to Socialism." In Richard Fagen, Carmen Diana Deere, and José Luis Corragio, eds., *Transition and Development: Problems in Third World Socialism*. New York: Monthly Review.

————. 1991. "The Crisis of Really Existing Socialism." *Monthly Review* 43, no. 1, May.

Luciak, Ilja A. 1987. "Popular Democracy in the New Nicaragua, the Case of a Rural Mass Organization." *Comparative Politics* 20, no. 1, October.

Lukacs, Georg. 1971. *History and Class Consciousness, Studies in Marxist Dialectics*. Translated by Rodney Livingston. Cambridge: MIT Press.

Macaulay, Neill. 1985. *The Sandino Affair*. 2nd ed. Durham, NC: Duke University Press.

McMichael, David. 1990. "U.S. Plays Contra Card." *The Nation*, February 5, 1990.

MacPherson, C. B. 1972. *Democratic Theory: Essays in Retrieval*. Oxford: Oxford University Press.

Malley, Nadia. 1985. "Relations with Western Europe and the Socialist International." In Thomas Walker, ed., *Nicaragua: The First Five Years*. New York: Praeger Press.

Marcus, Bruce, ed. 1985. *Nicaragua—The Sandinista People's Revolution*. New York: Pathfinder Press.

Markovic, Mihailo. 1982. *Democratic Socialism: Theory and Practice*. New York: St. Martin's Press.

Marx, Karl. 1960. *The Paris Commune*. New York: New York Labor News Co.

————. 1978. *The Civil War in France*. 2nd ed. In Robert C. Tucker, ed., *The Marx-Engels Reader*. New York: Norton.

Medvedev, Roy. 1975. *On Socialist Democracy*. Translated by Ellen de Kadt. New York: Alfred A. Knopf.

————. 1981. *Leninism and Western Socialism*. Translated by A. D. P. Briggs. London: Verso.

Megill, Kenneth A. 1970. *The New Democratic Theory*. New York: Free Press.

Mijeski, Kenneth, ed. 1991. *The Nicaraguan Constitution of 1987*. Athens: Ohio University Press.

Millet, Richard. 1977. *Guardians of the Dynasty*. Maryknoll, New York: Orbis Books.

Molyneux, Maxine. 1985a. "Mobilizing Without Emancipation? Women's Interests, the State, and Revolution in Nicaragua." *Feminist Studies* vol. 10, no. 2, Summer.

———. 1985b. "Women." In Thomas Walker, ed., *Nicaragua: The First Five Years.* New York: Praeger Press.

Mondragón, Rafael and Carlos Decker Molina. 1986. *Participación popular en Nicaragua.* Mexico City: Claves Latinoamericanos.

Morgan, Martha. 1990. "Founding Mothers: Women's Voices and Stories in the 1987 Nicaraguan Constitution." *Boston University Law Review* vol. 70, no. 1.

NACLA. 1987. "The Other Super Power, the USSR and Latin America, 1917–1987," *NACLA,* vol. 21, no. 1, January-February.

Newsweek. 1989. "Washington Wants to Buy Nicaraguan Election." September 5, 1989.

New York Times. 1992. "Fed Report Gives New Data on Gains by Richest in 80s." April 21, 1992.

Nichols, John Spicer. 1988. "La Prensa: The CIA Connection." *Columbia Journalism Review,* July-August.

Nolan, David. 1984. *FSLN. The Ideology of the Sandinistas and the Nicaraguan Revolution.* Coral Gables, Fla.: Institute for Interamerican Studies.

Northworthy, Kent and Tom Barry. 1990. *Nicaragua: A Country Guide.* Albuquerque: Central American Research Center.

Núñez, Carlos. 1980. *El papel de las organizaciones de masas en el proceso revolucionario.* Managua: SENAPEP, FSLN.

Núñez Soto, Orlando. 1982. "La ideología como fuerza material y la juventud como fuerza ideológica." *Estado y clases sociales en Nicaragua.* Managua: Collección Blas Real Espinales, CIERA.

Núñez Soto, Orlando and Roger Burbach. 1986. *Democracía y revolución en las Américas.* Managua: Vanguardia.

Oppenheimer, Martin. 1971. "The Limitations of Socialism." In C. George Benello and Dimitri Roussopoulos, eds., *The Case for Participatory Democracy.* New York: Grossman Publishers.

Oquist, Paul. 1990. *Dinámica socio-política de las elecciones Nicaragüenses—1990 análisis de los resultados globales.* Managua: Instituto de Estudios Nicaragüenses.

Ortega Saavedra, Humberto. 1980a. *50 años de lucha sandinista.* Managua: Colleción las Segovias, Ministerio de Interior.

———. 1980b. "La insurrección nacional victoriosa." *Nicarauac* 1, May-June.

———. 1980c. *La revolución a través de nuestra dirección nacional.* Managua: SENAPEP.

Osbun, Lee Ann. 1985. *The Problem of Participation.* Lanham, Md.: University Press of America.

Padover, Saul. 1956. *A Jefferson Profile.* New York: John Day Co.

Padover, Saul, ed. 1939. *Thomas Jefferson on Democracy.* New York: Mentor Books, the New American Library.

Parenti, Michael J. 1983. *Democracy for the Few.* New York: St. Martin's Press.

Pateman, Carol. 1970. *Participation and Democratic Theory.* Cambridge: Cambridge University Press.

Pérez Flores, Xiomara. 1989. "Notas sobra la participación de los trabajadores en la revolución sandinista, caso de la ATC y CST." Paper presented at the XV congress of the Latin American Studies Association, Miami, December 4–6, 1989.

Prevost, Gary. 1990. "Cuba and Nicaragua—A Special Relationship." *Latin American Perspectives,* Summer.

"Program of the Provisional Government of the National Reconstruction of Nicaragua." June 28, 1979. Managua.

Ramírez, Sergio. 1982. "Análisis histórico-social del movimiento sandinista." *Encuentro, Revista de la Universidad Centroamericana.*

Ramírez, Sergio, ed. 1979. *El pensamiento vivo de Sandino.* San José, Costa Rica: Editorial Universitaria Centroamericana.

Ramírez-Horton, Susan. 1982. "The Role of Women in the Nicaraguan Revolution." In Thomas Walker, ed., *Nicaragua in Revolution.* New York: Praeger Press.

Randall, Margaret. 1981. *Sandino's Daughters: Testimonies of Nicaraguan Women in Struggle.* Vancouver: New Star Books.

Reding, Andrew. 1984. "What Really Happened on November 4?" *Christianity in Crisis,* December 24, 1984.

———. 1985. "Under Construction: Nicaragua's New Polity." *Christianity and Crisis,* July 22, 1985.

———. 1986. "By the People: Constitution Making in Nicaragua." *Christianity and Crisis,* December 8, 1986.

———. 1987. "Nicaragua's New Constitution." *World Policy Journal.* Spring.

Robinson, William. 1990. "The Making of a Democratic Oppositon." *NACLA,* February.

Rousseau, Jean-Jacques. 1952. *The Social Contract.* In *Great Books of the Western World,* vol. 38. Chicago: Encyclopedia Brittanica.

Ruchwarger, Gary. 1987. *People in Power, Forging a Grass-roots Democracy in Nicaragua.* Massachusetts: Bergen and Garvey.

Ruíz, Henry. 1980. "La montaña era como un crisol donde se forjaba los mejores cuadros." *Nicarauac* 1, May-June.

Ryan, Randolph. 1990. "The Nicaraguan Playing Field." *The Boston Globe,* January 24, 1990.

Salvatore, Nick. 1982. *Eugene Debs: Citizen and Socialist.* Carbondale: University of Illinois Press.

Sandino, Augusto César. 1984. *El pensamiento vivo.* Vol. 2. Edited by Sergio Ramírez. Managua: Editorial Nueva Nicaragua.

Schumpter, Joseph. 1943. *Capitalism, Socialism and Democracy.* London: Allen & Unwin.

Schwab, Theodore and Harold Sims. 1985. "Relations with the Communist States." In Thomas Walker, ed., *Nicaragua: The First Five Years.* New York: Praeger Press.

Selser, Gregorio. 1981. *Sandino.* New York: Monthly Review Press.

Serra, Luís. 1985. "Grass Roots Organizations." In Thomas Walker, ed., *Nicaragua: The First Five Years.* New York: Praeger Press.

Sklar, Holly. 1989. "Washington Wants to Buy Nicaragua's Elections Again." *Z Magazine,* December.

Smith, Wayne. 1991. "Crisis in Cuba." Speech, University of South Florida, Tampa, October 18, 1991.

Somoza García, Anastasio. 1936. *El verdadero Sandino, o el caluvario de las Segovias.* Managua: Tipografía Robelo.

Spalding, Rose J., ed. 1986. *The Political Economy of Revolutionary Nicaragua.* New York: Unwin Hyman.

Taylor, Anne Marie. 1975. "*Cien años de soledad:* History and the Novel." *Latin American Perspectives 2.*

Thome, Joseph and David Kaimowitz. 1985. "Agrarian Reform." In Thomas Walker, ed., *Nicaragua: The First Five Years.* New York: Praeger Press.

Tirado López, Victor. 1979 [1980?]. *El pensamiento político de Carlos Fonseca*

Amador. Managua: Secretaría Nacional de Propaganda y Educación Política del FSLN.

Torres Pérez, Denis. 1989a. "La política exterior de la revolución sandinista (elementos para un balance)." *Cuadernos de sociología* 9–10, January-June.

———. 1989b. "La política exterior de la revolución popular sandinista." Ministerio de Relaciones Exterior, Managua.

Tünnerman, Carlos. 1990. "The Democratization of the FSLN." *Barricada International.* August 25, 1990.

Update. 1988. "From Property to Partner: New Divorce Law a Breakthrough for Nicaraguan Women," 7, 17, June 1, 1988.

U.S. Department of State. 1984. *Broken Promises: Sandinista Repression of Human Rights.* Washington, D.C.: Government Printing Office.

———. 1987. *Democracy in Latin America,* Special Report No. 158. Washington, D.C.: Bureau of Public Affairs.

Vanden, Harry E. 1982. "The Ideology of the Nicaraguan Revolution." *Monthly Review* 34, June.

———. 1986. *National Marxism in Latin America: José Carlos Mariátegui's Thought and Politics.* Boulder: Lynne Rienner.

———. 1990. "Law, State Policy and Terrorism." *New Political Science,* Fall/Winter.

———. 1991. "Foreign Policy." In Thomas Walker, ed., *Revolution and Counterrevolution in Nicaragua.* Boulder: Westview Press.

Vanden, Harry E. and Waltrud Queiser Morales. 1985. "Nicaragua's Relations with the Nonaligned." *Journal of Interamerican Studies and World Affairs* 27 Fall.

Vanden, Harry E. and Thomas Walker. 1991. "The Reimposition of U.S. Hegemony over Nicaragua." In Kenneth M. Coleman and George C. Herring, eds., *Understanding the Central American Crisis.* Wilmington: Scholarly Resources.

Vickers, George. 1990. "A Spider's Web." *NACLA Report on the Americas* 30, no. 1, June.

Vilas, Carlos. 1986. *The Sandinista Revolution.* New York: Monthly Review Press.

———. 1990a. "The Contribution of Economic Policy and International Negotiations to the Fall of the Sandinista Government." *New Political Science,* Fall.

———. 1990b. "What Went Wrong." *NACLA Report on the Americas* 30, no. 1, June.

Waksman Schinca, Daniel. 1979. "Entrevista con Tomás Borge." *Combate* (Stockholm), July-September.

Walker, Thomas, ed. 1982. *Nicaragua in Revolution.* New York: Praeger Press.

———, ed. 1985. *Nicaragua: The First Five Years.* New York: Praeger Press.

———, ed. 1991. *Revolution and Counterrevolution in Nicaragua, 1979–1990.* Boulder: Westview Press.

Weathers, Byrum E. 1988. "Factors Affecting the Emergence of Low-Intensity Conflict in Latin America." In Lewis B. Ware et al., *Low-Intensity Conflict in the Third World.* Maxwell, Ala.: Air University Press.

Wheelock, Jaime. 1980. *Nicaragua: imperialismo y dictadura.* Havana: Editorial de Ciencias Sociales.

———. 1984. *Nicaragua—The Great Challenge.* Managua: Alternative Views.

Wiebe, Robert. 1967. *The Search for Order.* New York: Hill and Wang.

Woodstock, George. 1971. "Democracy Heretical and Radical." In C. George Benello and Dimitri Roussopoulos, eds., *The Case for Participatory Democracy.* New York: Grossman Publishers.

❖ Index ❖

Afghanistan, 102
Agrarian Reform Law of 1981, 98
Agrarian Reform Tribunals, 87
Aguero, Fernando, 39
Aguirre, Danilo, 122
Algeria, 101, 102
Allende, Salvador, 4
America: What Went Wrong? (Barlett and Steele), 11
American Convention on Human Rights, 85
American Declaration of the Rights and Duties of Man, 85
American Popular Revolutionary Alliance (APRA), 27–28
Amparo, 87
AMPRONAC, 58
Anarchists, 16
Anarcho-communism, 27
Ancien regime, 52
Angola, 102
Anti-Imperialist League of the Americas, 27
Arce, Bayardo, 77, 97, 110, 112, 117, 119, 124
Arendt, Hannah, 16
Argentina, 140
Aristocracy, 8
Army to Defend National Sovereignty, 25, 27, 30
Authoritarianism: in Latin America, 3, 149; in the Soviet Union, 5, 55
Bahro, Rudolf, 3
Baker, James, 137
Baltodano, Mónica, 58
Baptist Convention, 93

Barlett, Donald, 11
Barricada, 56, 60, 100, 114, 122, 123
Batasuna, Herri, 126
Belgrade, 102
Bendaña, Alejandro, 119
Boaco (Nicaragua), 121
Bolaños, Enrique, 132
Bolívar, Símon, 49
Bolivia, 39
Bolshevik Grand Lodge (Mexico), 26
Bolshevik Party, 5
Booth, John, 73
Borge, Tomás, 6, 32, 33, 34, 36, 37, 39, 43, 45, 98, 99, 100, 110, 112, 118, 119, 124
Bourgeoisie, 24, 27, 34, 44, 50, 55, 141
Brandt, Willy, 77
Brazil, 3, 140
British colonialism, 24
Broad Opposition Front (FAO), 45
Burbach, Roger, 5
Bush, George, 131
Bush administration, 132, 136, 138, 142
Byzantine-Oriental societies, 16

Cadre schools, 115
Campesinos, 29
Capitalism, Socialism, and Democracy (Schumpter), 11
Cardenal, Ernesto and Fernando, 41
Caribbean Basin, 2
Carlos Fonseca Plaza, 80
Carrión, Luis, 42, 44, 110, 117, 118, 124, 125
Carter, Jimmy, 54, 137
Carter administration, 91

Casanova, Pablo González, 82
Castro, Fidel, 3, 34, 35, 36, 39, 78, 89
Castro, José Ramón Gutierrez, 32
Catholic Church, 24, 41, 60, 66. *See also*
    Christians; Church; Vatican II
Caudillos, 112
Center for International Studies (CEI),
    119
Central America, 25, 33, 57, 68, 101, 103,
    130; University of, 119
Central American Institute of Business
    Administration (INCAE), 139
Central American leaders, 19
Central American Peace Accords, 102
Central American peace process, 96,
    101, 130, 146
Central Intelligence Agency (CIA), 77,
    101
Chamorro, Carlos Fernando, 114
Chamorro, Pedro Joaquín, 45, 50, 72
Chamorro, Violeta Barrios, 50, 71, 72,
    73, 98, 131, 132, 140, 143, 148
Chamorro administration, 100, 125, 126,
    143, 149
Chamorro-Bryan Canal Treaty, 91
Chile, 4, 5, 137
China, 28, 40, 102
Chinendega, 121
Christian Democratic Party, 115
Christian democratic philosophy, 79
Christian(s), 41, 42, 66, 94; communities,
    15–16, 41, 66; movements, 40, 42, 29;
    organizations, 41; wing of the FSLN,
    85. *See also* Catholic Church; Church
Church, 47, 61
Church organiztions, 50
Civil War in France, The (Marx), 52, 115
Close, David, 72
Cold War, 90
Colombia, 41
Comintern, 5, 28–29; seventh congress
    of, 28; sixth congress of, 28
Committee in Solidarity With the
    People (CNSP), 115
Communism, 1, 7–8, 27, 76; "tropical
    communism," 35
Communist International, 27, 29, 32
Communist Manifesto (Marx), 8
Communist Party, 17; in Eastern
    Europe, 53, 54; of Nicaragua (PCdeN),
    79, 115, 132; in Soviet Union, 76, 115

Communists, 32; trade unions in
    Mexico, 26; in Western Europe, 28
Conservative Party, 24, 25, 31, 32, 34, 36,
    39, 50, 71, 79, 132
Constitution of Nicaragua, 60, 84–86, 93,
    94, 96; Article 23, 85
Constitutional Commission, 93, 94
Constitutionalist Liberals, 77
Contadora, 101. *See also* Central
    American peace process
Contra war, 95, 96, 104, 105
Contras, 65, 67, 68, 77, 78, 80, 86, 94,
    101, 102, 104, 130, 131, 137, 138, 140,
    142, 146
Coordinadora. See Democratic Coor-
    dinating Committee
Coordinating Bureau of the Nonaligned
    Countries of Latin America and the
    Caribbean, 101
Córdoba Rivas, Rafael, 73, 79
COSEP, 132, 139
Costa Rica, 76, 80
Council of Freely Elected Heads of
    State, 137
Council of Mutual Economic Assis-
    tance, 105
Council of State, 51, 52, 60, 72, 73, 74,
    75, 77, 78, 83, 95, 146
Counterinsurgency, 41. *See also* Low-in-
    tensity conflict
Cronin, Thomas, 10, 57, 143
Cruz, Arturo, 73, 77
Cruz, Rigoberto, 37
Cuba, 3, 5, 19, 34, 36, 40, 43, 44, 46, 53,
    54, 85, 90, 99, 100, 102, 105, 138, 139;
    democratic reforms in, 3–4; economic
    relations with Nicaragua, 104
Cuban Communist Party, 126
Cuban Revolution, 23, 32, 35, 36, 89
Cunningham, Frank, 67
Cyprus, 102

Dahl, Robert, 12, 13, 18
Darien Mountains, 39
Davis, L., 13
Democracy, 6, 7, 8, 9, 15, 16, 17, 50, 51,
    52, 53, 55, 64, 65, 66, 68, 82, 149; bour-
    geois democratic ideology, 28, 34;
    bourgeois democratic revolution, 3;
    bourgeois parliamentarianism, 7; clas-
    sical theories of, 9, 92; Communist

views of, 14; direct, 9, 10, 11, 14, 41, 58, 62, 129; full, 122, 126; grass-roots, 7, 10, 53, 58, 95; Jeffersonian, 2; in Latin America, 2–4, 9, 50, 54; Leninist views of, 14; liberal, 50, 53, 92; Marxism and, 1, 2, 16; in Nicaragua, 1, 49, 52, 71–72, 75, 83, 103; participatory, 3, 7, 14, 20, 49, 51, 53, 55, 63, 66, 68, 76, 83, 84, 88, 92, 129, 143; popular, 51, 52, 66, 82; and socialism, 1, 4, 5, 137, 138; Western representative; 2, 3, 7, 12, 13, 19, 49, 50, 51, 52, 53, 55, 56, 75, 82–83, 84, 88, 92, 95, 129, 130, 132, 143, 146, 147, 149. *See also Federalist Papers*
Democratic Conservative Party, 73, 79, 84, 93
Democratic Coordinating Committee, 74, 77, 78, 81, 82, 85, 131
Demos, 6, 7, 20, 30, 49–50, 53, 138
Denmark, 93, 104
Dependency theory, 44
D'Escota, Miguel, 41
Dewey, John, 13
Díaz, Adolfo, 24
Díaz, Mauricio, 79
Díaz, Porfirio, 26
Die Alternative (Bahro), 3
Djilas, Milovan, 18
Dubcek, Alexander, 3

Eastern Europe, 1, 2, 3, 6, 13, 14, 16, 19, 20, 53, 54, 82, 84, 96, 104; economic crisis in, 106
El Crucero, 120, 126, 148
El Nuevo Diario, 80, 122
El Salvador, 78, 80, 82, 106, 126
Electoral Law of 1984, 86
Engels, Fredrich, 2, 32, 115
Estelí, 63
Ethiopia, 102
Eurocommunism, 5
Europe, 9, 61, 103, 104
European Economic Community (EEC), 103, 104
Evertz, Adolfo, 79
Excelsior, 98
Extravision, 122

Fagen, Richard, 7
Farabundo Martí National Liberation Front (FMLN), 126

Federalist Papers, The, 10; *Federalist 57,* 10; *Federalist 55,* 10–11
Fidelistas, 36, 39
Figueres, José, 80
Finland, 102, 104
Flores Magón, Ricardo, 26
FNT, 121
Foco, 39
Fonseca Amador, Carlos, 5, 6, 29, 32, 33, 34, 35, 36, 39, 42, 43, 44, 45, 89, 106, 113; the "Carlos Fonseca Amador Northern Front," 45
Fonseca Teran, Carlos, 122
Freemasonry, 26, 27
Freire, Paulo, 41, 66
French Commune of 1792, 15
French Revolution of 1792, 16
FSLN. *See* Sandinista National Liberation Front
Fundamental Statute of August 22, 1979, 72

Gamez-Garmendia Cooperative, 63–64
García Márquez, Gabriel, 23
General Confederation of Workers (CGT), 26
"Generation of '44," 31
Georgino Andrade, 57, 58
German Democratic Republic, 3, 138
Germany, 28
Gilbert, Davis, 57, 112
Glasnost, 96
Godoy, Virgilio, 79, 81
Governing Junta of National Reconstruction, 50, 52, 72, 73, 74, 79
GPP. *See* Prolonged People's War
Gramsci, Antonio, 35, 55
Grass-roots organizations. *See* Mass organizations
Greece, 9, 13
Greens party, 53
Greider, William, 11
Grenada, 102
Group of Twelve, 45, 72
Guatemala, 32, 34, 36, 82, 101, 106
Guevara, Ché, 3, 34, 35, 36, 39, 89
Guevro, Noel, 36
Guido, Clemente, 79
Guido, Lea, 114
Gurr, Ted Robert, 11, 13
Guyana, 102

Hamilton, Alexander, 10, 11
Hands Off Nicaragua Committee, 28
Harvard Business School, 139
Hassán, Moisés, 50, 72
Havana, 100, 101, 104
Henríque, Juan Alberto, 79–80
Hispanicism, 24
Ho Chi Minh, 39, 89
Hodges, Donald, 26, 27
Honduras, 34, 36, 39, 101
Hooker, Ray, 78
Hungary, 2
Huntington, Samuel, 6

INAP, 138
Independent Liberal Party (PLI), 46, 72, 74, 79, 81, 82, 84
India, 101, 102
Indians (in Nicaragua), 23, 25, 29, 30, 33, 45, 46, 53
Indochina, 106
Industrial Workers of the World (IWW), 26
Institute for Human Advancement (IN-PRHU), 41, 66
Institute for Nicaraguan History, 117
Institute for Nicaraguan Studies (IEN), 119
Institute for the Development of Democracy (IPADE), 119
Institute for the Study of Sandinism (of FSLN), 113, 115, 117, 119
Interamerican Development Bank, 73
International Court of Justice, 102
International Covenant on Civil and Political Rights, 85
International Covenant on Economic, Social, and Cultural Rights, 85
International Monetary Fund, 144
Iran, 105
Italy, 104
Iturbe, Augustín de, 33

Jackson, Andrew, 9
Jefferson, Thomas, 1, 7, 8, 10, 13, 15, 16, 57, 68
Jinotega, 62
Jonas, Suzanne, 71
Julio Buttrago, 145
July 26th Movement (in Cuba), 34, 35, 44

Junta. *See* Governing Junta of National Reconstruction

Kratos, 6
Kroptkin, Peter, 26
Kuomintang, 28
La Prensa, 77, 94
Lara, Augustín, 52
Las Brisas, 145
Latin America, 23, 24, 25, 26, 36, 61, 75, 84, 87, 94, 99, 105, 129, 130, 137; Communist parties in, 28, 32, 35; democracy in, 2–4, 9, 50, 54; democratic socialism in, 4–5; guerrilla movements in, 37, 40; Marxism in, 5, 32, 34; revolutionary parties in, 42, 91
Latin American Studies Association, 76, 88
Law of Political Parties, 75
Lenin, Vladimir, 2, 5, 7, 12, 16, 17, 34, 89, 110, 115
Leninism, 55, 66
Leninist ideology, 19, 75, 109
León, 33, 34, 42
Liberal democrats, 14
Liberal Party, 31, 36, 50, 132
Liberal reform movement, 24, 79
Liberal Revolution of 1893, 24, 33
Liberation theology, 41, 89, 94
Libya, 105
"Light and truth" doctrine, 27. *See also* Magnetic spiritualism
Lincoln, Abraham, 6
Lobel, Jules, 83
Locke, John, 7
López, Santos, 33, 36
Low-intensity conflict, 67, 131, 138, 142. *See also* Counterinsurgency
Lowy, Michael, 4
Lukacs, George, 2, 18

Macaulay, Neill, 27
Madison, James, 10, 57
Magnetic spiritualism, 27
Malatesta, Errico, 26
Managua, 39, 42, 57, 60, 77, 80, 100, 101, 104, 122, 126; Department of, 121
Mao Tse Tsung, 39, 89
Maoists, 43
Mariátegui, José Carlos, 5, 6, 28, 29, 32, 35, 42

Markovic, Mihailo, 16
Martí, Austín Farabundo, 28
Martí, José, 31
Marx, Karl, 2, 7, 8, 14, 15, 18, 32, 52, 53, 54, 57, 115
Marxism, 1, 2, 5, 6, 16, 18, 32, 33, 42, 54, 68, 82, 89, 90, 115; conceptions of, 2; in Latin America, 5, 32; Marxist democratic regimes, 53; Marxist-Leninist ideology, 6, 7, 35, 44, 78, 79, 80; Marxist-Leninist parties, 14, 79; Marxist-Leninist states, 76; Marxist movements in Nicaragua, 41; Marxist parties in Latin America, 5; Marxist theory and method, 1, 3, 7, 18, 29, 32, 33, 41, 47, 82, 85, 100, 109, 130, 138; Marxist tradition, 2, 18; in Nicaragua, 35. *See also* Vladimir Lenin, Joseph Stalin, and vanguard party
Marxist-Leninist Party of Nicaragua, 29
Marxist-Leninist Popular Action Movement, 79
Masonic Grand Lodge, 27
Mass organizations, 51, 52, 53, 54, 55, 56, 58, 61, 62, 64, 65, 66, 72, 73, 77, 83, 84, 87, 94, 95, 96, 113, 129, 143, 146, 147, 149
Matagalpa, 32, 33, 39, 62
Mayorga, Silvio, 33, 36
Medellín, 41
Medvedev, Roy, 2, 5
Megill, Kenneth, 14, 18
Mestizos, 23, 33
Mexican Communist Party, 28, 29
Mexican government, 29
Mexican Revolution, 26
Mexico, 24, 27, 33, 101, 105
Meza, Samuel, 32
Mideast peace mission, 118
MiG incident, 82
Mill, John Stuart, 9
Ministry of Agriculture, 64
Miskito, 37. *See also* Indians
Molyneux, Maxine, 60
Monarchy, 8
Moncado, José M., 24–25
Monimbó, 45, 53, 54
Morales, Ricardo, 43, 44
Morales, Waltrud Q., 102
Morazán, Francisco, 33
Moscow, 105

Movement for Historic Fighters, 121
Movement for Revolutionary Unity, 93
Municipal Juntas for Reconstruction (JMRs), 74

Nagy, Imre, 2
Namibia, 101
National Assembly, 49, 61, 64, 68, 73, 75, 80, 82, 83, 84, 86, 87, 92, 93, 145, 146, 147; Governing Council of National Assembly, 93; special constitutional commission of, 83–84, 86
National Congress, 68
National Delegation (Paris), 15
National Endowment for Democracy, 137
National Guard (of Nicaragua), 30, 39, 45, 71
National Patriotic Front (FPN), 45–46, 74
National Union of Farmers and Ranchers (UNAG), 53, 62, 99, 113, 119, 147; national board of directors of, 62; organizational structure of, 63; regional assembly of, 62; regional board of directors of, 62; "plan of struggle" of, 62
Nazis, 28
Netherlands, 104
New Delhi, 101
New England: town meetings, 10, 53; townships, 8
New Jersey, 84
New Left, 5, 54
Newsweek, 142
Nicaragua, 2, 3, 5, 7, 10, 19, 24, 25, 31, 32, 33, 34, 36, 37, 41, 42, 44, 46, 47, 49, 50, 51, 52, 53, 55, 56, 61, 66, 67, 68, 74, 76, 77, 85, 89, 90, 91, 115; agrarian reform in, 98– 99; Atlantic Coast of, 24, 78, 115, 121; bourgeosie in, 34, 139; cooperatives, 34, 63; democracy in, 52, 71–72, 75, 83, 103; democratic socialism in, 1, 4–5; economy of, 97–100, 131, 138, 140, 146; educational system of, 56; foreign policy of, 54, 100–106; government structures in, 71, 72, 76, 86–88; literacy rate of, 55; political culture in, 55, 96, 129; political system of, 73, 87, 88, 92, 93, 130, 150; revolution in, 23, 46, 53, 67; society in,

94, 125, 130; war with contras, 86–87, 95, 96, 104, 105; women in, 58–62, 86, 125; workers movement in, 64
Nicaragua: hora cero (Fonseca Amador), 45
Nicaragua—The Great Challenge (Wheelock), 111
Nicaraguan Association of Women Luisa Amanda Espinosa (AMNLAE), 53, 58–62, 73, 84, 86, 95, 113, 121, 147
Nicaraguan Democratic Movement, 50
Nicaraguan in Moscow, A (Fonseca Amador), 33
Nicaraguan Ministry of Foreign Cooperation, 105
Nicaraguan Socialist Party (PSN), 5, 6, 31, 32, 33, 34, 35, 36, 37, 39, 46, 79, 104, 132
Niquinohomo, 25
Nonaligned Movement (NAM), 54, 100, 101, 102; Committee of Nine, 102; ninth summit of, 101; sixth summit of, 100, 101
North America, 7, 54, 61, 82, 91, 92
Norway, 104
Núñez, Carlos, 57, 93, 110, 117
Núñez Soto, Orlando, 5
Núñez, Rene, 117, 126

Oligarchy, 24, 71
One Hundred Years of Solitude (García Márquez), 23
Oquist, Paul, 119
Ordóñez, Cleto, 33
Organization of American States (OAS), 131, 137
Ortega, Daniel, 44, 50, 72, 73, 79, 86, 87, 100, 105, 106, 110, 112, 117, 118, 119, 124, 137, 145, 148
Ortega, Humberto, 23, 44, 46, 77, 110, 112, 117, 119, 126

Panama, 54, 43
Pancansán, 39, 40, 43, 45
Paraguay, 129
Paris, 7, 15, 16, 52
Paris Commune of 1871, 7, 8, 15, 16, 18, 52, 53, 54, 115
Parisians, 52
Pater familias, 84
Patria potestas, 84

Patriotic Youth, 35
Pavletich, Esteban, 6, 28
Peace Corps, 91
Pedagogy of the Oppressed (Freire), 41
People's Anti-Somicista tribunals, 87
Perestroika, 5, 96, 100
Pérez Estrada, Manuel, 79
Pérez, Rigoberto, 31
Periera, Constantino, 79, 82
Permanent Conference of Political Parties in Latin America (COPPAL), 119
Peru, 5, 6, 32
Poder popular, 54
Polisario Front, 101
Political Parties Law, 77–78
Political pluralism, 50, 90, 92, 93, 94, 95, 96
Polycentrism, 5
Popular consultations, 124, 149
Popular Social Christian Party, 46, 74, 79, 93
Populism, 9
Prague Spring of 1968, 3, 7
Proletariat, 8, 44
Prolonged People's War, 41, 44, 55
Puerto Rico, 101

Radio Sandino, 122
Ramírez, Sergio, 50, 72, 73, 79, 117, 124, 126
Raudales, Ramón, 32
Reagan administration, 77, 78, 82, 103, 104, 130, 131, 141
Reagan-Gorbachev Summit of 1985, 105
Reding, Andrew, 85, 86
Revolutionary Student Organization, 42
"Rigoberto Perez" column, 34, 35
Río Blanco, 41
Río Bocay, 40
Río Coco, 39
Rio de Janeiro, 77
Robelo, Alfonso, 50, 52, 72, 73
Rodríguez, Mercedes, 79
Roosevelt, Franklin Delano, 31
Rousseau, Jean-Jacques, 8, 9, 12, 13, 14, 16, 57
Ruíz, Henry, 40, 110, 112, 117, 119
Rural Workers' Association (ATC), 51, 53, 56, 62, 65–66, 94–95, 121
Russia, 14, 34; political culture in, 16. *See also* Soviet Union

Russian Revolution, 26

Sacasa, Crisanto, 33
San Antonio, 99
San Judas, 145
Sánchez, Domingo, 79
Sánchez, Luis, 140
Sandinismo, 23, 109
Sandinist ideology, 47
Sandinista Bario Committee, 57
Sandinista Defense Committees (CDS),
51, 52, 57, 58, 59, 74, 94– 95, 113, 114,
144
Sandinista National Lberation Front
(FSLN), 1, 5, 6, 19–20, 29, 30, 33, 35,
36, 37, 39, 40, 41, 42, 43, 44, 45, 46, 47,
49, 50, 51, 52, 53, 54, 55, 56, 57, 58, 59,
60, 61, 62, 65, 66, 67, 68, 72, 73, 74, 77,
78, 79, 80, 83, 84, 86, 87, 88, 89, 90, 93,
94, 95, 96, 97, 98, 99, 100, 103, 104, 105,
109, 120, 129; base committees of, 116,
124; Christian wing of, 85; Congress,
117, 118, 120, 122, 124, 125, 126, 149;
Department of Finances, 112–113, 115;
Department of International Relations, 112, 115, 119, 122; Department
of Organization, 112, 113, 114, 117;
Department of Political Education,
112, 114–115, 117, 119; Department of
Propoganda and Agitation, 112, 114,
122; Departmental Executive Committees, 121; elections, 78, 96, 129, 131,
132, 136, 137, 145; Executive Committee of the National Directorate, 87,
112, 118, 119; "first promotion" of,
113; foreign relations of, 100–106;
FSLN as vanguard party, 96, 123, 144;
Historic Program of, 49, 58, 90, 91, 92,
129; Insurrectionalist Tendency of, 44,
45, 46; media outlets, 122; National
Directorate of, 20, 36, 43, 51, 52, 67,
93, 96, 109, 110–112, 115, 116, 117, 119,
120, 121; Office of the Secretary
General, 112, 113, 117; Party Ethics
Commision, 120; party structure, 90,
111, 117, 121, 148, 149; philosophy of,
91, 92, 94, 138; Political Commissions,
112; Proletarian faction , 43, 44, 55,
110; Prolonged People's War faction,
43, 44, 110; recruitment, 114, 123;
regional committees, of, 116; Revolu-

tion, 2, 4, 19, 90, 112, 116, 119; Sandinista Assembly, 67, 113, 115–116,
117, 120, 122, 124, 125, 126, 148, 149;
"second promotion" of, 113;
Secretariat, 117, 123; Secretary
General, 118, 120; Terceristas, 43, 44,
91, 92, 110; trade unions, 125, 145;
worker federations, 65; zonal commit-
tees of, 116
Sandinista Popular Army, 114, 116
Sandinista Workers Central (CST), 51,
56, 59, 64–66, 95
Sandinista Youth, 53, 73, 113
Sandinists (original followers of San-
dino), 29, 30, 31, 32, 144
Sandino, Augusto César, 1, 6, 23–34, 35,
36, 39, 40, 44, 46, 47, 54, 55, 57, 71, 79,
89, 90, 100, 115, 144
Sandino, General de Hombres Libres
(Selser), 33
Schumpter, Joseph, 11
Segovias, 25, 30
Selser, Gregorio, 33
Social Christians, 74, 77, 78, 93, 132
Social Contract, The (Rousseau), 8
Social Democrats, 28, 74, 77, 78, 115, 132
Socialism, 5, 3, 7, 17, 53, 57, 90, 94, 97,
98, 125; bureaucratic, 2, 4, 6, 13, 19;
and democracy, 1, 4, 5, 137, 138;
socialist revolutions, 16; socialist
states, 1, 2, 4, 103, 105; socialists, 4, 7,
56; soviet model of, 33; in Spain, 16;
Stalinism and, 2; "with a human face,"
13. *See also* Communism
Socialist International, 77, 78
Somocismo, 144
Somocists, 43
Somoza Debayle, Anastasio, 4, 39, 41
Somoza dictatorship, 49, 50, 71, 72, 75,
76, 79, 90, 91, 94, 98, 109
Somoza economic apparatus, 88, 99
Somoza García, Anastasio, 30, 31, 32,
33, 34
Southern Africa, 106
Southwest African People's Organiza-
tion, 101
Soviets, 7, 16. *See also* Worker councils
Soviet Union, 1, 6, 16, 17, 32, 33, 34, 54,
76, 79, 90, 96, 138; constitution of 1977,
76; economic relation with Nicaragua,
104–106; intervention in Afghanistan,

102; intervention in Czechoslovakia, 2; intervention in Hungary, 2; Korean airliner incident, 102; Marxism in, 16, 18, 35, 76; New Economic Policy of, 100; writers in, 5. *See also* Russia

Spain, 104; Republican, 16

Spanish-American War, 29

Spanish Civil War, 16

Spanish colonialism, 46

Spanish conquest, 33

Spanish Socialist Workers Party (PSOE), 126

Spiritualism, 26, 27

St. Petersburg, 16

Stalin, Joseph, 2, 5, 6, 14, 16, 17, 18

Stalinism, 2, 17, 18, 32, 54, 149

Stalinists, 14, 35

State enterprises, 90

Steele, James B., 11

Stein, Nancy, 71

Stockholm Conference, 104

Stuttgart, 103

Superior Council of Private Enterprise (COSEP), 77–78, 85

Supreme Court of Justice (in Nicaragua), 86, 87

Supreme Electoral Council, 80, 81, 85, 86, 87, 131, 137

Sweden, 93, 100, 103, 104

Swiss Canton of Apenzell, 10

Tampico (Mexico), 26

Tegucigalpa, 36

Téllez, Dora María, 58, 109, 126, 149

Téllez, Isidora, 79

Third World, 4, 6, 46, 49, 144; Marxism, 5; relations with Nicaragua, 102, 103, 106; revolutionary movements in, 91, 110, 114; Nonaligned Movement in, 100

Tirado López, Victor, 36, 110, 119, 123, 124

Torre, Victor Raúl Haya de la, 28

Transition Agreement, 117

Trincado, Juaquín, 27

Trotsky, Leon, 17, 34

Ulloa, Sixto, 93

UNAP, 33

Unidad, 33

United Nations, 54, 101, 105, 131, 137, 140; General Assembly of, 102;

Security Council of, 101, 102

United Nicaraguan Opposition (UNO), 88, 89, 92, 93, 95, 132, 137, 138, 140, 142, 143, 144, 145, 148

United People's Movement (MPO), 45, 46

United States, 1, 2, 13, 19, 26, 30, 31, 33, 34, 45, 49, 54, 67, 71, 75, 77, 80, 84, 90, 91, 100, 101, 102, 104, 114, 129, 130, 132, 136, 147; Ambassador to Nicaragua, 43, 81–82; American Revolution, 9; Congress of, 137; Declaration of Independence, 8; democratic tradition, 9, 10; elections in, 11; embassy in Nicaragua, 40; foreign policy of, 3, 4, 20, 23–24; government of, 92, 94, 96; hegemony, 106, 131; House of Representatives of, 11; intervention, 71, 76, 101; Marines, 24, 27, 29, 33, 36; National Security Council of, 82; political system, 10, 13; press in, 82; public, 82; oil companies in Mexico, 26; State Department of, 96; supported political parties, 85, 137, 138; trade embargo against Nicaragua, 102, 104, 105, 130, 137, 138, 140, 143; trade with Nicaragua, 103; Washington, D.C., 24, 30, 71, 78; White House, 82. *See also* Bush administration; Carter, Jimmy; Central Intelligence Agency; Reagan administration

Universal Declaration of Human Rights, 85

University Christian Movement, 42

Vanguard party, 12, 16, 17

Vatican II, 41

Venezuela, 101, 105

Vickers, George, 83

Vietnam, 36, 40

Virginia, 8

Walker, William, 3, 23, 33

War of the Indians (1881), 33

Washington Post, 82

Waslala, 41

Weathers, Byrum, 138

West Germany, 77, 93

Western Europe, 7, 54, 84, 92, 130; economic relations with Nicaragua, 103, 104; political institutions of, 75,

85, 106
Western Hemisphere, 28, 29, 30, 106
Western Sahara, 101
What is Orthodox Marxism (Lukacs), 2
What Is to Be Done? (Lenin), 110
Wheelock, Jaime, 44, 98, 110, 111, 112, 118, 119, 124
Will, George, 11
Wiwili, 27
Workers council, 16. *See also* Soviets
World Bank, 138
World Court, 54
World Parliamentary Union, 102

"Yankee imperialism," 91
Yugoslavia, 53, 75, 129

Zaire, 101
Zambrana, Allan, 79
Zapata, Emiliano, 26
Zelaya, José Santos, 24, 33, 71
Zelaya, North and South, 121
Zeledón, General Benjamín, 25, 33
Zimbabwe, 101, 102
Zinica, 40

❖ About the Book and Authors ❖

Moving beyond Cold War rhetoric and stereotypical views of Third World Marxism, the authors convincingly argue that the democratic tradition and practice that was emerging in socialist Nicaragua could well have served as a model for other Third World states. They analyze concepts of democracy and the ideology of the FSLN and show that the Sandinista movement is not in any way stock Marxism-Leninism. Instead, this nationalist variant of Third World Marxism is—like most others—a function of indigenous realities.

Vanden and Prevost demonstrate that Nicaragua has seen the establishment of at least three different forms of democracy: popular, participatory democracy (manifested in mass organizations); Western-style representative democracy (as seen in the 1984 and 1990 elections and the resultant governmental structure); and Leninist vanguardism (shown in the functioning of the FSLN itself). After showing why participatory democracy did not triumph, they conclude with an assessment of the 1990 elections and their impact on the future of democracy in Nicaragua.

Harry E. Vanden is professor of political science and Chair of the Latin American and Caribbean Studies Committee at the University of South Florida. In addition to a number of articles and book chapters, he has written *Mariátegui: influencias en su formación ideológica, National Marxism in Latin America: José Carlos Mariátegui's Thought and Politics,* and *A Bibliography of Latin American Marxism.*

Gary Prevost is professor of government at St. John's University in Collegeville, Minnesota. He has written extensively on the politics of Spain, Central America, and the Caribbean. He is coeditor of *Politics and Change in Spain, Cuba—A Different America,* and *The 1990 Elections in Nicaragua and Their Aftermath.*